International Students' Multilingual Literacy Practices

NEW PERSPECTIVES ON LANGUAGE AND EDUCATION

Founding Editor: Viv Edwards, *University of Reading, UK*
Series Editors: Phan Le Ha, *University of Hawaii at Manoa, USA* and
Joel Windle, *Monash University, Australia.*

Two decades of research and development in language and literacy education have yielded a broad, multidisciplinary focus. Yet education systems face constant economic and technological change, with attendant issues of identity and power, community and culture. What are the implications for language education of new 'semiotic economies' and communications technologies? Of complex blendings of cultural and linguistic diversity in communities and institutions? Of new cultural, regional and national identities and practices? The New Perspectives on Language and Education series will feature critical and interpretive, disciplinary and multidisciplinary perspectives on teaching and learning, language and literacy in new times. New proposals, particularly for edited volumes, are expected to acknowledge and include perspectives from the Global South. Contributions from scholars from the Global South will be particularly sought out and welcomed, as well as those from marginalized communities within the Global North.

All books in this series are externally peer-reviewed.

Full details of all the books in this series and of all our other publications can be found on http://www.multilingual-matters.com, or by writing to Multilingual Matters, St Nicholas House, 31-34 High Street, Bristol, BS1 2AW, UK.

NEW PERSPECTIVES ON LANGUAGE AND EDUCATION: 109

International Students' Multilingual Literacy Practices

An Asset-based Approach to Understanding Academic Discourse Socialization

Edited by
Peter I. De Costa, Wendy Li and Jongbong Lee

MULTILINGUAL MATTERS
Bristol • Jackson

DOI https://doi.org/10.21832/DECOST5553
Names: De Costa, Peter, editor. | Li, Wendy, editor. | Lee, Jongbong, editor.
Title: International Students' Multilingual Literacy Practices: An
   Asset-based Approach to Understanding Academic Discourse Socialization/
   Edited by Peter I. De Costa, Wendy Li and Jongbong Lee.
Description: Bristol; Jackson: Multilingual Matters, [2022] |
   Series: New Perspectives on Language and Education: 109 | Includes
   bibliographical references and index. | Summary: 'This book presents the
   results of research that focused on international students receiving writing
   instruction on a US university campus. It explores how the students
   developed their foreign-student identities and their own ways of
   grappling with the unique issues they encountered as they worked to
   improve their academic literacy skills' – Provided by publisher.
Identifiers: LCCN 2022003118 (print) | LCCN 2022003119 (ebook) |
   ISBN 9781800415553 (hardback) | ISBN 9781800415546 (paperback) |
   ISBN 9781800415560 (pdf) | ISBN 9781800415577 (epub)
Subjects: LCSH: English language – Rhetoric – Study and teaching
   (Higher) – Social aspects – United States – Case studies. | English language –
   Study and teaching (Higher) – Foreign speakers – Case studies. |
   Literacy – Study and teaching (Higher) – United States – Case studies. |
   Multilingual education – United States – Case studies. | LCGFT: Case studies.
Classification: LCC PE1405.U6 I57 2022 (print) | LCC PE1405.U6 (ebook) |
   DDC 306.442/21073 – dc23/eng/20220420
LC record available at https://lccn.loc.gov/2022003118
LC ebook record available at https://lccn.loc.gov/2022003119

Library of Congress Cataloging in Publication Data
A catalog record for this book is available from the Library of Congress.

British Library Cataloguing in Publication Data
A catalogue entry for this book is available from the British Library.

ISBN-13: 978-1-80041-555-3 (hbk)
ISBN-13: 978-1-80041-554-6 (pbk)

Multilingual Matters
UK: St Nicholas House, 31-34 High Street, Bristol, BS1 2AW, UK.
USA: Ingram, Jackson, TN, USA.

Website: www.multilingual-matters.com
Twitter: Multi_Ling_Mat
Facebook: https://www.facebook.com/multilingualmatters
Blog: www.channelviewpublications.wordpress.com

The policy of Multilingual Matters/Channel View Publications is to use papers that are natural, renewable and recyclable products, made from wood grown in sustainable forests. In the manufacturing process of our books, and to further support our policy, preference is given to printers that have FSC and PEFC Chain of Custody certification. The FSC and/ or PEFC logos will appear on those books where full certification has been granted to the printer concerned.

Typeset by Riverside Publishing Solutions.

Contents

Contributors

Editors

Peter I. De Costa is an Associate Professor in the Department of Linguistics, Languages & Cultures and the Department of Teacher Education at Michigan State University. His research areas include emotions, identity, ideology and ethics in educational linguistics. He also studies social (in)justice issues. He is the co-editor of *TESOL Quarterly* and the First Vice-President of the American Association for Applied Linguistics.

Jongbong Lee is an Assistant Professor in the Department of English at Cyber Hankuk University of Foreign Studies. His main area of research interest is second language writing, particularly the interface between the fields of second language writing and second language acquisition. His work has appeared in journals such as *Cognition*, *Language Learning*, *Language Teaching*, *Studies in Second Language Acquisition* and *System*.

Wendy Li is an Assistant Professor at Duke Kunshan University. Her research interests include language teacher identity, agency, emotions, ethics in applied linguistics, second language socialization, and multilingual and multimodal literacy practices. Her work is published in *Language Teaching Research*, *English Today* and *Language Teaching*.

Authors

Joseph Cheatle is an Assistant Professor and Director of the Writing Center at the University of Southern Mississippi. His most recent scholarship focuses on how writing centers connect theory to practice and on creating collaborative approaches to improving services. His work is published in the *Writing Center Journal*, *The Journal of Writing Analytics* and *Praxis: A Writing Center Journal*.

Wenhao Diao is an Associate Professor in East Asian Studies and Second Language Acquisition and Teaching at the University of Arizona. She is interested in the identities, ideologies, and (in)equities that are (re)produced and (re)distributed through language teaching and learning. Her primary research focus has been the phenomenon of language learning and socialization during study abroad – particularly going to and from China. She co-edited the book *Language Learning in Study Abroad: The Multilingual Turn* (Multilingual Matters, 2021) and a special issue of the *L2 Journal* entitled *Study Abroad in the 21st Century* in 2016. She has also published numerous articles on applied linguistics journals and edited volumes.

Patricia (Patsy) Duff is a Professor of Applied Linguistics and Distinguished University Scholar in the Department of Language and Literacy Education at the University of British Columbia. Patsy's main scholarly interests are related to language socialization across multilingual settings, including academic discourse socialization at universities; qualitative research methods in applied linguistics; and issues in the teaching, learning and use of English, Mandarin and other international, heritage and Indigenous languages in transnational contexts. She has published widely on these topics.

Steven Fraiberg is an Associate Professor in the Department of Writing, Rhetoric and American Cultures at Michigan State University. His scholarship focuses on multilingual and multimodal literacy practices across classrooms, workplaces and communities. His publications include a co-authored book, *Inventing the World Grant University: Literacies, Mobilities, and Identities,* published by Utah State University Press.

Curtis Green-Eneix is a doctoral candidate in the Second Language Studies Program at Michigan State University. His research focuses on teacher development, identity, power dynamics in the classroom, language policy and planning pertaining to transnational education contexts, as well as socioeconomic position and online education. His research has been featured in *English Today*, *System* and *TESOL Journal*.

Scott Jarvie is an Assistant Professor in the Department of English and Comparative Literature at San Jose State University. His scholarship studying educational experience, particularly in secondary English classrooms, through perspectives drawn from the humanities, educational philosophy and curriculum theory, has appeared in journals such as *English Education, English Teaching: Practice and Critique* and *Changing English*.

Wenyue Ma is a PhD candidate in the Second Language Studies Program at Michigan State University. Her research interests mainly lie in language testing and assessment and quantitative research methods. Her research work has appeared in *Foreign Language Annals* and *Language Testing*.

Myeongeun Son is an Assistant Professor in the Department of English at Nagoya University of Commerce & Business. She recently finished her PhD in Second Language Studies at Michigan State University. Her research interests lie in second language (L2) acquisition and development and L2 language processing.

Bree Straayer-Gannon is a recent PhD graduate from the Rhetoric and Writing Program at Michigan State University. Her research focuses on how home cultures and discourse communities, particularly religious ones, impact learning, literacy and identity. Currently, she is a Director at The Literacy Center of West Michigan, working with language learning families.

Xiqiao Wang is an Assistant Professor in the University of Pittsburgh's Composition program. Her research on multilingual writing process in the context of global migration has appeared in professional journals such as *Research in the Teaching of English*, *College Composition and Communication*, *Journal of Second Language Writing* and *Language and Education*.

Xiaowan Zhang is the Test Development Manager at MetaMetrics, where she is responsible for the development, delivery and validation of language tests. She recently received her PhD in Second Language Studies from Michigan State University. While at Michigan State University, she taught second language acquisition, teaching methods and pedagogical grammar to TESOL undergraduates. She holds a master's degree in TESOL from the University of Illinois at Urbana-Champaign.

Foreword: Examining and Experiencing Academic Discourse Socialization through Collaborative Research

The nature and challenges of academic socialization – especially the multimodal literacies, genres, activities and practices inculcated across disciplines that newcomers must learn and negotiate – have attracted considerable interest in recent years. This work, now often referred to as *academic discourse socialization* (ADS), brings together and extends earlier research on (1) language socialization, which focused primarily on *oral language* development through social interaction in formal and informal contexts of learning (from pre-K to adult); (2) the development of academic literacies through formal education; and (3) multilingual socialization into various communities and cultural practices (e.g. academic, professional, vocational, recreational) across the lifespan (see, for example, Duff, 2007, 2010, 2017; Kobayashi *et al.*, 2017).

Several factors are associated with this increased attention to multimodal, multilingual (or translingual) academic discourse and the means by which people are socialized into it. First, the demographics in secondary and postsecondary education contexts are changing, with a greater proportion of multilingual transnational students being accommodated than ever before. Second, in many parts of the world, instructors and students are now involved in education and scholarship conducted through the medium of a language such as English that is neither their home language nor the language of their earlier schooling. They must therefore learn to engage meaningfully with the subject matter and curriculum, disciplinary discourses, and literacies in institutionally privileged languages and registers. In some cases, the education programs are designed precisely to increase students' possibilities and mobilities for subsequent transnational higher education and careers. Third, academic literacies and practices themselves continue to evolve with new technologies and social media, increasing recognition of the affordances of different semiotic repertoires and of changing norms about acceptable and valued practices within and across disciplines. However, these literacy practices do not exist within an affective, historical or ideological vacuum. They are wrapped up with learners' identities, assets, aspirations, agency, languages and program ideologies, and with their relationships, power dynamics, communities, and trajectories – all central aspects of contemporary sociocultural research in applied linguistics, including ADS. These multifaceted influences on development and performance should therefore be understood holistically across scales of time, space and place, to the extent possible. Finally, research has begun to explore doctoral and postdoctoral academic socialization itself as a site of high-stakes apprenticeship (and, possibly, contestation), as emerging scholars learn to navigate and gain command over complex, competitive, social, political and discursive cultures and practices. This book provides compelling examples of doctoral socialization into multiple genres of research activity and scholarship, as well as undergraduate students' experiences.

Changing educational contexts and issues, such as these, pose wonderful opportunities for applied linguists and writing specialists to examine critically the populations, texts, processes, practices, pedagogies, cultures and products of learning in their midst. To that end, this volume brings together the work of a team of researchers exploring their own and others' academic discourse socialization across multiple genres, languages, program contexts and communities at one US university. Supported by a Creating Inclusive Campus Grant (CICG), the project reveals a vibrant community of practice exploring academic socialization and mentoring among team members: doctoral students, writing center instructors, emerging scholars and new professors, as well as established professors and advisors. The authors present case studies of first-year undergraduate international students' experiences with various aspects of English writing instruction, including innovations some of these authors introduced into the curriculum. They frame the work in terms of activity systems (divisions of labor, rules, tools, participant structures, objects and outcomes featured in activity theory) or 'mobility systems,' and the kinds of scaffolding or mentoring that can strengthen writing courses and writing center interactions. Most importantly, the chapters in the book tell the stories of educators and students working within demanding interdisciplinary academic cultures mediated by English primarily. The research participants' and authors' resourcefulness and resilience in managing teaching/learning processes and participation in their learning communities, with crucial support from sponsors, peers, tutors, instructors and others (both near and far), remind readers of the challenges, opportunities and improvisation inherent in contemporary academic socialization.

Patricia A. Duff
University of British Columbia

References

Duff, P. (2007) Problematising academic discourse socialisation. In H. Marriott, T. Moore and R. Spence-Brown (eds) *Discourses of Learning and Learning of Discourses* (pp. 1–18). Victoria: Monash University e-Press/University of Sydney Press.

Duff, P. (2010) Language socialization into academic discourse communities. *Annual Review of Applied Linguistics* 30, 169–192.

Duff, P. (2017) Language socialization, higher education, and work. In P. Duff and S. May (eds) *Language Socialization* (3rd edn, pp. 255–272). Cham: Springer International.

Kobayashi, M., Zappa-Hollman, S. and Duff, P. (2017) Academic discourse socialization. In P. Duff and S. May (eds) *Language Socialization* (3rd edn, pp. 239–254). Cham: Springer International.

Introduction: Academic Socialization, International Students and Multilingual Literacies

1 Diversity Matters: Problematizing Academic Discourse Socialization in International Higher Education

Peter I. De Costa, Jongbong Lee and Wendy Li

The Greek philosopher Heraclitus rightly observed that the only constant in life is change. The truth in this dictum is borne out in the shifting tides of tertiary education and applies to the ebb and flow of international students at institutions of higher learning. After reaching a record high level in 2018–2019, the number of international students enrolled in US universities in the 2019–2020 academic year stood at 1,075,496 (Marklein, 2020), down about 20,000 students from the previous year. And in Fall 2020, that number declined a further 16%, solidifying the downward trajectory of international student enrollment in the US. However, this recent decline in student numbers is not particular to the US: Australia – another popular tertiary education destination among international students – has also experienced a sharp downturn and lost A\$1.8 billion in 2020, and is estimated to encounter a further A\$2 billion loss in revenue in 2021 (UA, 2021). That said, we anticipate this downward trend to be short-term, and we are confident that there will be a restoration of international student enrollment in the near future. Such a restoration, however, may take a different complexion in that, instead of targeting western, English-dominant countries, neighboring countries within a certain region may become the preferred destination for higher education aspirants. For example, in the north-east Asian context, recent studies (e.g. Mok *et al.*, 2021; Yu, 2021) conducted with Chinese students have indicated that these students may elect to study in Japan or Hong Kong, thereby indicating a growth in the intra-Asian higher education sector that offers more English-Medium Instruction (EMI) education options. The EMI programs in these countries thus become viable alternatives to programs that traditionally were only available in the west. Admittedly, the COVID-19 pandemic has played a pivotal role in hastening the dip in international student enrollment; however, in the US, this sharp decline has been exacerbated by travel restrictions and curtailed student visa issuances imposed by the former Trump administration.

We begin our introduction with these startling statistics to underscore the extent to which international student mobility is influenced by a host of factors, ranging from the fallout of a global health crisis to anti-immigrant measures and xenophobic sentiment. It is against this rapidly evolving educational landscape that we situate our volume, which is based on a year-long project conducted at a midwestern university – Great Lake University (GLU, a pseudonym). And while the aforementioned falling numbers are decidedly alarming and worrisome, we think it premature to cast the death knell on international education. As noted, change is a fixture in life, and one crucial aspect of change that we should not overlook is how international education is quickly taking on a different complexion as students opt for other countries in Asia (e.g. Japan, Malaysia, South Korea) and Europe (e.g. Germany and the Netherlands) in lieu of the traditional top destinations, namely the US, the UK, Canada and Australia (MacGregor, 2019), as Asia and Europe are increasingly perceived to be more welcoming and offer better educational value.

Apart from lower educational costs, these alternative destinations have also become increasingly attractive to international students because of the emergence of transnational English as a medium of instruction (EMI) campuses (De Costa et al., 2020), some of which are satellite branch campuses of major universities such as New York University (US), Nottingham University (UK) and Swinburne University (Australia). Such a destination recalibration is most keenly felt in the US, where Chinese international students have constituted the largest segment of the international student population, with Chinese students representing the largest percentage of international students (33.2%) during the 2017–2018 academic year (Institute of International Education, 2018).

GLU: A Microcosm of the US Higher Education System

As mentioned, our volume is based on a year-long project at GLU. The project was conducted during the 2017–2018 academic year, when the number of international students on campus was at its peak. At the time of our study, 6850 international students were enrolled at GLU, constituting 13.7% of its total enrollment. This percentage is representative of the international student composition on most US campuses. Importantly, and also common to most US universities, more than 70% of the GLU's international student population identified as Chinese when we conducted our study. To meet the needs of this population, GLU offered and continues to offer various academic and social resources, including English as a second language (ESL) language courses, English communication courses for international teaching assistants (ITAs), academic writing courses for international and domestic students, writing consultations offered through the university writing center, and a conversation partner program for international students, scholars and their family dependents.

While we focus on the international students' academic socialization at GLU in this volume, we are aware that the socialization experiences reported in this book are not limited to this university, or even to the US, because similar experiences have played out and continue to play out in comparable institutions across the globe that are characterized by the aforementioned complex support system found at GLU. Focusing on this established system and given this enduring interest in investigating the complex ecology in which international students are embedded, the first author of this introductory chapter (Peter) applied for and was awarded a grant to examine the academic socialization of international students at GLU. A tenured professor in the Department of Linguistics, Languages, and Cultures and the Department of Teacher Education, an affiliated faculty member of the English Language Center (ELC), and an advisory board member of GLU's writing center, Peter is himself a former international student (originally from Singapore) and a former ITA. Two years after he joined GLU in 2013, a colleague from the university's ELC and he conducted a series of workshops that brought faculty from across the campus to explore the phenomenon of academic discourse socialization. This effort culminated in Spring 2017 in the aforementioned grant that was funded by a center on campus. This center had been set up specifically to foster diversity and inclusion at GLU. As the principal investigator of the study, Peter subsequently invited three other faculty members (Steven Fraiberg, Xiqiao Wang and Joseph Cheatle) to join the project. All three colleagues held appointments in the Department of Writing, Rhetoric and American Cultures (WRAC), with Cheatle also serving as the associate director of GLU's writing center. Two advanced doctoral students, Jongbong Lee and Wendy Li, were hired as the project managers and several graduate students who were enrolled in Peter's qualitative methodology class in Fall 2017 became the field researchers for this project. While the students were enrolled in the master's in TESOL (Wenyue Ma) and doctoral Second Language Studies (Curtis Green-Eneix, Myeongeun Son, Xiaowan Zhang) programs, two other student authors, Bree Straayer-Gannon and Scott Jarvie, were doctoral students in the WRAC and Teacher Education departments, respectively.

Diversity Revisited and Extended

Over the course of a year, our research team met regularly each week to discuss our data collection and analyses as well as plan for subsequent conference presentations (see Chapter 2 for project details). Particularly noteworthy were the rich and rigorous discussions we had in our transdisciplinary team meetings, which brought individuals from different departments and programs. We hope that these discussions come to life in the three sections that follow Chapters 1 and 2, which set the stage for this volume.

In Part 1: Literacy Practices and Identity Development, the reader is introduced in Chapters 3 and 4 to the complex set of literacy practices in which our participants engaged across different spaces, including the writing classroom and the writing center, and is led to see how these practices shaped and, in turn, were shaped by their own identity development. For example, drawing on the notions of identity (Norton, 2013), agency (Duff, 2012) and language socialization (Duff, 2019) in Chapter 3, Zhang examines her focal participant's (Charles) language practices across the first-year writing classroom and the writing center. Specifically, Zhang reveals that Charles elected to rebuff the deficit-oriented ESL learner identity imposed on him by the writing center consultant and chose instead to recast himself in a more positive frame as a multilingual writer. Similarly, tracing international students' literacy practices across various literacy spaces, Straayer-Gannon and Wang (Chapter 4) draw insights from the notions of *translingualism* and *mobility literacies* in their telling of the story of a young woman from Ghana, who was able to achieve agency and access various semiotic and literacy resources, and thus navigate the institutional structures by cultivating mentorship and building networks in the local and translocal contexts. These two cases further support the need to resist the deficient perspective towards international students and point to the rich identity resources afforded by the adoption of an asset-based pedagogical approach in the classroom. In addition, these two cases highlighted the important role other socializing agents (e.g. writing center tutors, mentors) played in mediating students' academic discourse socialization experiences, which aligns with Friedman's (2021) call for future studies to examine students' language and literacy interactions outside the classroom and the impact on their academic discourse socialization.

Part 2: Navigating Resources and Services, which is composed of three chapters (Chapters 5 through 7), describes how our focal international student participants mobilized their communicative resources to make sense of the auxiliary services on the GLU campus and beyond. Informed by activity theory, Ma and Green-Eneix (Chapter 5) trace how their participants from China, Andy and Sarah, drew heavily on the Chinese student community on social media platform

WeChat and the writing center to help them socialize into the academic and social community. In addition to the social media resources, Son (Chapter 6) employs activity theory to demonstrate how her two focal participants (Minji from South Korea and Carter from Botswana) navigated the writing center service to facilitate their English academic writing development. Also focusing on the writing center, Cheatle and Jarvie (Chapter 7) provide readers with insights from a writing center tutor. Emphasizing the strengths of a linguistically responsive pedagogy, they recommend that writing center tutors adopt such a pedagogical stance when serving international students. These three cases highlight the importance of auxiliary services and complementary resources in socializing students into the target academic community.

Part 3: Theoretical and Pedagogical Orientations pushes the boundaries of academic discourse socialization by having us reimagine literacy and pedagogy in ways that take into account the translingual dispositions and practices of international students. For example, in Chapter 8, Fraiberg discusses how a transdisciplinary approach – i.e. a mobile literacy approach – is helpful in examining international students' literacy practices, which are continually woven into various semiotic webs. Regarding pedagogical orientations, in Chapter 9 Wang highlights how writing assignments such as *Translation Narrative, Writing Theory Cartoon* and *I Am from Poetry* open up spaces for students to draw on their multilingual and multimodal repertoires to support their acquisition of academic writing discourses. The discussion of those pedagogical practices also responds to Friedman's call for more investigation of practices that 'promote or discourage multicompetence in academic discourse' (Friedman, 2021: 10).

In the spirit of pursuing a diversity-driven agenda at our university research site, our project spawned several creative diversity-related endeavors to which we turn next. As illustrated across the various chapters, our contributing authors draw on a range of theories (i.e. activity theory, language socialization), as well as constructs such as translingualism and mobility literacies, multimodality, identity, agency and linguistically responsive pedagogy. The theoretical cross-fertilization demonstrated in this volume highlights the importance of bringing different theoretical stances into conversation with each other in order to unpack academic discourse socialization (see the Foreword by Duff and the Afterword by Diao), and the need to comprehend the possibilities and pitfalls associated with socialization processes.

Correspondingly, by embracing theoretical diversity, the chapters that follow also illustrate the significance of epistemological diversity as the reader is led to see the value of different types of knowledge that can emerge when a nonwestern-centric pedagogy (Singh & Han, 2017) is adopted to guide classroom practice. Relatedly, by examining the lived sociolinguistic realities of our focal international student participants, the chapters in this volume also serve as a valuable reminder for the need to consider local knowledge generated by students. In other words, the insider ethnographic accounts provided by our participants invite us to explore a reality that would otherwise have been opaque to some of us. For example, we learn from Ma and Green-Eneix (Chapter 5) about how WeChat was the social media platform most frequently used by Chinese students to exchange a myriad of resources in order to tackle not only academic problems but also everyday domestic problems such as selling or buying secondhand furniture or subletting an apartment. Crucial insights such as these should prod us into thinking about how we can leverage the affordances provided by WeChat to enhance the academic discourse socialization experiences of international students. Moreover, we are led to interrogate the notion of *nativeness* in this volume, as evidenced in Son (Chapter 6); her participants, Minji (South Korea) and Carter (Botswana), disclosed their preference for non-native English speaking writing center consultants because they felt that the latter could better address their writing concerns. Thus, the epistemological diversity of (i.e. both western and nonwestern-inflected insights gleaned from) this project gives us an alternate way of understanding the complexities surrounding international students' academic discourse socialization.

Furthermore, this project yielded multiple perspectives of understanding international students' experiences. These perspectives can be attributed to a wide range of data sources that includes surveys, interviews, observations and artefacts (e.g. class assignments, social media exchanges, literacy logs) that were either administered to or collected from the participants. These data sources also enabled us to examine the experiences of participants through a layered and nuanced approach that allowed us to honor and appreciate their individual life histories. In Chapter 5, for example, Ma and Green-Eneix trace how the prior high-school experiences of participants Andy (China) and Sarah (China) may have hampered their ability to subsequently fully integrate with the GLU domestic student community as both found comfort and solace in retreating into cocoon communities (Singh *et al.*, 2013) comprised of their co-nationals. By the same token, the rich multimodal analysis that accompanied the ethnographic investigations undertaken by Straayer-Gannon and Wang (Chapter 4) and Wang (Chapter 9) make us privy to the translingual performances enacted by their focal participants, Albina (Ghana) and Xiaoqi (China), respectively.

A fourth type of diversity in this volume takes the form of pedagogical innovations enacted by some of the writing instructors who participated in our project. These innovations, which stem from an asset-based orientation (i.e. one that honors the linguistic and cultural resources the international students bring with them to the writing classroom), include the translation narrative (Chapter 4, Straayer-Gannon & Wang; Chapter 9, Wang), graphic story (Chapter 8,

Fraiberg) and poetry (Chapter 9, Wang) assignments that incorporate translingual inquiry in the first-year writing classroom. Importantly, these teaching practices embody the Linguistically Responsive Pedagogy (Gallagher & Haan, 2018; Lucas *et al.*, 2008) that is espoused by Cheatle and Jarvie in Chapter 7. In putting forward such an alternative pedagogical approach, the authors also lead us to question the monolingual literacy theory bias that underpins Intensive English Programs (IEPs). Such programs have traditionally been established at universities – often mediated by English language centers – to teach the four canonical skills of reading, writing, listening and speaking in English (Kaplan, 1997) and to create revenue (Juffs, 2020), while attempting to pass as politically neutral entities (Piscioneri, 2011).

Looking Ahead

We started the introduction by reporting on the dwindling international student numbers. However, this decline is emblematic of broader shifts in higher education as college-age students have started to question the efficacy of a university education, especially in light of escalating tuition costs. The coronavirus pandemic has only amplified growing calls to arrest rising costs since many students, in particular high-fee paying international students, are grappling with financial problems. Others have found themselves wondering about the potential justification of having to pay exorbitant sums for online learning. Many international students feel shortchanged as they have been robbed of the opportunity to immerse themselves in the full international education experience. Perhaps more disconcerting is how the absence of face-to-face interaction with their instructors and peers has heightened the need to better understand the academic lives of this set of students. After all, the boundaries between school and home that characterize their lives, as the chapters in this volume illustrate, are porous (Collins & Muñoz, 2016; Wargo & De Costa, 2017).

Hence, as universities like GLU struggle to stay relevant and try to stem further hemorrhaging of international students, they need to figure out how to make the academic discourse socialization of their students in general, and international students in particular, smooth and meaningful. Demonizing social media platforms like WeChat and threatening to cut access to it is not the solution (https://www. washingtonpost.com/technology/2020/09/18/wechat-ban-faq/). Rather, universities need to experiment with how to capitalize on these resources with the intent to maximize instructional synergy (Fraiberg *et al.*, 2017). As this volume will demonstrate, an in-depth investigation of the lives of international students at GLU marks a first key step forward. Equally evident as you read the chapters is the pressing need to forge closer collaborations between key stakeholders such as the writing center, the English language center, international student office and course instructors as universities refine their internationalization agenda. In a globalized world, universities that want to remain competitive need to take concerted measures to attract talent at all levels. And that includes being able to draw good international students. At the end of the day, we need to remember, and as this volume reminds us, diversity, equity and inclusion matter. As educators, we have an ethical responsibility to make sure that these key priorities become a reality while not losing sight of the fact that the only constant in life is change.

References

Collins, L. and Muñoz, C. (2016) The foreign language classroom: Current perspectives and future considerations. *Modern Language Journal* 100 (S1), 133–147.

De Costa, P.I., Green-Eneix, C. and Li, W. (2020) Problematizing EMI language policy in a transnational world: China's entry into the global higher education market. *English Today* 1–8. doi: 10.1017/S026607842000005X.

Duff, P.A. (2012) Identity, agency, and second language acquisition. In S.M. Gass and A. Mackey (eds) *Handbook of Second Language Acquisition* (pp. 410–426). London: Routledge.

Duff, P.A. (2019) Social dimensions and processes in second language acquisition: Multilingual socialization in transnational contexts. *Modern Language Journal* 103, 6–22.

Fraiberg, S., Wang, X. and You, X. (2017) *Inventing the World Grant University: Chinese International Students' Mobilities, Literacies and Identities*. Logan, UT: Utah State University Press.

Friedman, D. (2021) Language socialization and academic discourse in English as a Foreign Language contexts: A research agenda. *Language Teaching* 1–15. doi: 10.1017/S0261444821000422.

Gallagher, C. and Haan, J. (2018) University faculty beliefs about emergent multilinguals and linguistically responsive instruction. *TESOL Quarterly* 52 (2), 304–330.

Institute of International Education (2018) International Student Enrollment Trends, 1948/49-2017/18. *Open Doors Report on International Education Exchange*. Retrieved from http://www.lie.org/opendoors.

Juffs, A. (2020) *Aspects of Language Development in an Intensive English Program*. New York: Routledge.

Kaplan, R.B. (1997) An IEP is a many-splendored thing. In M.A. Christison and F.L. Stoller (eds) *A Handbook for Language Program Administrators* (pp. 3–20). Burlingame, CA: Alta Book Center Publishers.

Lucas, T., Villegas, A.M. and Freedson-Gonzalez, M. (2008) Linguistically responsive teacher education: Preparing classroom teachers to teach English Language Learners. *Journal of Teacher Education* 59 (4), 361–373.

MacGregor, K. (2019, November 30) Chinese international students. The end of the affair. Retrieved from https://www.universityworldnews.com/post.php?story=20191129123948299.

Marklein, M.B. (2020, November 16) New international student enrolments drop by 43% in US. Retrieved from https://www.universityworldnews.com/post.php?story=20201116050900954.

Mok, K.H., Xiong, W., Ke, G. and Cheung, J.O.W. (2021) Impact of COVID-19 pandemic on international higher education and student mobility: Student perspectives from mainland China and Hong Kong. *International Journal of Educational Research* 105, 101718.

Norton, B. (2013) *Identity and Language Learning: Extending the Conversation* (2nd edn). Bristol: Multilingual Matters.

Piscioneri, M. (2011) Walking the tightrope: An inquiry into English for academic purposes. In P.L. Ha and B. Baurain (eds) *Voices, Identities, Negotiations, and Conflicts: Writing Academic English across Cultures* (pp. 195–212). Bingley: Emerald Group.

Singh, M. and Han, J. (2017) *Pedagogies for Internationalising Research Education: Intellectual Equality, Theoretic-linguistic Diversity and Knowledge chuàngxīn.* Singapore: Springer.

Singh, M., Harreveld, R.E. and Danaher, P.A. (2013) Transnational intellectual engagement via cocoon communities: Inter-university videoconferencing for local and international students. In M. Korpela and F. Dervin (eds) *Cocoon Communities: Togetherness in the 21st Century* (pp. 59–80). Cambridge: Cambridge Scholars Publishing.

Wargo, J.M. and De Costa, P.I. (2017) Tracing academic literacies across contemporary literacy sponsorscapes: Mobilities, ideologies, identities, and technologies. *London Review of Education* 15 (1), 101–114.

Universities Australia [UA] (2021) Budget 2021: Unis urge National Plan for Safe Return of International Students. Retrieved from https:// www.universitiesaustralia.edu.au/media-item/budget-2021-unis-urge-national-plan-for-safe-return-of-international-students/.

Yu, J. (2021) Lost in lockdown? The impact of COVID-19 on Chinese international student mobility. *Journal of International Students* 11 (S2), 1–18.

2 Academic Socialization in a Collaborative Research Project: Developing Identities as Emergent Scholars

Jongbong Lee and Wendy Li

Our discussion in this chapter is informed by the theoretical frameworks of the community of practice (Lave & Wenger, 1991) and the identity-inflected model of investment (Darvin & Norton, 2015). We suggest that our participation in such a collaborative project enabled us to gain various types of capital and knowledge desired in the academic community, and therefore facilitated our construction of identities as emergent researchers in this given community. By identifying gaps in the socialization process of novice researchers, our chapter will also contribute to an enhanced understanding of how graduate students who pursue academic careers are socialized into a new discourse community and will furthermore shed light on the training of future graduate students in doctoral programs.

Communities of Practice and the Model of Investment

Previous studies have drawn on diverse theoretical frameworks to explain the socialization of graduate students; among them, Lave and Wenger's (1991) community of practice is particularly appropriate to the academic context (see also Darvin & Norton, 2015; Morita, 2009). Lave and Wenger conceived of socialization as a process of legitimate peripheral participation in which newcomers take part in a community of practitioners. Legitimate peripheral participation is the first step in becoming members of a given community, with newcomers learning the skills and culture of the community as they participate in its practices. While participating in the community, newcomers take on new forms of participation and develop their identities, thereby evolving from newcomers to old-timers. In a graduate school context, graduate students as apprentice academics are considered newcomers, who need opportunities to participate in the community of practice. Later, they gain full participation, including having access to resources and gaining knowledge about the norms and conventions in the community, as they grow increasingly experienced in the community's practices.

Investment and the Shape of Identities

As they engage in socialization practices, graduate students shape and reinvent their identities, a process that can be understood through Darvin and Norton's (2015) model of investment. Although originally framed around language learning, this model can effectively investigate the constructs of capital, identity and ideology in relation to graduate students' socialization processes, and thus can be used to examine how graduate students invest in socialization in an academic community.

In this model of investment, the important concept of identity describes how a person understands his or her relationship to the world (Norton, 2013). According to Norton, personal identity can be construed in terms of being the subject of relationships (in a position of power) as well as subject to relationships (in a position of reduced power). In school settings, students construct their identities by positioning themselves as someone whom they want to be and by being affected by their social context. For instance, in De Costa's (2011) study, a Chinese immigrant student in a Singapore secondary school positioned herself as a successful student by interacting with peers and teachers; however, she was also positioned by her peers and teachers, who assigned a similar identity category. Thus, her interactions with the people around her, her positionings and the ideologies around her impacted her learning outcomes.

Identities are also affected by ideological structures (Darvin & Norton, 2015; Douglas Fir Group, 2016), and ideologies exert power and are reproduced by institutional norms and recursive hegemonic practices. In addition, ideologies influence how diverse forms of capital in a community are valued (Douglas Fir Group, 2016). Capital is often imbued with power, and capital can take different forms, namely, economic capital (e.g. wealth, income), cultural capital (e.g. knowledge, educational credentials) and social capital (e.g. connections to networks of power) (Bourdieu, 1986; Darvin & Norton, 2015). Capital is also distributed in communities, but how a given form of capital is valued depends on the community in which one is involved (Douglas Fir Group, 2016). In a school context, students positioned in the academic community of practice make use of, and compete to acquire, diverse forms of capital.

In the context of graduate school, diverse ideologies compete with one another as they affect and shape students' identities. What constitutes capital in graduate school is also subject to diverse values. To examine graduate students' socialization in an academic context, where they are surrounded by these aforementioned ideologies and forms of capital, it is useful to conceive of graduate students as legitimate peripheral participants who are engaged in academic socialization in a community of practice. As we will illustrate in this chapter, this certainly turned out to be the case for both of us.

Doctoral Graduate Students' Academic Socialization

Earlier studies have provided a detailed account of the development of academic discourse socialization (ADS) in the field of applied linguistics (Duff, 2010; Kobayashi *et al.*, 2017). Identifying ADS as a form of language socialization, Kobayashi *et al.* understood it to be 'concerned with the means by which newcomers and those they interact with learn to participate in various kinds of academic discourse in their communities and other social networks' (Kobayashi *et al.*, 2017: 239). Because it provides the necessary skills for an academic career, academic discourse socialization is crucial to a graduate student's future success. This form of socialization enables an aspiring scholar to become a member of an academic community by and through learning about the culture and expectations of the group (Austin, 2002; Corcoran & Clark, 1984). In graduate education, as many studies have shown (e.g. Anderson, 2017; Duff, 2010; Seloni, 2012; Weng, 2020), doctoral students accumulate the necessary capital – cultural, social and symbolic – by participating in practices such as acquiring disciplinary knowledge, presenting at conferences, publishing research, and reviewing journal articles so as to develop their identity as emergent scholars as well as to gain recognition and claim legitimacy in their disciplinary communities.

Previous studies (e.g. Austin, 2002; Corcoran & Clark, 1984; Darling & Staton, 1989; Darvin & Norton, 2019; Duff, 2010; Morita, 2000, 2009) have investigated how novice researchers or graduate students are socialized into new academic discourse communities. One of the main factors influencing students' socialization into academic discourses, according to the findings of many studies (e.g. Anderson, 2017; Seloni, 2012; Weng, 2020), is the interaction between students and their advisors and mentors. For example, Anderson (2017) examined the academic socialization experiences of seven Chinese doctoral students in a research intensive university in Canada. Her findings showed that the support of the students' advisors facilitated their acquisition of the skills and expertise that were needed in order to successfully become full members within their respective academic discourse community. In contrast, insufficient or even inappropriate mentorship not only deterred students from participating in the requisite practices but also positioned the students in deficient identity categories that hindered their access to the target communities.

In a similar vein, in a case study of two Chinese TESOL doctoral students' academic discourse socialization trajectories, Weng (2020) highlighted the important role the students' advisors played in shaping the participants' academic socialization experiences. Her findings showed that advisors' constructive feedback on the students' academic work, as well as the advisors' ability to provide social connections, supported the students' growing participation in the discourse community, thereby contributing to the recognition of their legitimate positions in the community. In addition, Weng's study reminds us that learning and socialization do not occur unidirectionally through advisors providing instruction or distributing knowledge to advisees: rather, success in socialization occurs only when the two parties construct knowledge together and forge healthy and meaningful mentorship relations together.

While community of practice remains a pivotal construct in language socialization studies, researchers also increasingly recognize its lack of explanatory power in accounting for the power dynamics embedded in processes of socialization, especially in interactions between newcomers and old-timers. Drawing on Bourdieu's constructs of capital, habitus and fields, Weng (2020) shows how the academic community is a power-laden environment where students experience various power dynamics with their advisors, thereby forming reciprocal or hierarchical mentorships. According to Weng, one of the focal participants, positioned as a co-worker and prospective researcher by her advisor, benefited from this cooperative relationship, which facilitated her growth as a legitimate member in the community. In contrast, another focal participant inhabited an identity as an order-abider (i.e. one who followed community rules), and positioned his advisor as the authority, which resulted in a hierarchical relationship and his subsequent marginalized status in the target community.

A similar reciprocal relationship between advisors and advisees can be found in Darvin and Norton's (2019) co-authored piece, where they detailed their experiences of co-authoring and co-publishing practices. Such practices created ample opportunities for Darvin (Norton's doctoral advisee) to engage in disciplinary practices and construct his identity as an emergent scholar in the field. Beneficial as the relationship was, they also recognized the power relations in the academic socialization process, which led to the development of their jointly produced model of investment (Darvin & Norton, 2015) to examine how students and advisors can invest in socialization practices. Defining academic socialization as learning 'the specialized ways of knowing and communicating in a given discipline, while negotiating multiple identities and relations of power' (Darvin & Norton, 2015: 178), they focused on collaborative writing. As Darvin and Norton (2019) pointed out, it was through collaborative writing that the novice scholar (Darvin) was recognized by Norton (the established scholar) as a legitimate member of the community. And it was through such recognition that Darvin was able to claim the right to speak (Norton, 2013), which was embodied in his academic writing.

Inspired by the previous work on academic discourse socialization, we drew from the theoretical frameworks of the community of practice (Lave & Wenger, 1991) and the identity-inflected model of investment (Darvin & Norton, 2015) to examine our academic discourse socialization experience in a collaborative research project. We were project managers for the two-year Creating Inclusive Campus Grant (CICG) project. As project managers of this large-scale cross-disciplinary collaborative research enterprise, we played multiple roles at different stages, when:

(1) constructing the grant proposal, we compiled information needed by the lead investigator, Dr Peter De Costa (our co-editor);
(2) designing the study, we worked as research assistants for the four main investigators (Drs De Costa, Xiqiao Wang, Steve Fraiberg and Joseph Cheatle), helping them to develop the methodology, including making decisions regarding participants, study contexts, materials, data sources and data analysis;
(3) collecting data, our main responsibilities were to assist the field researchers to secure and trace our focal participants and to facilitate communication between the field researchers and the investigators in updating and addressing issues that emerged in the field;
(4) analyzing the data analysis, we organized the data in a systematic way and assisted the investigators to develop plans for disseminating the findings;
(5) disseminating the data, we helped organize university-wide workshops and colloquia at different conferences (e.g. SLRF, TESOL, CCCC).[1]

Through sharing our experiences as we assumed these multiple roles, we intend to show how this collaborative research project constituted a valuable platform for fostering our academic socialization.

Context

When we began working as CICG project managers, we were both starting our third year of doctoral studies in a graduate program that specialized in second language learning and teaching at Great Lake University. As doctoral students (at the time of this study), in the process of socializing into the academic discourse community, we considered ourselves legitimate participants in the academic community. Moreover, given that the goal of this project was to examine how university-wide services can be connected to facilitate international students' academic learning, our identity as international students (Jongbong is originally from South Korea and Wendy from China) and L2 English students was an evident asset because: (1) it enabled us to easily relate to our participants' experiences; and (2) our home languages (Wendy speaks Chinese and Jongbong speaks Korean) helped enormously in recruiting co-national participants, especially the Chinese and Korean international students who constituted the majority of the international student population at our research site.

While working in the same research project, we had, however, somewhat divergent research interests. Wendy's research focuses on second language teachers' identities, emotions and agency. During her participation in the CICG project, she also developed a profound interest in international students' language socialization experiences and was developing her dissertation proposal on this topic. The lead investigator, Peter, was Wendy's doctoral advisor. Jongbong, on the other hand, does research on task-based language learning and teaching, with a special focus on language learners' writing activities. Both of us had participated in another of Peter's granted projects as field researchers. Upon the completion of that first project, we were invited by Peter to join the CICG project. Embarking upon this collaborative project, in which we worked primarily with four faculty members and nine graduate student peers (field researchers), we held a myriad of meetings related to writing a grant proposal, launching the project, recruiting participants from writing classes and matching the participants with the field researchers. We presented workshops on the MAXQDA software (qualitative analysis software), compiled the data, recorded meeting minutes, organized an in-house workshop for the writing department, wrote abstracts for conferences and a book, and managed funds. The major academic activities in which we participated are listed in Table 2.1.

In the following section, we describe how participating in these activities rendered us better able to communicate, think and act like academics.

Our Academic Socialization Trajectories as Project Managers

As project managers, we were involved in every step of the project, from the first information-gathering meeting with resource persons from different departments and programs on campus in 2017 to a very recent meeting with Peter to discuss the development of this edited volume in 2020. Throughout the project, transparency has been central to our cooperative relationship with the leading investigators, especially the principal investigator, Peter. Not only were we informed of the broad plans Peter had laid out for the project at the proposal writing stage, but he kept us involved in all conversations with other investigators,

Table 2.1 Academic activities in which we participated for the CICG Project

Time	Research Stage	Academic Activities
Summer 2017	Groundwork for the project	• meetings with investigators and resource persons • familiarizing ourselves with the operation of the writing center and academic activities in different neighborhood writing centers
Fall 2017–Spring 2018	Data collection stage	Before data collection • weekly meetings with investigators to fine tune data-collection tools • weekly meetings with field researchers to help them get familiar with the data collection tools • visiting the first-year writing classes to recruit participants and holding information meetings with potential participants to inform them of the details of the project and invite them to add their voices and insights to the project During data collection • weekly meetings with personnel to discuss ongoing issues during data collection • arranging financial compensation for focal participants and questionnaire participants After data collection • meetings to summarize the data collection stage and discuss preliminary findings
Fall 2018–Fall 2019	Findings-dissemination stage	University-based workshops • 2018 Fall semester first-year writing program workshop • 2019 Spring semester writing center workshop Conferences • colloquium panel at 2018 Watson Conference • colloquium panel at 2019 CCCC (Conference on College Composition & Communication) • colloquium panel at 2019 TESOL • colloquium panel at 2019 SLRF Pre-conference workshop at 2019 SLRF • 'Using MAXQDA to Analyze Qualitative Data'

field researchers and resource persons, as well as in all project-related meetings, email exchanges and the organization of workshops and conference panels. It is this transparency that provided us with ample opportunities to observe and participate in the behind-the-scenes academic practices that are not often addressed in graduate courses. In what follows, we will focus on three scholarly activities – written communication, meetings with investigators, and the dissemination of findings – in which we participated frequently, and we will demonstrate how these three activities socialized us into (1) communicating like an academic; (2) thinking like an academic; and (3) acting like an academic.

Written Communication with Project Personnel: Communicating Like an Academic

We shaped identities as emergent researchers and scholars as we invested in communication with project personnel and as we gained social capital (Bourdieu, 1986), i.e. valuable social networking opportunities, by doing so. In addition to countless emails to key personnel in the project, such as the investigators and field researchers, we also kept frequent email contact with department secretaries, grant managers, the university's human resources department and the focal participants, to make sure (1) the financial disbursement of the grant was justified and the funding was prudently distributed; (2) researchers were recruited ethically and paid fairly for their work; (3) focal participants were reimbursed in a timely manner; and (4) progress reports were submitted on time to meet stipulated deadlines.

In addition, at the findings-dissemination stage, we were involved in email communication with the first-year writing teachers and the writing center consultants, who were core constituents of our research project. They were invited to attend our workshops, as the findings of our project were thought to be beneficial to their work with international students. Furthermore, we also participated in email communication with established scholars working in similar areas in the field. Along with Peter, we engaged them in the discussion of our findings by inviting them to be panel discussants as well as commentators and reviewers on this edited volume. Reading and drafting these emails as well as conducting follow-up correspondences has been a great learning experience for us. In addition, with Peter's help, we practiced writing academic emails, using appropriate language, tone and levels of formality, to establish initial contacts; to send out requests; to ask for clarification, confirmation and collaboration; and to build contacts and forge good collaborative relationships with university staff and faculty as well as other scholars in the field. Through these email exchanges and interactions, we gained social capital (i.e. by building academic networks with faculty within the university and with scholars outside the university).

We also gained cultural capital (Bourdieu, 1986); that is, we accumulated knowledge about managing a research project and developed dispositions desirable to the academic discourse community. To start with, applying for research grants is a necessary element of any academic's scholarly activities. And while we had attended many courses and workshops about how to write grant proposals, similar opportunities to learn how to manage a grant project are rare. Therefore, by participating in this project, we gained otherwise previously unavailable experience and understanding of the complexity involving personnel and logistics that characterizes such a project. Gaining this type of capital has also contributed to our construction of identities as emergent researchers and scholars in the field.

In addition, our identities changed as we extended our commu-nication activities to abstract and proposal writing so as to pitch to different conferences, including the American Association for Applied Linguistics (AAAL), TESOL, SLRF and CCCC, as well as to the publisher of this edited volume, Multilingual Matters. While writing conference proposals is widely seen as a mandatory and essential academic practice for graduate students in academia, the chance to participate in writing colloquium or edited volume proposals is much rarer. In writing these proposals, we took on other identities, such as organizers of a colloquium or co-editors of an edited volume. Doing so helped us examine our contributors' work from different perspectives. For example, at the individual, micro level, we first needed to map out our contributors' work to their respective theoretical camps. Then, at the meso level, we learned to look for interconnectedness among the different contributors' work, which also led us to examine the interplay among their different theoretical camps. Last, at the macro level, and taking a bird's-eye view of all our contributors' work, we learned to situate our colloquia and edited volume within the field and to write about how the colloquia and edited volume might contribute to contemporary conversations about the topic. By doing so, we not only enhanced our understanding of current developments in the field but also departed further from the identity of being simply graduate students, and we therefore realized fuller participation as legitimate members of the academic community.

Meetings with the Leading Investigators and Field Researchers: Thinking Like an Academic

Across different stages of the project, meetings played a significant role in engaging us in the desired practices of our applied linguistics academic discourse community. The regular meetings required us to communicate ideas, provide progress updates, report problems encountered by team members, negotiate emergent conflicts, discuss challenges and search for solutions. During the stage of research design, we met with the faculty investigators (Drs Cheatle, De Costa, Fraiberg and Wang) regularly. In the beginning, in order to gain a comprehensive understanding of the transition experiences of international students on campus, Peter (Dr De Costa) invited faculty from different campus organizations, including the English language center, the first-year writing program, the writing center, and the Office of International Students and Scholars, to share their knowledge and help generate research ideas for the project. Later, when the data collection started, we continued to hold weekly meetings with the faculty investigators and field researchers to discuss the project research design and data collection tools, such as the questionnaire, semi-structured interviews, writing center observation protocols, and classroom observation guidelines. As we exchanged opinions about observation protocols and guidelines in subsequent meetings with the field researchers, we learned that listening to participant concerns, identifying problems, discussing possible solutions in a collaborative manner and coordinating perspectives are all key to executing successful meetings.

Through attending these meetings, we took on multiple roles. On the one hand, we were positioned as insiders within the international student community by the faculty investigators, who invited us to provide our feedback and insights regarding the research questions and the feasibility of data collection methods. Such practices pushed us to engage in reflexive practices (Guillemin & Gillam, 2004) by reflecting on our own encounters and challenges as international students, which in turn, enriched our discussions with the faculty investigators of this project. At our meetings, we often discussed how the international students were positioned and perceived, and what kinds of resources and services they mobilized to help their academic learning. Thus, our identity affordances kept us deeply engaged in the conversations with the investigators, which also contributed to our learning and internalization of the norms and practices of the academic discourse community. Furthermore, observing and participating in these discussions with established researchers in the field cultivated our research dispositions in that we learned to engage with theories and apply theoretical perspectives to understand seemingly mundane daily experiences.

Another crucial research disposition to which we were also often exposed at and through these meetings was inquiry-based thinking, which centers on (1) questioning and problematizing taken-for-granted thinking or practices, and (2) making visible hidden power relations or ideologies among our project team members and the student project participants, by critically examining them. For example, at one meeting, one of the faculty investigators brought up a concern about a normal practice at the writing center, in which writing center consultants would ask their clients to read their essays aloud. Both of us had been to the writing center before to get help with our own writing, and thus, we were familiar with the practice and had found it helpful in locating errors as well as identifying parts of our writing that did not flow well. Nevertheless, the first-year international students who participated in our project reported that they found the reading aloud activity unhelpful and even embarrassing, as they disliked hearing their own accented English pronunciation. This made us realize that, despite being international students ourselves, our advanced English proficiency exempted us from some experiences that undergraduate international students might often encounter. As this case illustrates, participating in such discussions trained us to reflect critically on certain institutional norms and widely accepted practices. Such critical reflection thus enabled us to interrogate hidden university curriculum agendas and ideologies, leading us to ask, for example, who benefits from such norms and practices, and who is excluded or marginalized by them. Because critical inquiry is an integral part of training for future researchers and scholars, our engagement in these inquiry-based meetings gave us opportunities to be socialized into thinking like academics.

On the other hand, for the field researchers, we were positioned as insiders in the project leadership team because we often served as intermediaries between the faculty investigators and the field researchers; the former required us to give the latter instructions, update them on the project's new developments, and collect their feedback on behalf of the leading investigators. Moreover, given the complex power dynamics between professors and graduate students (the field researchers were graduate students enrolled in one of Peter's courses), we often became their go-to people when they encountered problems during data collection. Nevertheless, this insider identity, enacted during our interactions with the field researchers, was mitigated by the fact that we were their student peers in the same graduate program. Therefore, embedded in these interactions that shaped how we were positioned were different power relations, namely: (1) the power relations between Peter and us; (2) the power relations between the other faculty investigators and us; and (3) the power relations between us and the field researchers. Therefore, a significant part of our academic socialization entailed us learning to negotiate our own identities as graduate students and as fellow researchers, while also carrying out research responsibilities in an ethical manner (De Costa *et al.*, 2020).

Serving the Community through Sharing our Findings: Acting Like an Academic

As Weng (2020) rightly observed, serving the public constitutes an important part of one's academic repertoire. Therefore, the important part of our participation in the project has been to share the project's findings in different venues and to advance the understanding of the topic in the field, and thus fulfill the role of being a citizen scholar. As mentioned, the goals of our research project were to (1) provide a better understanding of how undergraduate international students deploy the strategies and resources at their disposal to meet their first-year writing course demands; and (2) shed light on how first-year writing instructors and writing center consultants could work together to better help international students with their academic writing. To fulfill these goals, we first organized workshops for both the first-year writing program and the writing center program on campus. We recognized that at these workshops, and in contrast to conference presentations, sharing our findings should not be the only goal: rather, teachers and consultants coming to the workshops expected to see how the findings could be applied to their teaching and consultation work. Therefore, we invited our presenters to focus on the pedagogical implications of the project. In addition, we also understood that the workshops could be transformed into a space for professional development, i.e. instructors and consultants could share their in-class interaction experiences with these students.

The findings of the project, due to its longitudinal and ethnographic nature, could illuminate another part of the international student experience: reporting what these students were doing outside the classroom. Such illumination contributed to a more comprehensive understanding of international students' learning experiences. In light of the number of international students at US universities, we also expected the findings of our project to be of interest to scholars and teachers in other higher education contexts. Therefore, we submitted colloquium proposals to different US-based conferences (CCCC, SLRF, TESOL and Watson), which we discussed earlier. Fortunately, our proposals were accepted by all these conferences, and we have been able to share our findings with broader audiences.

Attending the conferences provided ample opportunities to be socialized into the academic community. First, Peter, who was the co-organizer of the colloquia, always treated us as fellow organizers and as fellow scholars. Therefore, we were also often perceived as emerging scholars rather than as graduate students by our academic peers at these conferences. Such positioning also empowered us to have our own voices as academics while engaging in constructive discussion and dialogue. Second, as we led colloquia, we felt keenly the purpose of sharing our findings at conferences. When leading these colloquia, we were often approached by instructors from different institutions with inquiries about international students in their respective classrooms and campuses. Our research was also of interest to scholars working in similar areas. For example, the author of the Afterword to this edited volume, Dr Wenhao Diao, was invited to be a discussant in our 2019 SLRF colloquium. At this event, she not only synthesized each of the presentations but also extended current discussions on second language socialization to include *lingua franca* socialization in multilingual academic contexts. She also rightly pointed out that second language socialization often occurs through peer socialization, often observed when non-native speakers socialize with other non-native speakers through practices of translanguaging (Diao, 2016). This insight became a great inspiration to us and was incorporated into the research of one of the contributors to the volume. Thus, as colloquia organizers, we were privileged to engage in various academic conversations with other scholars, develop our own academic networks, and most importantly develop our understanding of academic practices. As graduate students, we were encouraged to present our research at conferences and to publish our findings. But it is the experience of being the project managers of a large collaborative project, and organizers of multiple colloquia, that helped us understand how the act of dissemination gives rise to innovative and insightful ideas that advance current discussions in the field. In addition, these experiences have been inspiring, encouraging us to engage in similar activities in the future.

Discussion

Throughout this project, we engaged in academic socialization as we gained and expanded our social and cultural capital. As novice researchers, we participated in the community of practice, gaining knowledge about the norms and conventions in the academic community (e.g. Darvin & Norton, 2015; Morita, 2009). As noted, Peter hired us as project managers, mentored us when we wrote to other scholars, and guided us to take leading roles in meetings. He extended his own social capital to us when he introduced us to other scholars and faculty members, further enabling our ability to become emergent scholars and to develop our own academic networks. By soliciting our feedback on the grant proposal he wrote, he helped us learn how to organize a grant proposal. When we worked on the book proposal, Peter shared exemplary book proposals he had previously submitted to other publishers, and he explained the key features of the book proposal writing genre to us. This practice helped us gain experience in proposal writing. The processes of submitting grant proposals and abstracts for conferences are informed by the ideologies of reviewers, authors, book editors and publishers. Because a collaborative project involves the negotiation of institutional and disciplinary ideologies, writing collaboratively is a socialization process (Corcoran & Clark, 1984; Darling & Staton, 1989; Darvin & Norton, 2019; Duff, 2010). When writing abstracts for conferences and the book, we drafted them and sought feedback from our project faculty investigators, thus enabling us to participate in another kind of academic discourse (Kobayashi *et al.*, 2017). The extent to which we accepted the suggestions of established members of the community subsequently determined and shaped what we wrote.

The dynamics surrounding the negotiation of identities in the community of practice were manifested in how we developed our identities in our applied linguistics academic discourse community. Our identities have been shaped through our social interactions with others (e.g. De Costa, 2011; Norton, 2013). Beginning as legitimate peripheral participants, we learned how to organize meetings, lead workshops and write proposals. As we transitioned from being graduate students to project managers, and subsequently to co-authors and co-editors, we found ourselves taking different roles depending on the circumstances. Particularly when leading workshops and co-authoring papers with other faculty members, we applied our newly acquired symbolic capital of authorship and leadership in our academic community (e.g. Darvin & Norton, 2015).

In our academic socialization, a complex dynamic of power emerged from the competing ideologies of faculty members and field researchers (i.e. our fellow graduate students). Similar to the participants in Wang in Chapter 9 of this volume, we sought help from the faculty members and students by having conversations about managing and negotiating different tasks in this collaborative project. As a means of academic socialization, a collaborative project can be a space that is characterized by asymmetrical distributions of power, particularly between faculty members and students. Being able to hear voices from both sides, as project managers, we tried our best to communicate concerns between faculty and students as effectively and equitably as possible. Like the workings of power, ideologies are unbalanced in academic society (Weng, 2020). Nevertheless, we strove for balance in order to achieve the goals of our project, and to contribute to the negotiation of ideologies in the academic community by playing the role of brokers between faculty members and the student field researchers.

To shape our identities as scholars, we invested in our academic socialization throughout the process of this project. We were third-year graduate students when the project began but we felt that we were ready to start our formal academic careers. As we eagerly participated in this project, we switched our identity from that of a graduate student to that of beginning scholars, in ways that reflected the experiences of doctoral students reported in previous studies (e.g. Morita, 2000, 2009). In other words, we developed both a better understanding of academic careers in applied linguistics and the role of faculty in our field. Our experience as project managers serves as an example both of academic socialization and the importance of engagement with the academic community through the variety of roles and tasks we took throughout the process of this project.

Conclusion

As we engaged in academic socialization, our identities constituted, and were constituted by, interactions with faculty members, peers and many others in this project. By extending his capital (economic, social and cultural), Peter helped us to develop our identities by having us communicate, think and act like academics. This, in turn, enabled us to secure a legitimate place in academic society. At the same time, he contributed to our growth as emergent scholars in an applied linguistics community of practice, a community in which we now have a greater and more invested membership.

Note

(1)   SLRF = Second Language Research Forum; TESOL = Teaching English for Speakers of Other Language; CCCC = Conference on College Composition and Communication.

References

Anderson, T. (2017) The doctoral gaze: Foreign PhD students' internal and external academic discourse socialization. *Linguistics and Education* 37, 1–10.
Austin, A.E. (2002) Preparing the next generation of faculty: Graduate school as socialization to the academic career. *The Journal of Higher Education* 73 (1), 94–122.

Bourdieu, P. (1986) The forms of capital. In J.F. Richardson (ed.) *Handbook of Theory and Research for the Sociology of Education* (pp. 241–258). New York: Greenwood Press.

Corcoran, M. and Clark, S.M. (1984) Professional socialization and contemporary career attitudes of three faculty generations. *Research in Higher Education* 20, 131–153.

Darling, A.L. and Staton, A.Q. (1989) Socialization of graduate teaching assistants: A case study in an American university. *International Journal of Qualitative Studies in Education* 2 (3), 221–235.

Darvin, R. and Norton, B. (2015) Identity and a model of investment in applied linguistics. *Annual Review of Applied Linguistics* 35, 36–56.

Darvin, R. and Norton, B. (2019) Collaborative writing, academic socialization, and the negotiation of identity: Authors, mentors, and gatekeepers. In P. Habibie and K. Hyland (eds) *Novice Writers and Scholarly Publication: Authors, Mentors, Gatekeepers* (pp. 177–194). London: Palgrave Macmillan.

De Costa, P.I. (2011) Using language ideology and positioning to broaden the SLA learner beliefs landscape: The case of an ESL learner from China. *System* 39 (3), 347–358.

De Costa, P.I., Lee, J., Rawal, H. and Li, W. (2020) Ethics in applied linguistics research. In J. McKinley and H. Rose (eds) *The Routledge Handbook of Research in Applied Linguistics* (pp. 122–130). New York: Routledge.

Diao, W. (2016) Peer socialization into gendered L2 Mandarin practices in a study abroad context: Talk in the dorm. *Applied Linguistics* 37 (5), 599–620.

Douglas Fir Group (2016) A transdisciplinary framework for SLA in a multilingual world. *The Modern Language Journal* 100 (S1), 19–47.

Duff, P.A. (2010) Language socialization into academic discourse communities. *Annual Review of Applied Linguistics* 30, 169–192.

Guillemin, M. and Gillam, L. (2004) Ethics, reflexivity, and 'ethically important moments' in research. *Qualitative Inquiry* 10 (2), 261–280.

Kobayashi, M., Zappa-Hollman, S. and Duff, P. (2017) Academic discourse socialization. *Language Socialization* 8, 239–254.

Lave, J. and Wenger, E. (1991) *Situated Learning: Legitimate Peripheral Participation*. Cambridge: Cambridge University Press.

Morita, N. (2000) Discourse socialization through oral classroom activities in a TESL graduate program. *TESOL Quarterly* 34 (2), 279–310.

Morita, N. (2009) Language, culture, gender, and academic socialization. *Language and Education* 23, 443–460.

Norton, B. (2013) *Identity and Language Learning: Extending the Conversation* (2nd edn). Bristol: Multilingual Matters.

Seloni, L. (2012) Academic literacy socialization of first year doctoral students in US: A micro-ethnographic perspective. *English for Specific Purposes* 31 (1), 47–59.

Weng, T.H. (2020) On becoming a doctoral student: Chinese doctoral students' socialization of capital and habitus in academia. *British Journal of Sociology of Education* 41 (4), 1–19.

Part 1: Literacy Practices and Identity Development

3 Second Language Academic Discourse Socialization, Identity and Agency: The Case of a Chinese International Student

Xiaowan Zhang

Introduction

In response to the rapid increase in Chinese international students attending US postsecondary institutions (Huang, 2016), many institutions provide a variety of academic and social resources – e.g. English as a second language (ESL) courses, writing center services, academic writing courses, and student-to-student conversation programs – to Chinese and other international students to facilitate their academic participation and success (Martirosyan *et al.*, 2019). Despite such efforts, research has shown that international students, particularly Chinese students, experience considerable difficulty acquiring English academic discourses, literacies and cultures (e.g. De Costa *et al.*, 2016).

A growing body of research has sought to understand international students' academic and social experiences in postsecondary institutions from a language socialization perspective. Much of this research has focused on how international students, particularly those who speak English as a second language (L2), participate in L2 academic discourses of their target communities through interactions with more experienced members of the community and through engagement in various affordances and resources in the L2 learning environment (e.g. Anderson, 2016; Duff, 2002; Morita, 2004, 2009; Okuda & Anderson, 2018; Waterstone, 2008). Despite the rise in L2 socialization studies, few have investigated L2 students' academic discourse socialization experiences beyond a single context (e.g. the classroom), which thus limits the understanding of the role of context in L2 socialization. With this study, I contribute to existing L2 socialization research by examining the L2 academic discourse socialization experience of a Chinese undergraduate, Charles. Specifically, I explore how this socialization took place in a variety of academic and social contexts, including the university writing center, a writing classroom, and several out-of-class contexts, such as the dorm and basketball court. I have also sought to understand how Charles constructed and negotiated his roles, positionalities and agentive stances in these contexts as well as how his identity and agency influenced his L2 socialization process. To do so, I traced longitudinally Charles' L2 socialization trajectory for four months, from September through December 2017, using an ethnographic case study approach.

Academic Discourse Socialization, Identity and Agency

As postsecondary institutions in North America become more culturally and linguistically diverse, a growing body of research has focused on the processes by which L2 learners from non-English-speaking backgrounds become socialized into English-dominant academic discourses and practices. This process, more generally known as 'L2 academic discourse socialization,' is concerned with how L2 learners acquire oral and written academic discourses and gain participation, competence and membership in a given L2 academic discourse community. From a sociocultural perspective, academic discourse is not just 'an entity' but 'a social, cognitive, and rhetorical process and an accomplishment, a form of enculturation, social practice, positioning, representation, and stance-taking' (Duff, 2010: 170). All these social features inherent in academic discourse make it a potentially rich site of 'identity work' and of 'negotiation of institutional and disciplinary ideologies and epistemologies' (Duff, 2010: 170) as L2 learners are socialized through, and to, the use of L2 academic discourses.

Early research on L2 academic discourse socialization drew heavily on traditional language socialization theory, which broadly examined how newcomers to a culture (typically, young children) acquire the linguistic and cultural practices of the community for greater participation and competence (Ochs & Schieffelin, 2008; see Morita & Kobayashi, 2008 for a review of studies on L2 academic discourse socialization). An important distinction made in traditional language socialization models is that between *experts* and *newcomers* in a given community: while *experts*, or more experienced members in the community, are the primary agent in the socialization process, *newcomers*, or less experienced individuals who seek community membership, are passive and complicit recipients of the expert's transmission of linguistic and cultural practices (Duff & Doherty, 2015). Language socialization, by the traditional definitions of *newcomers* and *experts*, occurs in a unidirectional, deterministic and prescriptive manner.

Such a traditional view of language socialization has been increasingly challenged by the emerging research on L2 socialization on various grounds (e.g. Anderson, 2016; Duff, 2002; Morita, 2004, 2009; Okuda & Anderson, 2018; Waterstone, 2008). Importantly, recent work on L2 academic discourse socialization has revealed that newcomer L2 learners engage in complex and dynamic socialization processes facilitated by negotiations of identities (i.e. the learner's 'subjectives' or 'subject positions' in relation to other participants in the community; Duff, 2012: 415) and the exercise of agentive power (i.e. the power to 'make informed choices, exert influence, resist, or comply' despite the constraints imposed by the social context; Duff, 2012: 413). In addition, L2 learners also actively draw from their home languages and literacies to help navigate the academic demands and challenges, and to facilitate their L2 socialization (see Straayer-Gannon & Wang, Chapter 4, this volume; and Wang, Chapter 9, this volume, for a detailed discussion). For example, Morita (2004, 2009) examined the L2 academic discourse socialization of a group of Japanese students studying in a Canadian university. Her findings highlighted the tensions between the newcomer students and their expert teachers in various social aspects of L2 socialization, as well as the agency possessed by the students to negotiate their participation and positionalities. Morita (2004), for example, found a 27-year-old female master's student, Rie, actively resisted her marginalized status in a doctoral-level course. Rie attempted to re-position herself as a legitimate participant by (1) vocally articulating the difficulty she encountered when attempting to participate in class, and (2) requesting the instructor to make adjustments in her teaching. Her requests, however, were rejected by the instructor, who positioned Rie as a deficient non-English speaker with language barriers. While the instructor believed Rie's language barrier was her 'personal problem' that she should work on, Rie believed it was part of the instructor's responsibility to accommodate different learners and meet their unique needs. Such unsuccessful negotiation led Rie to cope with her marginalized status through a form of 'nonparticipation' (Norton, 2001), which, as Morita commented, is 'nevertheless a way of coping and exercising her personal agency' (Morita, 2004: 594).

Another interesting case is reported by Waterstone (2008), who interviewed a 27-year-old Ukrainian undergraduate student, Susan, regarding her opinions about being positioned as an ESL learner. Susan resisted being called an ESL learner, because such a positionality denied her complex experiences with English and her identities as a good student, a past English major and a former English teacher. Meanwhile, Susan internalized such a positionality and wanted to speak and write English as a native speaker. How Susan accepted or rejected the feedback from her writing consultant illustrated her contradictory identifications:

on the one hand, Susan wanted to revise her papers following the writing consultant's suggestions, so as to be accepted by native speakers of English; on the other hand, she exercised her agency as a good student by critically evaluating the suggested edits and rejecting those she disagreed with.

A more recent cross-case study by Okuda and Anderson (2018) further revealed that not all experts, such as supervisors and writing center consultants, are good, competent L2 socializers. The authors focused on the academic discourse socialization experiences of three Chinese graduate students, who all reported having encountered considerable challenges integrating into the academic discourse community at a Canadian university. While each student actively sought to improve their L2 writing skills, only one of them, Blenda, was successful in doing so by strategically negotiating her linguistic needs and expectations with her writing consultant. Okuda and Anderson pointed out that students' supervisors, who were supposed to provide adequate mentoring and written feedback, failed to fulfill their responsibility of socializing L2 students. The writing center also failed to serve as an effective L2 socializer as its *nonproofreading* philosophy prevented writing consultants from providing form-focused guidance that was aligned to the needs of the participants (see Son, Chapter 6, this volume, who also discusses international students' experiences at the writing center).

In sum, the studies described above have provided rich evidence that challenges the traditional, deterministic view of language socialization. Collectively, these studies have suggested that newcomers are not necessarily passive receivers in L2 socialization; nor are experts necessarily competent socializers. Moreover, the studies have highlighted the dynamic, socially situated interplays between identity position, agency and L2 learning: rather than passively accept the knowledge, practices and ideologies transmitted by the experts, newcomer L2 learners may negotiate their academic and linguistic needs and expectations through exertion of agency (e.g. Rie's non-participation and Susan's evaluation of the consultant's feedback) to achieve their own academic and linguistic goals; in addition, L2 learners may negotiate their roles, positionalities and identities relative to experts to gain better access to opportunities in a given L2 academic discourse community.

While these studies have provided valuable information about the relationship between L2 academic socialization, identity and agency, few of them have extended their investigation beyond a single (and somewhat isolated) social or academic context of L2 socialization (e.g. the writing center in Okuda & Anderson, 2018) (see Straayer-Gannon & Wang, Chapter 4, this volume, who also examined international students' literacy practices across different academic contexts). This hence limits the contribution of these studies to understanding (1) how L2 students engage in multiple socialization resources, and (2) how L2 socialization shapes and is shaped by locally constructed identities and agentive stances in different social and academic contexts. Given that most postsecondary institutions nowadays provide a variety of multi-sited academic and social resources to support L2 students' academic discourse socialization (Martirosyan *et al.*, 2019), there is a need for research that investigates L2 academic discourse socialization across a wider variety of learning events and contexts (Kobayashi *et al.*, 2017).

I address this gap by examining the L2 academic discourse socialization experience of a Chinese international student, Charles, in two academic contexts, the writing center and an introductory writing course (FYW 100, as will be described in the next section), and multiple social contexts outside of the classroom, such as the dorm and basketball court. Similar to the focal students in the studies cited above (e.g. Rie and Susan), Charles was a newcomer L2 learner to an American university who sought to succeed in the English academic community. The purpose of this study is two-fold: (1) to examine whether and to what extent Charles made use of various resources surrounding him in his L2 academic discourse socialization (including the writing center, FYW 100, and the social networks he was exposed to in the community); and (2) to understand the roles, positionalities and agentive stances that Charles negotiated in different L2 socialization contexts. To help achieve this, I draw on more recent language socialization models (Duff, 2010; Duff & Doherty, 2015) that describe language socialization as a dynamic, complex, and bi-/multi-directional process, and that foreground *newcomers'* agentive power both to selectively appropriate the L2 community's dominant discourses and to internalize, challenge or resist identities and roles imposed onto them.

This study was guided by three research questions:

(1) How was Charles' L2 academic discourse socialization mediated by the surrounding resources – the writing center, an introductory writing course and various social networks – to which he had access?
(2) What roles or positionalities did Charles negotiate in various social and academic contexts (e.g. the writing center, the FYW 100 classroom and his dorm)?
(3) What are the relationships between agency, positionality and context in Charles' L2 academic discourse socialization?

Methodology

Participants and context

In this study, I will focus on two major types of writing resource available to all students at Great Lake University: an introductory writing course, i.e. the FYW 100, and the university writing center. The objective of FYW 100 was to prepare students for smooth transitions to college-level writing, reading and researching. A second course, FYW 101, had the same course objective but covered more advanced content than FYW 100.

The university writing center aimed at providing convenient writing help and service to students and was an important writing resource available to Great Lake University's students. The majority of the writing center's consultants, as listed on its website, were undergraduate students with liberal arts backgrounds. At the time of the study, no consultants listed any educational or instructional backgrounds or TESOL qualifications.

The focal participant of this study, Charles, was recruited from a FYW 100 section in Fall 2017. Charles was a male freshman student from mainland China. He was born and raised in China and had graduated from a public high school in China right before he started his first semester at Great Lake University in Fall 2017. Charles was admitted to Great Lake University with a composite TOEFL score of 85. At Great Lake University, freshmen seeking admissions to a degree-granting college would only be accepted after accomplishing a designated combination or sequence of courses (totaling a minimum of 28 credits) required by the target college. Since Charles indicated supply chain management (which was under the business college) as his preferred major, he enrolled in five courses in fall 2017 to fulfill the pre-entrance course requirement set by the business college. In addition to FYW 100, Charles took one course in math, one in biology, one in social studies and one in kinetics. It is worth noting that admissions to the business college was extremely competitive at Great Lake University and was contingent on a high cumulative grade point average (GPA), rich experiences in extracurricular activities, as well as a demonstration of desirable personal traits. In light of these demanding admissions requirements, Charles worked hard over the course of his study to become a qualified candidate for his dream program in supply chain management.

Data sources

Data were collected over a four-month period from September through December 2017 regarding Charles' experiences with the two types of academic writing resources – FYW 100 and the writing center – and his social networks inside and outside the academic contexts. To enable data triangulation, I collected multiple sources of data through a background survey, two interviews, two classroom observations (FYW 100 only), and two writing center observations. All interviews and observations (except for the observation of Charles' first writing center visit) were audio-recorded. Because the two interviews were conducted in Chinese, I translated them into English after data collection had finished. Each interview lasted for about 40 minutes. Other data collected included

Table 3.1 Data sources and data collection timeline

Method	Data	Data collection time (2017)
Offline observation	Writer center: Field notes and audio-recorded consultations	09/24* and 11/01
	FYW 100: Field notes and audio-recorded classroom interactions	10/20 and 11/14
Survey	Background information such as TOEFL scores, high school education background, travel experiences, etc.	10/10
Interview	Two audio-recorded interviews with the participant	10/10 and 11/21
Artifact	Writing assignments, course syllabi, assignment instructions	9/24 through 12/31
Online observation	Social media interactions (WeChat, QQ, Facebook, Twitter, Instagram and Weibo)	9/24 through 12/31

*The observation was not recorded due to Institutional Review Board (IRB) restrictions.

Charles' social media posts, artifacts and literacy logs. Table 3.1 displays a complete list of data sources and a timeline of data collection.

Data analysis

I conducted data analysis inductively and iteratively by examining all data sources concurrently and recursively for categories and themes that informed Charles' L2 socialization process. I first read through the data to obtain a holistic understanding of the academic and social resources Charles had access to. During my second reading, I highlighted the parts that described Charles' L2 discourse socialization experiences in relation to his use of various resources at his disposal. In a third reading, I then generated a list of initial categories based on recurring themes in the data, including identity negotiation, personal agency, resistance, language ideology and legitimacy. I expanded this initial list upon subsequent readings following the suggestions of Duff (2012) for investigating agency and identity in second language acquisition. Specifically, I paid special attention to the pronouns and categorical noun phrases used by Charles in his descriptions of different people for the purpose of understanding his identities; in addition, I made special notes for (1) the linguistic markers Charles used to differentiate between voluntary choices and requirements (e.g. 'chose' vs. 'required to'); (2) the decisions he made regarding the preferred means of socialization (e.g. 'went to the teacher for questions'); and (3) the critical incidents and interactions he had with other participants in the same community where he complied with, resisted or contested his identities, positionalities or roles. A final list of categories was compiled based on the themes and categories generated in this stage with similar themes and categories collapsed or combined.

Researcher's role

Charles and I shared similar linguistic, cultural and educational backgrounds: both of us were born and raised in mainland China, we both spoke Chinese as our first language (L1), we received kindergarten through 12th-grade education in China and were studying at Great Lake University as international students. Although I was a master's student when I first came to the United States, I had similar experiences as Charles did in attempting to integrate into an English-dominant academic discourse community. I empathized with Charles' eager desire to achieve academic success and also understood the struggles and difficulties he faced in an unfamiliar environment where he needed to rely on an L2 to survive or prosper academically. Our shared backgrounds promoted good rapports between us, thanks to which Charles was willing to share his thoughts with me during and outside our interviews. Throughout this study, I maintained my role as a reflexive researcher, while I also positioned myself as a friend and resource to Charles and helped him whenever I could with any questions that he had about academic or personal issues.

Results

In this section, I will present Charles' L2 academic discourse socialization experiences in relation to his use of three types of academic and social resources of interest: the university writing center, the FYW 100 course, and the social networks he was exposed to inside and outside the classroom. While the first two types of resources provided Charles with primarily academic support, the third one had the potential to facilitate Charles' L2 socialization both academically and socially.

Writing center

Charles started participating in this study about a month into his first semester at Great Lake University. At that time, he had just finished writing a draft of his first writing assignment for FYW 100. Out of good intentions, the instructor of FYW 100, Ms Huang (pseudonym), required all her students, including Charles, to visit the writing center at least twice to edit their draft essays for their first and second writing assignments. I observed Charles' two writing center visits and had an interview with him after each of his visits.

Although Charles had two different consultants in his two writing-center visits, the procedures of these two consultations were not significantly different. Both consultants asked if Charles was willing to read his essay aloud from the beginning to the end. While Charles was doing so, the consultants frequently stopped him after he read every one to two sentences to point out errors. They provided corrections orally and waited for Charles to make the corrections, and then asked Charles to resume reading aloud. The consultants did a meticulous job in identifying and addressing the micro-level writing issues in Charles' essays, including punctuation, spelling, word choices and grammatical mistakes, but neither paid attention to the content of Charles' essays or the message that Charles tried to convey through his essays. The whole editing process was dominated by the consultants, who gave intensive form-focused corrective feedback (Ellis, 2017) with little explanation about why a correction should be supplied. Almost no questions were asked by the consultants or by Charles throughout the consultations.

Excerpt 1 presents part of the conversation between Charles and his second writing consultant. The way in which the consultant provided corrective feedback in Excerpt 1 was representative of the remainder of the consultation.

Excerpt 1 (from the recording of Charles' second writing center visit):

1 **Charles:** (reading aloud his essay) When the …(unintelligible word) comes to China, the people in the China spent a lot of time becoming practitioner due to they are longing for their own purification.

2 **Tutor:** OK, so 'due to they are,' so 'due to they are' doesn't quite flow. But there is a…(not finished)

3 **Charles:** 'Due to' is just an alternative of 'because.'

4 **Tutor:** Yeah, I was gonna say, 'let's use because.' That'll work better in this situation.

5 **Charles:** (Typing the correction on his laptop)

In Excerpt 1, the consultant tried to correct Charles' use of 'due to.' When the consultant was about to offer a correction in Turn 2, Charles cut him short by explaining that 'due to' was an alternative to 'because,' asserting implicitly that he was confident about what he wanted to convey through this phrase. Turn 2 can also be interpreted as an attempt by Charles to negotiate his participation and positionality: while the consultant positioned Charles as an L2 learner who was not able to make correct word choices and a passive error corrector, Charles attempted to re-position himself as a legitimate writer who was able to make rational word choices and who was an active contributor to the consultation. Unfortunately, the consultant ignored the 'negotiation' request from Charles and continued his pursuit of correction in Turn 4. Even worse, the consultant did not explain to Charles why 'because' was a better word choice than 'due to.' Charles gave up his negotiation after Turn 4 and silently replaced 'due to' with 'because.'

It is worth noting here that, although Charles did not speak much during his writing center visits, he was always eager to express his own understanding of English writing during our interviews. Viewing English writing was 'an art,' Charles preferred 'concise and simple' writing styles over 'complex and sophisticated' ones. Moreover, Charles believed Chinese writing and English writing were 'transferable,' as he explained to me in our first interview:

Excerpt 2

Although the Chinese classes I took in high school do not seem to be relevant to English writing, [they are actually quite relevant]. My Chinese teachers would always spare some time in class for us to practice writing. Sometimes we would devote a whole class to writing practices. We discussed different types of genres and readings in each Chinese writing class. To me, writing development more or less involves reading development and the accumulation of knowledge through reading. Although I did not accumulate much during my high school years, there is still something that can help me in writing. All languages have something in common because they are a product of human culture. No matter what languages you are learning as a second language, whether it is English, Japanese, or Korean, as long as you write, your writing experiences in your native language will always contribute to your second language writing.

The impression Charles left on me during the interviews – as an enthusiastic and devoted English writer – stood in stark contrast to his passiveness and reticence at the writing center, where he was treated as an English learner with writing problems that needed to be corrected. I was not surprised to hear Charles say he was disappointed with the academic support provided by the writing center. When I asked Charles whether the consultants' corrective feedback had helped him solve his language problems, Charles answered 'No' and expressed strong resistance to the label of an English learner with language problems. He said:

Excerpt 3

I don't need help with language problems because I do not have any. I achieved good TOEFL scores. I was exempted from taking ESL courses. And I was not admitted to the university on a conditional offer.

To Charles, 'ESL' was a stigmatizing label suggesting an English language deficit, which was opposite to his own evaluation of his English proficiency level. Charles told me he had always been an excellent student in his high school English classes and was even exempted by his teacher from doing homework because of his good English skills. Charles' confidence in his English proficiency led him to position himself as a legitimate English writer. For this reason, he expected to be advised by the writing consultants on 'macro-level issues' such as 'essay structure and sentence variety' that any writer may struggle with. Because what he received at the writing center was feedback on 'small things like punctuation,' Charles dismissed such feedback as 'meaningless' and 'a waste of time.' Facetiously, he compared the writing consultants to the 'Word' software, saying their function was to 'underline the errors in an essay and suggest corrections.' Charles explained why he did not need corrective feedback (Excerpt 4):

Excerpt 4

I made those mistakes because I was not being careful... Of course I knew how to write in the correct way. I don't think these corrections they made would help me in any real sense because I will naturally pick up these things after I receive more exposure to English.

Charles' resistance to the writing center also manifested itself in his investment in the consultations: while he booked a one-hour consultation for his first visit, he intentionally booked a shorter session of half an hour for his second visit in order to minimize his time investment in the writing center. Moreover, Charles refused to schedule additional appointments beyond the two visits required by Ms Huang, despite an invitation from the second consultant for Charles to go back and work on the unfinished part.

FYW 100

Unlike Charles' resistance to the writing center, his attitudes towards FYW 100 were contrastively positive. According to Charles, what he learned from the FYW 100 was strikingly different from, and much more helpful than, what he was offered at the writing center. He made the following comparison between the writing center and FYW 100:

Excerpt 5

What we are being taught in FYW 100 is concrete stuff ranging from writing introduction to discipline-related writing techniques. The teacher also provided us with plenty of examples. All these things make me feel there have been some real changes in my understanding of English writing, such as how I should write and what I can add to make my essay look more colorful and refined. But for the writing center, the only function it has is to waste my time. So I would advise other students not to go there.

In contrast to the form-focused corrective feedback offered by the writing center, the content of FYW 100 placed greater emphasis on 'concrete' writing skills, such as techniques for refining an essay.

The focus of FYW 100 on more macro aspects of writing was closely aligned with what Charles believed he needed to work on in his English writing.

In FYW 100, Charles was never positioned as an English learner with language problems. He told me that Ms Huang rarely corrected him on grammar or other small issues:

Excerpt 6

Our (FYW 100) teacher does not teach grammar at all because we have been learning and practicing grammar since the middle and high school grades… she won't correct my grammatical errors when she grades my essays because those are all small things that have little to do with the overall structure of the essay. For example, if someone writes an article in a messy order… misplacing each word in a sentence. I meant when someone is writing in Chinese, even though every word is placed in an unconventional order, people can still understand what the author means… you would be awed at how amazing the author is when you finally get the gist of his writing… grammar is just too trivial as compared with the organization of an article.

Moreover, Ms Huang encouraged Charles and other international students in her class to draw on their L1 linguistic and cultural knowledge in English writing. A majority of the writing assignments Ms Huang gave to her students were designed to engage them in reflecting on the differences between English-dominant cultures and other cultures. Charles and other international students were therefore given an opportunity to write in English about the culture in which they were born and raised. Not only was Charles' knowledge about Chinese culture validated in FYW 100 but, also, his knowledge of the Chinese language. Being a Chinese–English bilingual herself, Ms Huang was able and willing to communicate with Charles and other Chinese students in both Chinese and English. Charles told me he would speak Chinese to Ms Huang outside class, and Ms Huang would use either English or Chinese to respond to him. Additionally, Charles and his Chinese group mates were allowed to use Chinese and English to talk with each other in small group discussions. In other words, Charles was positioned in FYW 100 as an emerging Chinese–English bilingual writer. Such a positionality resonated deeply with Charles' self-positioning. When I asked Charles about his views on him using Chinese in an English writing class, he answered:

Excerpt 7

We are not ESL students but are all qualified undergraduate students. We do not have any problems with English. So they [Ms Huang and other instructors in Great Lake University] do not have to require us to speak in English.

Charles' response demonstrated his strong resistance to being positioned as an English learner with language problems. He also justified his use of Chinese in FYW 100 by positioning himself as opposite to a deficient English learner.

Positioning himself as an adequate instead of a deficient English user, Charles spoke of himself as being an agent who actively made investment in FYW 100 inside and outside the classroom. He told me he worked much harder in FYW 100 than he did in his high school English classes. When he was in high school, Charles often slept through English classes and ignored the homework but, in FYW 100, he maintained excellent punctuality and attendance, listened carefully in class, spent extra time to chew on each assignment, and tried his best to incorporate what he learned in class in his essays. Charles also developed a habit of previewing the FYW 100 textbook: he would underline each new word in the textbook and looked it up in the dictionary. When he could not figure out the meaning of a word on his own, he would ask for help from his native English-speaking dormmates. Charles would also read the essays written by those students who received higher scores in writing, looking for their strengths, and he learned from their writing styles. These conscious efforts that Charles devoted to FYW 100 all stood in striking contrast with his minimized investment in the writing center.

Social networks

Charles told me at our first meeting that he did not have many Chinese friends. Soon I realized that Charles' lack of Chinese friends was not a result of social marginalization by his co-national peers but was, rather, a result of self social network selection. In our first interview, Charles expressed a strong aversion to his co-national peers from China, particularly those from a wealthy background, whom he described as 'rich, good-for-nothing students who took pride in skipping classes and purchasing luxurious goods.' Due to his disapproval of these rich Chinese students' acts, stances and activities, Charles said he deliberately steered away from other Chinese students on almost all social occasions, whether inside or outside the classroom. Charles also tried hard to distinguish himself from other Chinese students by identifying himself as a good, highly motivated and hard-working student.

One agentive act that Charles took to minimize his socialization with other Chinese students was to live in a residential hall that hosted fewer Chinese students. In addition, Charles chose to share a dorm room with three native speakers of English from the United States. Unlike many US international students, who found it hard to make friends with native speakers (e.g. see Zappa-Hollman & Duff, 2015), Charles said he and his three roommates got along well, probably because they had the same interests in sports and Japanese animations. They often watched sports games and Japanese animations together in the dorm and ate together in the cafeteria. Charles would also go to his roommates when he had questions related to English. Furthermore, Charles maintained a good relationship with several black students in his dorm building (including the student superintendent of his residential hall), with whom Charles often played video games and basketball.

Contrary to his friendly attitude towards domestic English-speaking students, Charles intentionally kept a distance from Chinese students whenever they were around him. Next, I illustrate this observation based on my observation of Charles' behavior in FYW 100.

Figure 3.1 is a seating chart that I created based on the field notes from my first classroom observation. Each oval represents a student. While more than 80% of the students in Charles' FYW 100 class were Chinese (15 out of 18), he only knew the two Chinese group mates in his small group. In the class I observed, Charles (Student 1) sat in the left front corner surrounded by me and his two male group mates (Students 2 and 3). In contrast, the majority of other Chinese students sat at the back of the room, occupying the last two rows. As one can see in Figure 3.1, the seat Charles picked was isolated from the rest of the class, which made it hard for Charles to communicate with students outside his small group. Based on my observation, the seven Chinese

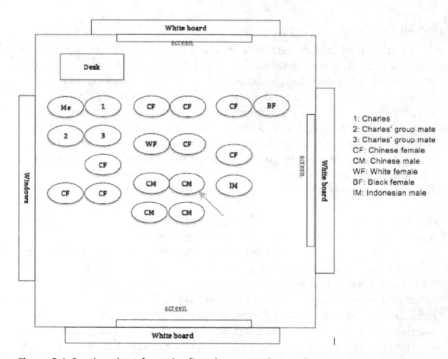

Figure 3.1 Seating chart from the first classroom observation

male students in Charles' class constituted two distinct camps: the front-row camp of three students, represented by Charles and his group mates who were punctual, well-disciplined and highly engaged in class, whereas the back-row camp of four students (the block of four Chinese males in the middle of the classroom), under the leadership of an American-high-school graduate (identified by the arrow in Figure 3.1), had poor class attendance and frequently disturbed classroom order by talking loudly among themselves or with the Indonesian male student sitting next to them. I observed no verbal or non-verbal exchanges between these two camps of Chinese male students throughout – and even after – the class, which further indicated they belonged to two different camps. When I asked Charles why he did not talk to the Chinese students sitting at the back, he simply said he did not know them and added that he did not feel the need to get to know them either. Charles also disclosed to me that it was not a random decision to stay within his small group: he did so deliberately because his group mates shared his attitudes toward wealthy Chinese students.

Charles even carried his indifference towards other Chinese students over to the basketball court. As an enthusiastic fan of basketball, Charles spent around three hours on the basketball court at least four days a week. He told me he made many good friends on the basketball court, including one 60-year-old player who used to represent Great Lake University's basketball team. Basketball also provided Charles with an opportunity to use English, as he described in the following excerpt:

Excerpt 8

Basketball is all about team communication. For example, the defense for this round can be two-three zone defense, three-two defense, one-three-one zone defense, or man-to-man defense. Regarding offence, it may be pick-and-roll or two-man screening. Each strategy needs to be clear among team members; if not, the team would be scattered around, and there could be a big chance of losing the game.

However, when I asked Charles whether he played basketball with other Chinese students, he gave me an unequivocal 'No' and said that he did not enjoy playing basketball with other Chinese students (Excerpt 9).

Excerpt 9 (from Interview 1):

1 XZ: So most of your friends are American?

2 Charles: Yes, most of them are American.

3 XZ: Except for your three American roommates, do you have other friends?

4 Charles: There are a lot of funny Americans on the same floor where my dorm is.

5 XZ:	So you also have opportunities to meet other Americans outside your dorm room?
6 Charles:	Yes.
7 XZ:	Any other opportunities to speak with Americans?
8 Charles:	Yeah, on the basketball court, and the interaction is mostly daily talk. I don't like playing basketball with Chinese students because they are poor players.
9 XZ:	So you normally play basketball with Americans.
10 Charles:	Yes, I only play with them.

In Excerpt 9, Charles talked about his friends at Great Lake University: he enjoyed having his social network revolving around 'fun' Americans, and he refused to socialize with other Chinese students, who, in his eyes, were 'poor' basketball players. The adjectives Charles used to describe Americans and Chinese clearly reflected his different attitudes towards these two groups. Based on the evidence presented in this section, one can surmise that Charles was resistant to positioning himself as a Chinese student at Great Lake University: instead, he positioned himself as a good, motivated and hard-working student who was different from the majority of the Chinese students on campus.

Discussion

In this study, I investigated the L2 academic discourse socialization experience of Charles, a newcomer Chinese student to the US post-secondary academic community. I did so by following his interactions with other members in the same community across various academic and social contexts, including the university writing center, an introductory writing course (FYW 100), his dormitory building and the basketball court. I provided an in-depth, longitudinal examination of Charles' access to and use of the various academic and social resources surrounding him, through interviews and observations.

Charles' experiences indicated that identity negotiation was an integral part of his L2 academic discourse socialization, a finding that corroborates several previous studies (e.g. Morita, 2004, 2009, 2012; Waterstone, 2008). How Charles was positioned by the writing center and the instructor of FYW 100 considerably shaped his experiences with these two types of academic writing resource. At the writing center, Charles was treated as an ESL learner with language problems and was provided with intensive feedback on grammar, spelling, punctuation and other linguistic aspects of English. Charles strongly resisted such a positionality and the service provided by the writing center because, in his eyes, an ESL learner was a stigmatized label that suggested language deficit and incompetence. Such a positioning was opposite to Charles' own evaluation of his English proficiency (e.g. he was admitted to Great Lake University with a satisfactory TOEFL score) and his positionality of himself as a legitimate English writer, which therefore led Charles to reject and avoid the academic socialization support from the writing center. In contrast to Charles' resistance to the writing center was his acceptance of FYW 100, where he was positioned by the Chinese–English bilingual instructor as an emerging bilingual writer. In FYW 100, Charles was never picked on for his L2 grammar and he was encouraged by the instructor (Ms Huang) to draw on his L1 language and literacy skills to support his L2 writing. Because the way he was positioned by Ms Huang closely aligned with his self-positioning, Charles wholeheartedly embraced his L2 socialization experiences in FYW 100. The contrastive positionalities being imposed on Charles by the writing center and Ms Huang, and Charles' contrastive attitudes towards these positionalities, underline the importance of examining L2 socialization in multiple contexts. Doing so is important because postsecondary institutions like Great Lake University may offer multiple resources for L2 socialization that operate under different, even opposite, philosophies, with some casting a positive but others casting a less positive light on L2 learners' identities. As a result, L2 learners may hold different attitudes towards these L2 resources and utilize them differently, depending on how they are positioned. Situating L2 socialization investigations merely within a single context will thus result in an incomplete and probably skewed picture of L2 learners' socialization experiences.

My findings from this study further highlighted the complexity and situatedness of identity construction and negotiation and showed that an individual learner may take multiple and contradictory identities within and across contexts of L2 academic socialization (Morita, 2004, 2009, 2012; Waterstone, 2008). During our interviews, Charles revealed to me a variety of identities and roles that he sought to mobilize and balance in life: a Chinese–English bilingual, a legitimate English writer, a good and motivated student and a Chinese student who did not want to be identified with the wider Chinese student group. Despite his Chinese ethnic, linguistic and cultural backgrounds, Charles resisted socializing with his co-national peers due to his negative perception of his Chinese peers in the same academic community, particularly those from a wealthy background. This act of positioning, however, was in frequent contradiction to his identities that were contingent on his Chinese ethnicity. For example, in FYW 100, Charles had to socialize with other Chinese students in order to capitalize on his identity as a Chinese–English bilingual writer during group work. In order to balance his conflicting identities, Charles intentionally chose to stick with his small Chinese group (who had similar identities to Charles) throughout the course. These findings highlight the complexity of identity construction, suggesting that L2 learners may or may not identify with the ethnic, racial or other social identity category labels they are born with and may actively seek to reconcile themselves with the labels imposed on them that they subsequently resist. Importantly, this study underscores how L2 learners' construction of identities is situated: they may settle with different, sometimes contradictory identities in and through different L2 socialization contexts. It is therefore important that researchers and educators who work with L2 learners recognize the complexity and situatedness of identity given that L2 learners are often classified into presumably homogenous groups based on their ethnic/gender/linguistic/cultural backgrounds. Such oversimplified classifications may obliterate important differences within L2 learner subgroups. For instance, Charles and his group in FYW 100 may behave significantly differently from the other group of male Chinese students sitting in the back of the room (see Figure 3.1) despite their shared gender and ethnic backgrounds.

Agency was also foregrounded in different forms throughout Charles' L2 academic discourse socialization journey, exhibiting complex relationships with identity, positioning, investment and L2 learning (Duff, 2012). Charles' own agency enabled him to take control of his L2 writing socialization process by differentiating his investments in the writing center and FYW 100. Positioning himself as a legitimate English writer, Charles made a clear distinction between 'large, important' issues related to writing, such as structure and sentence variety, and 'small, meaningless' issues related to language, such as grammar, spelling and punctuation. Because writing center consultants advised him exclusively on 'small' language-related issues as if he were an ESL learner, Charles agentively resisted their practices, ideologies and positionalities of him as an ESL learner by minimizing his investment in the writing center. Not only did he shorten his second of the two required writing center visits on purpose, but he also discontinued the use of the writing center completely after the two mandatory visits. In contrast, Charles channeled considerably more investment into FYW 100, where he was given ample opportunities to learn 'large' writing-related issues as a legitimate bilingual writer. Charles' active investment in FYW 100 included but was not limited to excellent class attendance and punctuality, high-level attentiveness, active participation, careful homework completion and voluntary class preparation outside the classroom. Furthermore, agency enabled Charles to position himself as different from other Chinese students studying in the same academic community. Charles made various conscious and highly agentive efforts to keep a distance from his co-national peers. For instance, Charles chose to stay with three native-speaker roommates in the dorm, he distanced himself from the majority of Chinese students in class and he avoided playing basketball with other Chinese students. Through these agentive acts, Charles actively designed his L2 socialization path and selected the primary participants involved in his L2 socialization process.

Although he exercised his agency in a powerful manner, Charles' agency largely took a form of 'avoidance' and 'nonparticipation' (Norton, 2001), rather than active and strategic negotiations. For example, while he frequently negotiated his needs, expectations and identities in his interviews with me after his writing center visits, Charles seldom attempted to do so with the writing center consultants. Charles told me he did not care to do so because he could obtain the writing advice he needed from other sources, such as his FYW 100 instructor. However, what if Charles were not enrolled in FYW 100? Or what if he had not had a Chinese–English bilingual as his writing instructor? In those situations, Charles' agentive 'nonparticipation' might have resulted in no or little L2 learning and socialization, which could have yielded highly deleterious results. Future researchers interested in L2 socialization may want to pay more attention to agentive 'nonparticipation' and investigate the mechanism behind this type of agentive act as well as its ramifications on L2 socialization.

Pedagogical Implications

This study has two important implications for postsecondary institutions that struggle to provide effective resources to support their growing L2 student populations.

First, it is important that universities provide resources that are aligned with the needs and expectations of L2 learners. Taking writing centers as an example, the findings of this study and previous research on writing centers suggest that one type of writing service does not fit all student clients. While the three Chinese graduate students in Okuda and Anderson (2018) wanted and needed linguistic feedback but were not provided with such feedback at the writing center, Charles was provided with intensive linguistic feedback but dismissed it as 'useless.' This raises questions about the efficacy of training writing consultants to provide unified, standardized services to all student clients regardless of their needs. To more effectively help L2 students, who may have different writing needs than native-speaker students, writing centers should train consultants to listen to L2 learners' needs and carefully tailor their services to better accommodate these needs. It is important that consultants maintain effective communication with their L2 student clients throughout the consultation. In particular, consultants should give their L2 clients more opportunities to express their needs and expectations by asking more questions and by encouraging their clients to ask them questions.

Second, postsecondary institutions and their staff and faculty members should learn to view L2 students more positively by validating their L1 knowledge and identities. L2 students bring valuable linguistic and cultural assets into postsecondary institutions in North America. Their presence and participation in social and academic activities often serve as a great resource for native English-speaking students who want to expand their horizons and learn about other languages and cultures. Cross-cultural communications between L1 and L2 students will not only promote mutual understanding but will also prompt these students to discover the strengths and weaknesses of their own cultures, values and worldviews. However, healthy cross-cultural exchanges are only possible if L2 students are positioned positively and when their L1 language and literacy skills are validated and valued. Thus, pedagogical models that position L2 students as ESL learners with language deficits will likely demoralize L2 students and discourage them and cause them to refrain from integrating into the L2 community. This is notable in the case of Charles, who made an active investment in L2 writing when he was positively positioned as a bilingual writer but refused to do so when he was positioned as an ESL learner. Therefore, an asset-based approach is empowering because it considers students' home languages and literacies as assets and it explores how these assets can be utilized to facilitate their learning. As shown in Charles' case, he was encouraged to draw on his multilingual repertoires by Ms Huang, which contributed to his identity construction as a bilingual writer and also empowered him to resist the deficient positioning (see a detailed discussion of the asset-based pedagogy in Chapter 9 of this volume).

References

Anderson, T. (2016) Negotiating academic discourse practices, ideologies, and identities: The socialization of Chinese PhD students. Unpublished doctoral dissertation, University of British Columbia.

De Costa, P.I., Tigchelaar, M. and Cui, Y. (2016) Reflexivity and transnational habitus: The case of a 'poor' affluent Chinese international student. *AILA Review* 29, 173–198. https://doi.org/10.1075/aila.29.07dec.

Duff, P.A. (2002) The discursive co-construction of knowledge, identity, and difference: An ethnography of communication in the high school mainstream. *Applied Linguistics* 23 (3), 289–322. https://doi.org/10.1093/applin/23.3.289.

Duff, P.A. (2010) Language socialization into academic discourse communities. *Annual Review of Applied Linguistics* 30, 169–192. https://doi.org/10.1017/S0267190510000048.

Duff, P.A. (2012) Identity, agency, and second language acquisition. In S.M. Gass and A. Mackey (eds) *Handbook of Second Language Acquisition* (pp. 410–426). Abingdon: Routledge.

Duff, P.A. and Doherty, L. (2015) Examining agency in (second) language socialization research. In P. Deters, X. Gao, E.R. Miller and G. Vitanova (eds) *Theorizing and Analyzing Agency in Second Language Learning: Interdisciplinary Approaches* (pp. 54–72). Bristol: Multilingual Matters.

Ellis, R. (2017) Oral corrective feedback in language teaching: A historical perspective. *Avances En Educación y Humanidades* 2 (2), 7–22. https://doi.org/10.21897/25394185.1482.

Huang, X. (2016) Transnational Chinese students' literacy and networking practices. *Journal of Adolescent and Adult Literacy* 60 (6), 687–696. https://doi.org/10.1002/jaal.623.

Kobayashi, M., Zappa-Hollman, S. and Duff, P.A. (2017) Academic discourse socialization. In P.A. Duff and S. May (eds) *Language Socialization* (3rd edn, pp. 1–17). New York: Springer.

Martirosyan, N.M., Bustamante, R.M. and Saxon, D.P. (2019) Academic and social support services for international students: Current practices. *Journal of International Students* 9 (1), 172–191. https://doi.org/10.32674/jis.v9i1.275.

Morita, N. (2004) Negotiating participation and identity in second language academic communities. *TESOL Quarterly* 38 (4), 573–603. https://doi.org/10.2307/3588281.

Morita, N. (2009) Language, culture, gender, and academic socialization. *Language and Education* 23 (5), 443–460. https://doi.org/10.1080/09500780902752081.

Morita, N. (2012) Identity: The situated construction of identity and positionality in multilingual classrooms. In S. Mercer, S. Ryan and M. Williams (eds) *Psychology for Language Learning: Insights from Research, Theory, and Practice* (pp. 26–41). London: Palgrave Macmillan.

Morita, N. and Kobayashi, M. (2008) Academic discourse socialization in a second language. In P.A. Duff and N. Hornberger (eds) *Language Socialization* (2nd edn, pp. 243–55). New York: Springer.

Norton, B. (2001) Non-participation, imagined communities and the language classroom. In M.P. Breen (ed.) *Learner Contributions to Language Learning: New Directions in Research* (pp. 159–171). London: Pearson Education.

Ochs, E. and Schieffelin, B. (2008) Language socialization: An historical overview. In P.A. Duff and N.H. Hornberger (eds) *Language Socialization* (2nd edn, pp. 3–15). New York: Springer.

Okuda, T. and Anderson, T. (2018) Second language graduate students' experiences at the writing center: A language socialization perspective. *TESOL Quarterly* 52 (2), 391–413. https://doi.org/10.1002/tesq.406.

Waterstone, B. (2008) 'I hate the ESL idea!': A case study in identity and academic literacy. *TESL Canada Journal* 26 (1), 52. https://doi.org/10.18806/tesl.v26i1.390.

Zappa-Hollman, S. and Duff, P.A. (2015) Academic English socialization through individual networks of practice. *TESOL Quarterly* 49 (2), 333–368. https://doi.org/10.1002/tesq.188.

4 Reinventing Transnational Identities and Sponsors

Bree Straayer-Gannon and Xiqiao Wang

Research on transnational students' literacies has illuminated the ways in which literacy takes place under the influence of intersecting global and local forces. As transnational students negotiate myriad academic, social and career challenges, they draw on literacy, spatial and identity resources developed in spaces that span multiple geographical territories (Lam, 2009; Lorimer Leonard, 2017; Wang, 2019). Whereas previous research on transnational students' literacy and networking practices have focused on how students leverage existing and new networks in local and translocal contexts to perform agentive literacy identities, access linguistic, semiotic and literacy resources, and navigate institutional structures (Fraiberg *et al.*, 2017; Lam, 2009; Vieira, 2011; Wang, 2017), such research has yet to fully explore the experiences of transnational students with little access to existing networks due to their status as lone representatives of their cultural and linguistic backgrounds. This empirical study, drawing on interviews, participant observation and student artifacts, reports on the networking practices of Albina, a young woman from Ghana, concerning her literacy experiences across a bridge writing class (i.e. the FYW 100), a first-year writing class (i.e. the FYW 101) and a writing center (see Zhang, Chapter 3, this volume, who also traced a transnational student's academic socialization experiences across multiple sites).

Drawing on a mobility framework (Fraiberg *et al.*, 2017; Lorimer Leonard, 2017), we discuss the strategic moves and agentive stance the student deploys to develop an expanding and translocal network of literacy sponsors (Brandt, 2001). In so doing, we describe how such networks allow the mobilization of multiple linguistic, literacy and professional resources that mediate her transnationally grounded, activist agenda and identity (see Fraiberg, Chapter 8, this volume, who adopted a mobility system to understand transnational students' experience). Brandt's (2001) literacy sponsors framework allows for noting the complicated ways the act of networking is intertwined with economic access, gender and privilege. It creates space for the 'range of human experiences and ideological pressures that turn up at the scene of learning' as learners negotiate developing agentive stances while simultaneously responding to economic pressures and social expectations (Brandt, 2001: 20). By focusing on exceptions rather than the mainstream (the most visible and dense student populations), we further complicate existing scholarship on mobility by presenting a nuanced picture of the inherently heterogeneous population of transnational students, who operate with distinct literacy and professional trajectories, identity scripts, and languages and semiotic resources. We observe how such trajectories, identities and semiotic resources are configured and reconfigured in response to personal, institutional and transnational exigencies and how such reconfigurations produce certain consequences.

Mobility Framework

While the field of composition studies has a long history of teaching and researching composing processes, it has largely directed its analytical gaze at human agency and the production of print-based texts in academic, disciplinary and workspace contexts. Such research efforts have just begun to examine literacy as unfolding in an assemblage of agents, modalities, artifacts, practices and processes of composing, which remains fluid, mobile and negotiated as it circulates and reconfigures across spaces and times (Stornaiuolo *et al.*, 2017; Vieira, 2016; Wang, 2020). Increasingly, writing scholars have called for a dynamic conceptual framework that attends to composing processes as inherently heterogeneous, complexly layered, and fundamentally distributed across human and non-human agents that come to shape and be shaped by multiple authorial intentions, meaning potentials, semiotic affordances, historical trajectories and mobile capabilities (Fraiberg *et al.*, 2017; Lam, 2009; Roozen, 2009; Shipka, 2011; Yi, 2010). Furthermore, such research has underscored the importance of understanding composition as innovative enactments of multilingual and multimodal repertoires, through which multiple linguistic and semiotic resources are variously mobilized to not only facilitate the movements of meanings, texts and identities across time and spaces, but also to create opportunities for physical, intellectual and imaginative movements.

While writing research on literacy mobility has thus far framed mobility as a phenomenon of fluidity, with a majority of research providing celebratory accounts of writers moving across ever-loosening borders and boundaries with flexibility and dexterity, accruing agency along the way, others have called attention to moments of fixity enabled by 'regimes of mobility' (Schiller & Salazar, 2013), pointing to the multilingual, transnational individuals' literacy lives as inflected with inequality, struggles and suppression (Fraiberg *et al.*, 2017; Lorimer Leonard, 2013). Weaving together and extending such scholarship, this study provides a layered account of one transnational multilingual writer's networking practices across times and spaces, which enable access to academic and professional resources located at local and translocal scales (Wang, 2019), which help her develop academic discourse skills and, in turn, facilitate her academic socialization. In particular, we attend to her expanding networking practices as a critical strategy for managing her geographic, literacy and professional mobilities, which are inflected with powerful regional, national and global forces that simultaneously enable and regulate mobility.

Study Context

The study followed Albina (a pseudonym) across two semesters as she moved from a bridge class (FYW 100) to her first-year college writing class (FYW 101). The FYW 100 course is the only remaining remedial course at the university and served approximately 900 first generation, heritage language and English language learners annually at the time of the study. Close to 80% of this student population were Chinese international students, along with a scattering of international students from countries such as Saudi Arabia, South Korea, Colombia, Zimbabwe as well as domestic students. For most students, completion of the course is required prior to taking a regular first-year writing course. In the past seven years, a team of teacher scholars has engaged in sustained pedagogical innovation, which resulted in a revised curriculum that embraced principles of translingual theory (see Chapter 1 of this volume for a detailed discussion of the curriculum). A curriculum that invited students' languages, cultures and reflections was essential in supporting Albina's negotiation of language and cultural differences in her first years at the university.

Data for the study were gathered by Bree through interviews, observations, writing logs and writing samples. Albina was interviewed twice each semester. These recorded and transcribed interviews encompassed inquiries around her developing writing practices, resources accessed, including the writing center and internet-based resources, and follow up on classroom and writing center observations. The interviews also allowed space for more informal conversation regarding Albina's overall international student experience as she adjusted to life on campus and in the United States. Recorded and transcribed classroom and writing center observations were conducted once during the first semester. She also submitted samples of her work during both semesters, demonstrating the revision choices she made between her various drafts, and she described the various resources used in that revision process. This robust body of data was analyzed with a grounded theory approach, observing different themes emerging in response to our inquiry. Feminist theory and indigenous methodologies also undergird this approach, which scholars note has become increasingly characteristic of grounded theory in the last decade (Clarke 2019; Gómez & Zapata-Sepulveda, 2016).

Participant

At the time of the study, Albina was a freshman student majoring in Gender Studies. Born and raised in a small village in Ghana, Albina speaks multiple languages. She speaks Cwi, a tribal language seldom used beyond her village; her primary language of learning is English, which was used throughout her education in Ghana and South Africa; and she also speaks Gonja, the dominant language of her country.

Albina's education trajectory is an increasingly transnational one as she strategically leverages various forms of scholarship and mentorship programs to access academic and professional resources located at local and translocal scales. Identified by a non-profit organization early on as a brilliant student in need of financial and academic support, Albina was awarded with a scholarship that supported her basic education in Ghana, her participation in various professional development experiences offered in neighboring African countries, and her studies during her senior year at a high school in South Africa. This transnational academic trajectory was further extended through the ABC Credit Card Foundation Scholarship Program (a pseudonym), for which she was the only awardee from her home country to receive full financial support for her studies in the US university.

Even though her high achievements measured through standardized testing exempted her from the need to take the TOEFL exam and the FYW 100 course, Albina opted to take the writing class to better prepare herself for the formal language practices expected at the university. As a gender studies major, Albina is intensely interested in issues around gender equality and women's education, particularly in African countries similar to and including Ghana. Such interests manifest in the student organizations she participates in, the courses she has taken (two women's studies courses in her second semester) and her professional activities (tutoring refugees and organizing workshops for young women). She intended to complete her education in the United States and engage in advocacy work in Ghana. In anticipation of a requirement of her ABC Credit Card Foundation Scholarship Program, she was actively applying for an internship in non-profit organizations in Ghana.

Researcher Positioning

Xiqiao was the course instructor for the FYW 100 class that Albina opted to take during her first semester as a freshman student. Informing Xiqiao's understanding of Albina's literacies were her own background as an international student from China, a biliterate scholar and a writer struggling to add English to her linguistic repertoire. The translingual curriculum offered in the FYW 100 class was the result of sustained, collaborative pedagogical innovation involving the collaborative effort of six teacher scholars and it centered students' languages and cultures as sites of inquiry and objects of analysis (see Chapter 1 of this volume for additional information). As we will discuss, such a curriculum was essential for surfacing and exploring Albina's literacy practices.

Bree was the primary field researcher to observe Albina's classroom and writing center activities as well as interviewing her over the course of two semesters. Bree has never had an international educational experience but she has taught writing to English language learners in various contexts, both in and out of institutional spaces. In addition, her work as the First Year Writing program assistant, as well as her rhetorical research background in gender and identity, inform her observations and analysis of Albina's experiences.

Findings

I am from farming **hoes.**

From ancient versatile and agricultural hand tool.

I am from a compound house painted in red and yellow colors.

From fairly, quiet, and small neighborhood, where residents are well acquainted with one other.

I am from the beautiful **yellow tassels of corn cob,** at all corners of the market.

From buyers bargaining for low prices and sellers practicing black market.

I'm from moon-time stories of folklores and riddles from Nafisah and Amina.

I am from cooking, house keeping, and guest hosting, from 'a way to a man's heart is through his stomach' and 'don't play with boys'.

I am from **Sunni Islam,** from women wearing **hijabs and men wearing hats.** From being peaceful with myself and those around me.

From encouraging alms givings, offering daily prayers in **a masjid,** and fasting during the holy month of Ramadan.

I am from Damongo and the **Jakpa kingdom, the** solid balls of **Touzafi and Banku.**

From the beautiful dance of **Damba** and the colorful **traditional smocks.**

From my granny, who always sings and dances whenever we visit her from my elder sister leaving home at a young age for the city in search of greener pastures, and me leaving home at dawn to errands for my neighbors and receiving nothing in return but 'thank you' and 'may God bless you'.

On the walls of my dad's room is a stack of photos of my dad's **enskinment,** initiating my family into royalty.

I am from these diverse pictures of which each has a unique meaning in my family's history.

The beautiful different pieces of my culture make up who I am and where I come from.

The poem, composed as part of a FYW 100 writing class, provides Albina with an opportunity to explore myriad cultural narratives and tropes that inform her social, academic and professional identities. She tapped into a wealth of rhetorical strategies, linguistic structures and cultural tropes developed in her home language to reflect on and represent her Ghanaian roots. In so doing, she explored the multifaceted and dynamic nature of her identity. Parts of the poem (highlighted in bold) were embedded with hyperlinked images that visually illustrated important themes in her poetry. In what follows, we discuss Albina's dynamic negotiation of her identities, literacies and sponsors in a transnational network of resources.

Rewrite Gender Scripts

As Albina's poem beautifully illustrates, her hometown, a small rural village in the southern part of Ghana, follows an agrarian lifestyle, where the majority of residents engage in farming and trading. In this rural area, most residents still held 'local beliefs' about 'a woman's place is in a man's kitchen,' as illustrated in two lines in her poetry, which highlight sayings that embody family values: 'a way to a man's heart is through his stomach' and 'don't play with boys.' Born and raised alongside 10 siblings, Albina remembers learning to perform household chores from an early age. In a culture where young women are ultimately placed within the boundaries of the domicile, parents are especially reluctant to send young women to attend schools, believing that education does not play an important role in the lives of women. As Albina reflects:

Girls who are still at home don't get anyone to encourage them, but always listen to what the parents said, their place is in the kitchen. No matter how much education you acquire, you will still end up in a man's house in the kitchen. So they feel like, no, I will not waste my time in school and at the end of it be in a man's house, so I better go to a man's house. So that is what I better do. (Personal communication, 3 December 2017)

Young girls in Albina's hometown had often internalized such discourse and, therefore, felt ambivalent about their own education, even with financial sponsorship that made it possible for them to attend school. In elementary school Albïna was identified by a non-profit organization that sponsored young African women's education as a 'needy, but brilliant student,' along with a cohort of 84 other young women. This organization provided financially for Albina's entire education, and she was also able to travel to South Africa for the last two years of high school, where she received more one-on-one teaching. Even though Albina did not talk about the individuals who financially undergirded her sponsoring organization, she felt their influence on her life:

> I was like if these people saw potentials in me, then it will be bad on my side to disappoint them, so I have to keep pushing hard to maybe like make them proud and also to make my community and my parents proud. (Personal communication, 3 December 2017)

The organization provided for the 'needy' part of her identification while Albina felt the imperative to fulfill the 'brilliant student' part.

But with the internalized discourse regarding young women, her cohort of 84 was not able to acquire a certificate through a national exam, which was a prerequisite for college application and admission. She was the only one who qualified and continued with the organization, which also sponsored her college education abroad. Bearing witness to most of her childhood friends being rushed into marriages upon graduation from high school, Albina felt especially fortunate that her father was 'very serious about [his children's] education' and supported her academic pursuit. Her family celebrated her accomplishments.

While Albina is expected to succeed academically, she is also perceived, as women are generally, as vulnerable. Reflecting on her first moment of culture shock upon arrival in the US, Albina described the empowering feeling of being in control of her own life. To illustrate, she described a conflict between her and her father, which is emblematic of the overall lack of agency she feels. In preparation for Albina's travel to the US, her father insisted that Albina followed the travel itinerary he determined, which went to into specific details such as which bus Albina could take to get to the airport. When Albina queried the possibility of taking an alternative bus route, she was asked to follow the 'plan.' As a first-year student, Albina was amazed and slightly overwhelmed about the decisions that she needed to make, from which classes to take to when to take a break.

Albina's identity as an aspirational young adult in global marketplace was mediated by semiotics and identity resources located at different scales. At the backdrop of her transnational mobility were broader social narratives that render young women hidden and stuck geographically and socially (in men's kitchens and having to follow a script for managing mobility). Although such identity scripts, located at a local scale, seem to constrain young women's mobilities (social, academic and geographical), they respond to other linguistic and identity resources existing at transnational scales to create opportunities for innovation and agency. This is most tellingly illustrated by the presence of the NGO as a transnational literacy sponsor, which supports Albina's mobilities by disrupting local discourses of identity.

Taken together, such analysis facilitates a holistic understanding of identity as dynamically negotiated through assemblages of narratives and sponsors which react to one another in resonating and dissonant ways. On the surface, Albina's mobility is marked by fluidity, with her moving across ever-loosening borders with flexibility and dexterity. Such a lens recognizes the indeterminacies of her identity as emergent, where 'meaning bubbles up in interactions among people, texts, and things' and 'the emergent, felt, mobile dimensions of literate practice' (Stornaiuolo *et al.*, 2017: 77). That is, bits and pieces of her social and literacy lives travel across space and time to shape and reshape important aspects of literacy experiences and identities at a US university. On the other hand, her experience is suggestive of the profound influence of fixity, where her mobility takes shape against boundary-enforcing forces that restrict and regulate it. Indeed, scholars have observed the 'paradox of mobility' as a central feature of mobility, pointing to multilingual transnational individuals' literacy lives as inflected with inequality, struggles and suppression (Lorimer Leonard, 2017).

Reinventing Gender Identity

Albina was also engaged in the dynamic performance of her identity in various literacy tasks expected in her first-year writing classroom. In the translingual curriculum offered in the class, one assignment invited students to bring and 'translate' a lullaby for diverse audiences. Albina's team member, Jun, a young ethnic minority woman from China, chose a lullaby that speaks directly to romantic rituals in her culture – where young women used delicately hand-crafted silk balls to choose their husband during an annual match-making festival. Albina, obviously fascinated by the freedom the young women enjoy in choosing their own life partner, reciprocates a cultural ritual in her own culture:

> In my village, on a given day in the dry season (we only have two seasons, dry season and wet season), young men who are interested in courting the daughter in a household all come early in the morning. They try to show their skills by cleaning the father's house. The father observes who does the best job and that is the man chosen for his

daughter. But the daughter does not get to make that decision. (Class conversation transcript, 23 October 2017)

A curriculum that centers students' languages and cultures makes visible the challenges of communicating across linguistic, cultural and ethnic lines. The use of 'I am from poetry' and 'Translation Narrative' assignments positioned Albina and her fellow students as experts, whose knowledge of cultural rituals, tropes and narratives becomes a resource for learning and inquiry. For students like Albina, who strategically leverages academic and professional resources to find her own position in the world, such assignments provide a space to reflect on an interweaving web of academic, professional and life experiences accumulated across her transnational journey.

As the following classroom observation makes clear, Albina seizes every opportunity to engage with issues of gender inequality. The interaction occurs in the midst of an assignment that invites students to explore and examine literacy practices in a professional field they so choose. Students were invited to draft and perform a skit that captures the everyday activities of a young professional. While the majority of the international students in the class are business majors, Albina and her teammate decided to depict an interaction between an advocacy professional and a victim of domestic abuse. Situating the interaction in the office of the advocate, the students provide a heart-gripping representation of the tragic circumstances of a young woman. Ensuing a short exchange that involves the advocate attempting to comfort and encourage the victim to reveal the abuse that left many bruises and much redness on her face, the victim, performed by Albina, produced the following monologue:

> I didn't want to discuss with anyone because I thought no one would understand me, but you seem to be someone who understands what I am going through. I have been married for five years now and I do all the house chores. I am just a housewife. My husband doesn't allow me to work. I have a certificate. Everything is good. I know I am very good for a job, but he doesn't want me to go out. All I do is to cook for him and when I don't cook on time, he beats me. (Classroom observation transcript, 27 November 2017)

After the skit, Xiqiao led the class discussion, which invited students' interpretation of the interaction. The ensuing conversation brought together culturally inflected gender ideologies, with quite a few young men from China noting that the victim should not leave her husband because of the serious financial and emotional cost of a divorce. A few young women, on the other hand, argued that departure is a legitimate response to physical violence. The nature and consequences of domestic violence were further unpacked, as various students offered nuanced cultural understanding of gender roles in connection to professional opportunities, domestic violence and solutions to such social problems:

> **Teacher (T):** What could happen when she does divorce him?
>
> **Male Classmate (MC):** Like the money. Fortune. She could be like…
>
> **T:** You mean like splitting the family fortune?
>
> **MC:** Yeah, I do not know if you have child or not. A child be expensive. What about the children if you get a divorce? Your life could be worse but the child do not deserve to get a divorce.
>
> **T:** But she has her own life.
>
> **Female Classmate (FC):** If she had a child, that would be a better reason to get a divorce.
>
> **MC:** If she had a child, that is not a reason to get a divorce.
>
> **FC:** But if she had a child and was getting abused, that would make it even more harmful. It would be better to get a divorce because that child wouldn't be around the abuse.
>
> **MC:** That is her own choice, but I feel it's expensive to raise a child by herself.
>
> **T:** But did you guys notice she was talking about that she had a certificate. She was ready to work but her husband wouldn't let her go out of the house and work.
>
> **MC:** Yeah, so this is another reason she cannot have a job.
>
> **T:** She can get a job.
>
> **Albina:** But I could get a job at any time because I have a good certificate.
>
> **T:** Because her husband doesn't let her go.
>
> **MC:** You are free to go (lots of laughter). Find another husband.
>
> **T:** Find another husband?
>
> **MC:** Yeah.

With the teacher's prompting, Albina continued with an improvised response to such queries at length, making clear her self-identification as a women's advocate:

> Yeah, so I was going to like say I support the fight for women, the fight about being happy, fighting for happiness in your marriages, but I don't have the courage to stand up and fight for myself because I am afraid of my husband. And I am afraid of what I will face in the world if I leave my husband and go out. Like I am not sure if another man will be willing to marry me because I am like, it's like a stigma on me. Someone who has been divorced by their husband.
>
> (Classroom observation transcripts, 27 November 2017)

As the conversation continued, Albina further unpacked a cultural norm that limits women's lives and career possibilities through the socially inscribed stigma attached to divorce:

> I think in America it is different but where I come from if another man wants to marry you, and he finds out that you have been divorced by another man, he might not have any problem with it, but maybe his religion would, like you want to marry a secondhand (wow – teacher) a secondhand, so… That's why most women do not want to speak up when they are being abused in their homes like they prefer to just swallow everything and remain in their marriage.
>
> (Classroom observation transcripts, 27 November 2017)

What is particularly noteworthy from this extensive intercultural exchange is the complex ways in which gender scripts were maintained or disrupted to shape women's educational and vocational opportunities. It is helpful to remember that this conversation took place at a large American university in 2017 with a group of young freshman students coming from diverse cultural and linguistic backgrounds (the majority being Chinese, with individual students from Korea, Saudi Arabia and Ghana). In particular, the male student, who vocalized the view that that domestic violence might need to be tolerated for financial security, received much encouragement and support through his peers' laughter and exclamation. Albina also shared her country's views of women being considered 'secondhand' when they divorce, even in the context of domestic violence.

Jones (2016) notes there is a 'need for applied linguists doing language and identity studies to carefully consider the role that gender plays in educational, or other institutional, contexts' (2016: 216). She goes on to say that these gender norms impact student learning: 'In classroom contexts, gender norms are likely to play a role in how different children learn or succeed in the classroom and in the identities that they inhabit or are ascribed even in contexts that do not appear to be gendered' (2016: 217). Albina noted that her character was educated and had a 'good certificate' but was not allowed to use it for gainful employment. She also responded that her character felt depressed and humiliated, which highlights the embedded emotional challenges in rewriting gender scripts and harkens back to the discouragement that Albina's peers face in Ghana as they work hard to complete an education only to end up in a 'man's kitchen.' Jones encourages: 'For applied linguistics, then an understanding of how gender roles are produced and drawn upon is important when trying to understand patterns of language use in real-world contexts' (2016: 217). This classroom discussion around gender roles, drawing from diverse cultural backgrounds, reveals the ways in which student success and motivations are impacted by home gender scripts even when students are pursuing an education physically distant from their home communities (Tanyas, 2016).

From a mobility perspective, this exchange also points to the complex ways in which cultural and rhetorical knowledge developed through lived experiences transform identities in powerful ways. This performance of her identity as a women's rights advocate unfolds not inside one domain, space or time, but across many moments in the lives of the multiple students involved in making sense of it. Such meaning-making happens in spaces that are never pure or settled, 'where discourses and knowledge are necessarily heterogeneous, and where multiple semiotic resources are so deeply entangled that distinct modes simply don't make sense' (Prior, 2018: n.p.). Indeed, the complex negotiation surrounding the skit mobilized many moments embedded in students' learning to be across social and cultural contexts, communicating for different purposes and audiences, and subjected to different valuation systems. In this recursive process of defining meaning, negotiating differences and seeking clarity, students not only repurposed knowledge and strategies developed through previous social lives but also developed strategies to engage with a diverse audience in simultaneously stable and innovative ways (Roozen, 2009).

Reinventing Literacy Sponsorship

The previous section makes clear the value of an asset-based curriculum in making visible, and enabling students' engagement with, issues of gender identity and inequality. Such engagement further encouraged Albina's reflection on the struggles of other young women in her cohort who failed to achieve academic success despite NGO support. In particular, she attributes her peers' struggles with educational success to a lack of mentorship by women who have achieved career and academic success. Although a mentor was provided to Albina's cohort by the NGO, she understood that this mentor was overwhelmed with having to care for 85 students. Because the mentor was so busy, she never truly made herself available for all scholarship participants. With this knowledge, Albina actively built a friendship with the mentor, knowing full well that such friendship might not lead to immediate benefits. She noted: 'I always go to her with questions. Even though she does not come to us, I always go to her' (personal communication, 3 December 2017). Albina would invent questions to ask her mentor and would occasionally stop by her office. Over time, through the mentor, she gained access to successful alumni and their wealth of knowledge about navigating the scholarship program to her own benefit.

When the opportunity to participate in a camp for girls interested in science, math and technology presented itself, the mentor recommended Albina for the program because of their close friendship. The camp connected Albina to a larger cohort of young women coming from diverse but similar backgrounds, who shared with her lessons and stories about how young women could leverage the scholarship to gain additional educational and academic resources, such as pursuing one's study in western countries. Albina was profoundly inspired by such stories, which opened her eyes to more opportunities. She noted:

> I went there and I met other girls on this same scholarship who the scholarship helped go abroad to study medicine. They told us about how the scholarship supported them and background some were even poorer than me and they were able to make it to the UK and I was like if this person is able to make it in, why can't I? (Personal communication, 3 December 2017)

In addition to the past scholars who attended, the camp also invited alumni to speak to young women about their stories of success, which helped to construct a broader narrative mapping the trajectory of academic and professional growth that young women from under-privileged backgrounds could emulate.

Albina identifies this camp experience as perhaps the single most powerful moment that led to pursuing education abroad. She did not indicate whether any of the people she met continued in relationships with her but, seeing examples of women who 'made it', she was able to picture fully a path away from the gendered discourse of her community. She also saw how mentorship had woven aspects of her life together and was aware that seeking out her program's mentor led to the camp opportunity.

Albina makes complex connections between mentorship and success. She is acutely aware that it was her direct intervention that brought about sponsorship and mentoring opportunities and knows she is unusual in that trait. She feels that mentors should seek out young women, particularly because they are embedded in gendered discourse. She attributes this lack of mentorship as the single largest factor in why her cohort did not achieve to the level she did. She notes:

> You're supporting the neediest students who are not ready to learn, and if they are not ready to learn, you don't just leave them. You have to put together initiatives that will make them rise up and set expectations of you, but if they just give the resources and then they go, then they [students] feel disappointed. (Personal communication, 3 December 2017)

The lack of mentoring has negatively impacted achievement in her school so much that Albina's younger sister said the organization is most likely going to pull the aid from their school.

At the university, Albina began to shift her identity from mentee to that of a mentor, advocating for other young women and rewriting the gender scripts in her community and others like hers. As part of her college sponsorship, she is required to have an internship with a non-profit in Africa, which she hopes to fulfill with the same organization that sponsored her education. She noted that although people in the organization know how to identify students and offer valuable resources, they do not always know what students such as herself intrinsically need for success. Her passion and career goal is to return to Ghana and mentor other young women. During the latter years of her high school education in South Africa, she traveled back to Ghana and started a workshop with young women in her community. She did not talk about elements we might imagine when we consider education. Instead, she talked about time management, hygiene and money. She emphasized the community parts of education that were lacking with no parental support. They might be taught math, science and history by teachers but they are not taught life skills to make it outside of the home. She believes that in order for a mentorship to truly succeed in a way to override the scripts young women live in, they need to meet with a mentor regularly. When asked what a good incentive would be for someone to work harder, she replied:

> I think inspiration is a very good thing. They should try as much as possible to meet with the students regularly at least twice a week... they are teenagers like me, so they need that direction. If you don't direct us and you leave us on our own, this is where we tend to mess up. (Personal communication, 3 December 2017)

Albina identifies that it is not simply resources that students need: they need to be shown 'this is the path you can follow to be successful.' Even here in the US, she mentors young people by tutoring at the Islamic center.

Albina's drive to cultivate develop and leverage relationships with potential sponsors has not changed since coming to the US, but the things she learns are different:

> People here inspire me to some extent even though there are no struggles in their stories. But they are sharing how they are making it in their classes and what is the dream for their futures to be. I try to compare their dreams to mine, and I think I can also dream big. (Personal communication, 3 December 2017)

Albina recognizes the ways in which her university peers, who grow up in relative privilege naturally dream larger, and this inspires her to push her dreams to a level that comes to her peers easily without as much struggle.

With Albina lacking the privileges of her university peers, one might assume her focus would be to cultivate economic networks, mentors and sponsors for herself and for her activist work. Brandt (2001) notes we can trace the paths of literacy through economic channels with literacy sponsorship often carrying financial and professional resource access but, also, at times, lacking relational connection and often carrying obligations and expectations for the learner that can shape their literacy trajectory (Brandt, 2001: 19). Albina is unique in that she recognized early on that financial sponsorship alone does not guarantee success. Instead, she subverts the notion of economic access as key to success with her effectiveness rooted in cultivating relationships and connections. Her activist work focuses on hands-on mentorship and development of life skills and 'inspiration.' She notes: 'I believe in connections.' She talks to people at the bus stop and joins multiple clubs that explore different religions, simply to understand more of American culture and how people around her strive for meaning. She seeks not only to be understood but to understand. Zhu and Kramsch note that transnational student success is 'based on ability to gain sociocultural knowledge and linguistic capital' (2016: 378). Clearly, Albina is able to figure out how to situate herself in different situations to her advantage and much of how she gains important sociocultural knowledge is through her focus on intentional social connections. 'Unlike economic capital, symbolic capital is all the more powerful as it is invisible. The strategies we put in place to gain distinction strive to make symbolic power invisible by making it seem natural' (Zhu & Kramsch, 2016: 380). At the end of the year-long project, Albina asked Bree if she knew of other research studies she could get involved in, or if she knew of other people on campus who had the same interests as herself, particularly in the experience of African women. In this question, Bree realized the 'natural' and skilled way Albina had cultivated connection with her, and that Albina's participation in the study was a connection point, and that Bree herself was cultivated by Albina as a source of sociocultural knowledge and symbolic capital. In this way, Bree was not only able to hear Albina's interview depictions of her intentional mentor and sponsor connections but, as a researcher, she was able to experience firsthand the skilled, nuanced and effective ways in which Albina enacts her networking and sponsor-seeking practices, further affirming the narrative given in the interview and Albina's belief in 'connections.'

Conclusion

Although Albina did not have existing mentoring networks available to her in her home country, Ghana, she strategically cultivated new means of mentorship through intentionally making 'connections,' beginning in childhood in Ghana and continuing to her university study abroad in the US. Through her mentors, she was able to situate herself in a place of access to successful individuals who had overcome their local gender scripts as well as severe economic challenges. Listening to stories from those successful individuals, alongside her growing awareness of the importance of herself cultivated mentoring, she gained agency in continuing to increase her network and she began seeing herself as an advocate, mentor and resource for other young women in her home country. Although Albina is a unique individual, her story reveals the opportunity available in self-cultivated mentoring and making connections, even when resources are very limited and no natural networks exist. She joins clubs in an effort to understand different cultures and consciously cultivates relationships even when she is stressed from her academic workload. Her belief in the power of mentorship, particularly for those with economic and social challenges, is so dynamic that she has formed her career trajectory around her fulfilling that role for women in her community.

Teachers could provide sustained instruction, explicit modeling, and directed reflection on students' individual experiences with literacy sponsors and mentors. Such a move might require that writing teachers foreground students' cultures and cultural ways of networking to build higher levels of understanding and critical awareness of how one can leverage existing old networks and forge new ones. As seen in Albina's story, Xiqiao's strategic implementation of a curriculum that centers students' languages and cultures helped make visible powerful gender scripts, creating an opportunity for reflection and negotiation. Albina's classroom explanations regarding her viewpoint on divorce and domestic violence challenged other students' gender scripts prescribing women's place in the domestic space even while experiencing violence and in spite of having an education. This opportunity for public rewriting enhanced Albina's commitment to a career trajectory involving advocacy for women's education and opportunity.

References

Brandt, B. (2001) *Literacy in American Lives*. Cambridge: Cambridge University Press.

Clarke, A. (2019) Situating grounded theory and situational analysis in interpretive qualitative inquiry. In A. Bryant and K. Charmaz (eds) *The SAGE Handbook of Current Developments in Grounded Theory* (pp. 3–48). London: Sage Publications. https://doi.org/10.4135/9781526485656.n3.

Fraiberg, S., Wang, X. and You, X. (2017) *Inventing the World Grant University: Chinese International Students' Mobilities, Literacies and Identities*. Logan, UT: Utah State University Press.

Gómez, A. and Zapata-Sepulveda, P. (2016) Ten years of critical qualitative research at the International Congress of Qualitative Inquiry. *International Review of Qualitative Research* 9 (2), 137–139. https://doi.org/10.1525/irqr.2016.9.2.137.

Jones, L. (2016) Language and gender identities. In S. Preece (ed.) *The Routledge Handbook of Language and Identity* (pp. 210–224). London: Routledge.

Lam, W.S.E. (2009) Multiliteracies on instant messaging in negotiating local, translocal, and transnational affiliations: A case of an adolescent immigrant. *Reading Research Quarterly* 44 (4), 377–397. https://doi.org/10.1598/RRQ.44.4.5.

Lorimer Leonard, R. (2013) Travelling literacies: Multilingual writing on the move. *Research in the Teaching of English* 48, 13–39. https://ncte.org/resources/journals/research-in-the-teaching-of-english/.

Lorimer Leonard, R. (2017) *Writing on the Move: Migrant Women and the Value of Literacy*. Pittsburgh, PA: University of Pittsburgh Press.

Prior, P. (2018) How do moments add up to lives: Trajectories of semiotic becoming vs. tales of school learning in four modes. Paper presented at the Thomas Watson Conference, Louisville, KY.

Roozen, K. (2009) 'Fan fic-ing' English studies: A case study exploring the interplay of vernacular literacies and disciplinary engagement. *Research in the Teaching of English* 44 (2), 136–169.

Schiller, G.N. and Salazar, B.N. (2013) Regimes of mobility across the globe. *Journal of Ethnic and Migration Studies* 39 (2), 183–200. https://doi.org/10.1080/1369183x.2013.723253.

Shipka, J. (2011) *Toward a Composition Made Whole*. Pittsburgh, PA: University of Pittsburgh Press.

Stornaiuolo, A., Smith, A. and Phillips, N.C. (2017) Developing a transliteracies framework for a connected world. *Journal of Literacy Research* 49 (1), 68–91. https://ncte.org/resources/journals/research-in-the-teaching-ofenglish/.

Tanyas, B. (2016) Gendering migration narratives: A qualitative inquiry on language use and agency in adaptation stories. *Gender and Language* 10 (1), 85–105. https://doi.org/10.1558/genl.v10i1.17495.

Vieira K. (2011) Undocumented in a documentary society: Textual borders and transnational religious literacies. *Written Communication* 28, 436–461. https://doi.org/10.1177/0741088311421468.

Vieira K. (2016) Writing remittances: Migration-driven literacy learning in a Brazilian homeland. *Research in the Teaching of English* 50 (4), 422–449. https://ncte.org/resources/journals/research-in-the-teaching-of-english.

Wang, X. (2017) Spatial and literacy practices of Chinese international students across a college bridge writing classroom and WeChat. *Language and Education* 31 (6), 561–579. https://doi.org/10.1080/09500782.2017.1337128.

Wang, X. (2019) Observing literacy learning across WeChat and first-year writing: A scalar analysis of one transnational student's multilingualism. *Computers and Composition* 52, 253–271. https://doi.org/10.1016/j.compcom.2019.02.002.

Wang, X. (2020) Becoming multilingual writers through translation. *Research in the Teaching of English* 54 (3), 206–230. https://ncte.org/resources/journals/research-in-the-teaching-of-english.

Yi, Y. (2010) Adolescent multilingual writers' transitions across in- and out-of-school writing contexts. *Journal of Second Language Writing* 19 (1), 17–32. https://doi.org/10.1016/j.jslw.2009.10.001.

Zhu, H. and Kramsch, C. (2016) Symbolic power and conversational inequality in intercultural communication: An introduction. *Applied Linguistics Review* 7 (4), 375–383. https://doi.org/10.1515/applirev-2016-0016.

Part 2: Navigating Resources and Services

5 International Chinese Students' Navigation of Linguistic and Learning Resources

Wenyue (Melody) Ma and Curtis Green-Eneix

Introduction

As the higher education landscape transforms to an international and borderless market (Altbach, 2012), the number of international students continues to grow within the United States, increasing by 67% since the turn of the century (Bound *et al.*, 2016: 2). According to the Institute of International Education (2019), China sends the largest number of international students to the US, with Chinese students accounting for 33.7% (369,548 students) of all international enrollments (1,095,299 students[1]) in the US. To meet the demand of this large influx of Chinese citizens wishing to receive education abroad, many international high schools and international education programs in public high schools have been established in the last twenty years. These schools prepare students explicitly for the college application process and for higher education by exposing them to the curricula found in the US and in Britain (S. Liu, 2018), which cater to both students' desires and parents wanting their child(ren) to study abroad. Driven by the need to understand how pre-study abroad education received in Chinese international high schools impacts the life and academic achievement of Chinese international students studying in the US, and how they employ their linguistic and learning resources to overcome adversity, the current study focuses on two tertiary students who attended international high school in China before entering a university within the United States. Adopting an activity theory framework (Engeström, 1987, 2001), we analyzed data from multiple sources (e.g. background survey, interviews, observations of both classrooms and writing center consultations, media artifacts) to understand how the educational experiences of these two Chinese international students shaped the ways in which they went about navigating social encounters at their US university.

Literature Review

As a growing number of Chinese citizens study abroad in the United States, China's enthusiasm for study abroad has resulted in the country's education sector expanding its international high schools and international departments in public high schools in recent years. This surge in Chinese international students is consistent with the booming Chinese economy (D. Liu, 2016). Additionally, it has been due to China's school reform occurring at a time that focused on meeting the knowledge-based society on the global stage (S. Liu, 2018). Outside institutions engaging in neoliberal recruitment practices, there are usually three main reasons why individuals from China study abroad: (1) to receive a better quality of education and better research opportunities; (2) to interact with people from diverse cultural and linguistic backgrounds; and (3) to improve their job prospects once they have received their overseas degree (Dimmock & Ong Soon Leong, 2010). However, research and media reports have documented that many Chinese international students in the US are now facing a variety of difficulties and challenges while pursuing higher education. Many students eventually find themselves in predominantly English-speaking countries, marginalized and having difficulties engaging in social activities with their Western peers (Kumaravadivelu, 2003; Sato & Hodge, 2009; Zhang, 2016). In addition, Straker (2016) has observed that this student population lacks both opportunities and the communicative skills for interacting within the classroom. He noted that was because of either language proficiency, cultural background, and/or their ideologies on how to interact within the classroom. As a consequence, these students are often grouped as 'one massive, undifferentiated category (or problem)—English language learners—[thereby] obscuring tremendous differences in their backgrounds, resources, goals, abilities, and trajectories' (Duff, 2015: 66).

Education scholars (e.g. Heng, 2018; Wang, 2016) have sought to dispel the deficiency myths surrounding Chinese international students by considering how they navigate the space in which they find themselves along with how their life histories shape their interactions while abroad (Wargo & De Costa, 2017). For instance, Heng found that Chinese undergraduates often faced two primary expectations. The first expectation centers around speaking and 'thinking like a "Westerner"' (Heng, 2018: 28). The second ties to fitting into the sociocultural context they are within by relearning certain academic skills. On the other hand, Wang (2016) has highlighted that Chinese international students' use of the social networking platform WeChat is an essential mediational tool for mobilizing their academic literacy within their respective sociocultural context (see Blommaert & Horner, 2017). Additionally, WeChat allows them to maintain their relationships with friends and family back home in China (e.g. De Costa *et al.*, 2016). However, the tool also causes them to self-segregate into what Dervin and Korpela refer to as *Cocoon Communities* – communities that form for a 'specific purpose, around imaginaries or for contextual reasons' and that are composed of 'voluntary and informal members' who may share the same or similar discourses and practices (Dervin & Korpela, 2013: 4). While these studies have furthered researchers' understanding of how international students navigate their context abroad, most of the discussions have not considered how students participate, or withhold participation, within this community through the use of their available resources. In addition, the importance of pre-study abroad education and its impact on students' subsequent educational experiences has largely been under-investigated, if not overlooked completely.

Activity Theory and International Student Participation

To fully examine how Chinese international students' high school experience informed their participation in a foreign English-speaking country, we use Activity Theory (Engeström, 1987, 2001; Leont'ev, 1978) as it provides us with a useful lens to unpack the interactions students are part of within the socioenvironmental contexts. Leont'ev (1978) developed activity theory based on Vygotsky's (1978) ideas regarding how an individual interacted with their social reality in relation to their mental understanding. This understanding occurs through mediated action. Mediated action takes place through a dialectical relationship with an object of interest and tools (e.g. language and other cultural artifacts) as they relate to the social and material environment (Lantolf *et al.*, 2015). This was represented by Vygotsky (1978: 40) as a triangle composed of three components: subject, mediating artifact, and object.

Leont'ev (1978) built upon Vygotsky's initial idea but shifted the focus of these socially motivated interactions away from the mind of a single individual. Rather, he focused on the social interaction with one or multiple individuals (in the form of division of labor) found in the community space, which was constantly driven by social influences. This shift resulted in the explicit understanding of how a group of (two or more) individuals went about achieving an activity, resulting in the second generation of activity theory. Figure 5.1 illustrates the components within Leont'ev's activity theory, which comprises of an activity system.

The top three components – *subject, mediating artifacts* and *object* – are built upon Vygotsky's idea of mediation in which individuals (the subject) use an assortment of psychological, symbolic, and material tools and artifacts such as language (the mediating artifact) to interact

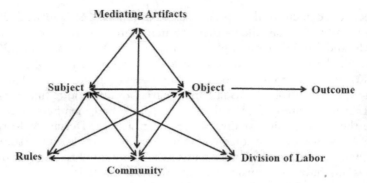

Figure 5.1 Activity theory triangle (Engeström, 1987: 27)

with objects, people and concepts to achieve a particular goal, such as learning a language (Kozulin, 2018). Mediation, as Kozulin (2018: 24) explains, is a 'process related to the formation, development, enhancement, or deterioration of human mental functions'. Or, how we relate our psychological understanding to the social activity and community that an individual finds themself within. Leont'ev (1978) built upon this to consider the cultural and individual components that shape the object/goal of the activity by including *community, rules, division of labor* and an *outcome*.

Community is considered a group of members who willingly self-govern themselves by agreed upon rules that shape their use of mediating tools in order to achieve and share similar goals and experiences (Swain *et al.*, 2015). A community in this sense can be composed of a single classroom or be as expansive to include members around the world (see Sauro's [2014] study on using Harry Potter fandoms to learn a language). *Rules* can be considered the norms or the expectations of interactions within the community. Lastly, *division of labor* is how individuals (attempt to) work together to achieve the goal. But, as Swain *et al.* (2015: 99) explain, the division of labor 'both shapes and is shaped by the rules of this particular action, the subject, the goals and the mediating artifacts [used]'. Leont'ev's (1978) version of activity theory explicitly concerns how individuals interact with one another to achieve an activity. However, Leont'ev's activity theory does not consider how the object necessarily transforms into the outcome and whether activities can change and morph into other activities over time (Engeström, 1987, 1999).

While Leont'ev's (1978) second generation of activity theory mainly focused on how an individual's motivation shaped their actions and behavior within a sociocultural context, Engeström (1987, 1999, 2001) expounded further upon activity theory. Engeström introduced the role of time, dialogue, and activity within this third generation of activity theory. Engeström's (1987) activity theory focus includes the same components that Leont'ev (1978) singular activity system did but diagrams them for the first time. However, Engeström (1999, 2001) elaborated that the activity system develops and changes over time. Additionally, these components may change due to contradictions that occur. *Contradictions*, as Engeström (2001: 137) elaborates, are 'historically accumulating structural tensions within and between activity systems'. These contradictions and tensions occur when 'an activity system adopts a new element from the outside (for example, a new technology or a new object), [with the result that] some old element (for example, the rules or the division of labor) collides with the new one', resulting in both tension and 'innovative attempts to change the activity' over time (2001: 137).

Another change between the second and third generation of activity theory is that Leont'ev (1978) focused on a singular activity where individuals participated within. Engeström (1999, 2001) expanded this to include individuals having their own goals and, in turn, their own activities. This third generation of activity theory highlighted that individuals negotiate and have dialogue to achieve the objective, resulting in the objective being transformed into a negotiated outcome. This outcome may be different from what individuals have expected. These multiple perspectives and activity systems that an individual participate within may also lead to 'discontinuity in action or interaction' (Akkerman & Bakker, 2011: 133) within the boundaries of that activity. These boundaries are not impervious, however. Akkerman and Bakker (2011) further elaborate that the boundaries that define activity systems can be crossed, since they are constantly developing. As the authors explain: '[B]oundary crossing should not be seen as a process of moving from initial diversity and multiplicity to homogeneity and unity but rather as a process of establishing continuity in a situation of sociocultural difference' (2011: 152). Boundary crossing has, in fact, been found to occur in varying forms in previous research. For example, J. Liu (2015) observed that as Chinese international graduate students in the UK experienced a change in their learning environment, they initiated a shift in their goals, used different mediating tools, and divided labor within an activity differently. This indicates that as individuals spatially move to a new context and/or place – be it physical or virtual – the way in which they use resources and participate within an activity changes as well.

This analytical perspective assists in de-centralizing the Western values and ideologies detailed in the prior section which ascribe Chinese international students as deficient actors in the classroom (Straker, 2016). Activity theory thus provides a useful means to interrogate the participation of international students and their national peers in Western academic communities (see also Chapter 6, this volume). For example, Albusaidi's (2019) study used activity theory to understand how a female international student participating in a 12-month program in the United Kingdom used available tools to engage with the dynamic and shifting learning opportunities within the international classroom. They found that participation was not only constituted by overt actions (e.g. raising one's hand and speaking) but also by covert actions and decisions (e.g. formulating a goal for an interaction, use of body language, observing others) that occurred in relation to peers and individuals found within and around the community. Moreover, this theory affords researchers a framework to question how participation between individuals may clash, be negotiated and/or be mutually co-constructed in relation to the affordances – both physical and virtual – at people's disposal. This is highlighted by Zhu and Mitchell's (2012) study that focused on participation in peer interaction within a US university ESL writing classroom. Adopting activity theory, the authors described how two Latin American international graduate students adapted the teacher's goal for the writing peer response activity to their own personal learning goals and motives by changing the ways they used their full linguistic and semiotic resources.

In understanding the different generations of activity theory, we chose to adopt Engeström's approach since it allows us to better understand how international students navigate and participate within the US higher education context. Additionally, we are able to note how students are using their available mediated resources to acquire and refine learning strategies in this new and foreign context. Therefore, our study aims to understand how Chinese international students' past experiences informed the ways they navigated and participated in the interactions they encountered at a US university through their deployment of their linguistic, cultural, semiotic and multimodal resources. To address this aim, our study was guided by the following questions:

(1) How did the education at Chinese high schools, as well as past experiences in China, impact the academic studies and life of Chinese international students in the US?
(2) What strategies and learning resources did these students employ to cope with the challenges they encountered in and outside the classroom?

Methodology

This study was part of a larger research project that was funded by Great Lake University, located in the midwestern part of the United States. This public research university is a four-year university and predominantly serves domestic students. However, its Chinese international students make up a large proportion of its international student population. The central aim of the study was to observe a group of first-semester Chinese international students at Great Lake University with regard to what navigational strategies they used throughout the university. All project participants were offered financial compensation for their six-month cooperation. Specifically, our study focuses on two participants who were currently enrolled within this university. We chose these students for this study due to their seemingly similar backgrounds and because they negotiated academic and social challenges in unique and interesting ways different from the other students in the broader study.

Participants

Our two participants, Andy and Sarah (pseudonyms), were enrolled in different sections of the same mandatory university first-year writing course (i.e. FYW 100).

Andy. Andy was born in Hangzhou, the capital of Zhejiang province in China, but spent most of his life in Shanghai. Before coming to the US, he spent the first two years in a public school and then transferred to an international high school for his last two years. However, Andy did not want to transfer to the international high school or study abroad: but he was compelled to study in the US because his 户口 (*hukou*, a household registration system established in the 1950s to control population movements) has his permanent residence placed in Hangzhou (for more information on *hukou*, see Swider, 2014). This resulted in him being unable to take the 高考 (*gaokao*, a high stakes college entrance exam in China) in Shanghai, where he received his high school education. Andy would have been disadvantaged by the differentiated selection criteria and the quota policy had he not taken the *gaokao* in Shanghai. Therefore, he transferred once again to an international high school that prepared him to study abroad at a US university.

At the time of this study, Andy was a first-year undergraduate who was undecided about his major. He had a higher than average TOEFL score that exceeded the cut-off score (i.e. 80 on TOEFL iBT) the attending university required of international students. This allowed him to skip preparatory ESL courses before directly enrolling in regular undergraduate classes. During the data-collection phase of our study, he was taking four courses: first-year writing (i.e. FYW 100), statistics, mathematics, and biology. Andy intends to return to China and get a job related to business, where he can use English per his father's suggestion.

Sarah. Sarah is from Chengdu, the capital of Sichuan province in China, where she did her high school education in the study abroad track. Due to the tremendous pressure from *gaokao* on test takers, she decided to avoid the test by studying abroad. Because she had never lived in an English-speaking country before attending the university in the US, there was a point of contention between her parents regarding whether to send Sarah abroad. Her father felt that it was important and meaningful to study in the US, whereas her mother was worried since their only child had never lived away from her parents before. This was eventually settled and both supported her studying abroad.

Sarah was 18 years old and a first-year undergraduate who did not decide her major. Like Andy, she had higher than average TOEFL scores that exceeded the cut-off score allowing her to skip the preparatory ESL courses (i.e. 80 on TOEFL iBT). During the data-collection phase of our study, Sarah was taking four courses: first-year writing (i.e. FYW 100), media information, computer science, and biology. She was undecided regarding what she would do after she graduated.

Collecting and analyzing the data

We opted to collect multiple data sources from both participants. The first author (Ma) primarily collected the data in which she interviewed both Andy and Sarah in their first language, Mandarin Chinese, and collected the data sources listed in Table 5.1. The procedure of our data analysis also encompasses a two-cycle coding approach (Saldaña, 2016), which is illustrated in Figure 5.2.

Once the first interviews were collected, the first author (Ma) transcribed and translated the interviews from Mandarin Chinese into English, in which she and the second author (Green-Eneix) did initial coding separately, which encompassed concept-driven coding by assigning codes based on the activity theory framework (Engeström, 1999). In terms of using activity theory for coding, we followed the example of Kessler (2020) and the advice of Yamagata-Lynch (2010).

Table 5.1 Data collection process within the first phase

Methodology	Sources	Method used
Survey	Primary participants	Two surveys completed at the beginning and the end of their first semester respectively
Interviews	Primary participants	Conducted two separate face-to-face semi-structured interviews in Mandarin Chinese with both primary participants
Non-participatory observations	Observed participants' interactions within the writing classroom	Multiple non-participatory observations in the writing classroom Sketched classroom layouts along with extensive field notes
Documents	Collected all assignments, social media artifacts and literacy logs from the participants	Read all materials and did content analysis

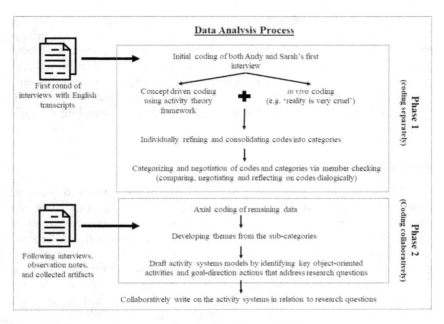

Figure 5.2 Data analysis process (inspired by Carcary, 2009)

The coding criteria followed the activity theory framework, which identified the subjects, mediating artifacts, objects, rules, community, division of labor and the outcome of the activity. During this cycle of coding in which we read the transcript line-by-line, we also incorporated *in-vivo coding* (i.e. using the words and or phrases of the participant to mark data; Saldaña, 2016) to stay open to all theoretical directions as we coded the initial interviews for both Andy and Sarah.

In doing the initial coding cycle (Friedman, 2012; Yamagata-Lynch, 2010) on Andy and Sarah's data, we then separately refined our codes before we compared with one another. After we had finalized our own codes, we member checked in the form of an intensive discussion instead of quantifying for reliability for multiple reasons. The first and most important reason was to understand our interpretations by comparing the first author's emic (i.e. insider) and the second author's etic (i.e. outsider) perspective to the data. The second was to further refine and identify sub-categories that would be used for the second cycle of coding. These mutually agreed upon criteria were used to analyze the remaining collected interviews, observation notes and collected artifacts in the form of axial coding in which we coded the rest of the data. Once we had completed the coding together, we discussed again how the sub-categories related to one another as we developed the themes. Moreover, we also worked together to identify the activity system as we began to engage in collaborative process writing. This process writing allowed both of us to co-construct a mutual understanding concerning the activity systems in relation to the questions and the themes created to address each component of the activity system. Just like Yamagata-Lynch (2010: 75), these activity systems would 'continue to be drafts until [we] write the thick description of the data in a narrative format'. Such a description enabled us to develop an in-depth understanding of each activity system.

Findings and Discussion

Our central goal in this chapter is to better understand and examine how both Andy and Sarah's educational background and their life histories informed how they used their available resources as they (attempted) to participate within the various communities in and around a US university. Our analysis of the data yielded the following themes: pre-study abroad, impacts on their life and studies, and transcending the US and China's border through WeChat. In the following section, we first describe Andy and Sarah's high school experiences before studying abroad (i.e. the pre-study abroad context). This is then followed with an exploration of the ways in which their experiences informed how they used their resources to participate in various activities within and outside the writing classroom as well as in the physical and virtual space.

Pre-study abroad

Before coming to the US, both Andy and Sarah took a number of English courses that were intended to help them get high grades on the TOEFL test and prepare them for upcoming college life in the US. However, as noted above, unlike Sarah who had actively pursued studying abroad and consciously chose a high school for this purpose, Andy could not get into a top-ranked international high school due to education policy changes and his lack of English proficiency. Rather than seeing the international high school he attended as a place to receive instruction and become well-prepared for study in the US, he saw it merely as a stepping stone to receiving a high school diploma and to help him get into a university in the US. Unsurprisingly, when he was asked about his experiences in his prior international high school, and how helpful he found the instruction, the conversation was as follows:

Excerpt 1 Reality is very cruel

[E]verybody was fooling around in my high school. [...] Foreign teachers would give you the kind of classes you would have in American high schools. The textbooks and courses are exactly the same, but, after all, the school [that I attended] is not the kind of good international high school, so both students and teachers were just fooling around. Do you know what I mean? [...]I would do whatever I am asked to do. It does no harm to me, so it does not really matter. [...] There might still be some help [for my English proficiency]. After all, there are foreign high school teachers, so your English would be certainly a little [better], but it is totally different from what you expected. Reality is very cruel. (Andy, Interview 1)

Although Andy's international high school took up a Western curriculum, he felt his international high school hardly prepared him for his studies in the US. This is even though he, along with a few others, achieved the ideal TOEFL scores for applying to colleges in the United States. This unsatisfactory result probably stemmed partly from his reluctance to go abroad in the first place, which may have been exacerbated by his peers' low motivation and his teachers' half-hearted attitude.

Similarly, Sarah's opinions regarding her international high school experience were not very positive either. When asked what kind of instruction she had in the high school and if she found the instruction helpful for her studies in the US, she responded:

Excerpt 2   Teachers simply hope you could get a good TOEFL score

Nothing special. I think it might've just been of some help for my language skills. I feel the teachers simply hope you could get a good TOEFL score. The instruction was not that helpful for your overall English language proficiency. [...] [T]here were some classes taught by foreign teachers, but the lessons were very boring. (Sarah, Interview 1)

From Sarah's perspective, although the TOEFL instruction offered in her high school was adequate and effective for her to get an acceptable TOEFL score to get into a university in the US, she did not find it very helpful for her adaptation and integration into the new environment. The word 'boring' used to describe the lessons taught by the foreign teachers indicated that she neither enjoyed nor appreciated the way they taught the courses.

From an activity theory perspective, the excerpts shown above collectively illustrate that although the pre-study abroad education was deemed adequate – given that both participants were eventually admitted to college – the instruction they received before studying abroad was not conducive to learning and thriving in an English-dominant environment (*Outcome*: see Figure 5.3). To some extent, they found the TOEFL instruction to be effective in terms of helping them get the scores they wanted. This was not surprising given that the instruction that our participants received was mainly test-oriented (see *Rules* in Figure 5.3). It was therefore not intended to improve their overall English proficiency, which would have been more practical and meaningful for them for coping with real-life problems in an English-speaking country (S. Liu, 2018).

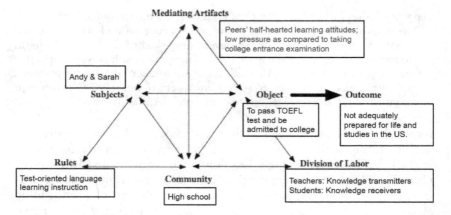

Figure 5.3 International high school activity model

Specifically, Andy felt disadvantaged because of the lack of discipline at his high school. However, his motivation to learn seemed strong, since he was one of only two students who received acceptable scores on the TOEFL and successfully got into a university in the US. This was quite unexpected to us, especially given that he did not want to study abroad in the first place, and his high motivation seemed unaffected by his less-motivated peers (*Mediating Artifacts:* see Figure 5.3). In Sarah's case, she felt the TOEFL courses might have been helpful in terms of passing the test but that they were not very effective for her language development in the long run (*Outcome:* see Figure 5.3). As for the instruction offered by English native-speaking teachers, she found it neither helpful nor enjoyable. However, because teaching is often conceived as a unidirectional transfer of knowledge activity in Chinese class (Heng, 2018), it is possible that both participants were used to taking on the role of merely being a knowledge receiver (*Division of labor:* see Figure 5.3). Andy's passive acceptance (i.e. 'I would do whatever I am asked to do. It does no harm to me, so it does not really matter.') also lent some support to this speculation. Despite both participants' discontent with the ineffective instruction, they chose to adopt a more receptive role in their learning.

Impact on their life and academic studies

In understanding both Andy and Sarah's educational backgrounds and how they felt under-prepared to study abroad, we shift to the second half of our first research question: How did these past experiences inform the way Andy and Sarah navigated and participated in their new academic and social community? Within a classroom context, Andy and Sarah quickly immersed themselves into a cocoon community (Dervin & Korpela, 2013). This is illustrated by the writing classroom layout (Figure 5.4),

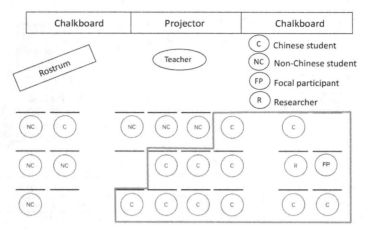

Figure 5.4 Writing classroom layout

which we sketched during our first in-class observation of Andy's writing class.

Figure 5.4 presents a clear division between the Chinese and non-Chinese students in the writing classroom. Andy is the furthest away the non-Chinese students. This classroom layout could in turn inform why Chinese international students are positioned as 'deficient' in Western contexts (Duff, 2015; Straker, 2016). Specifically, this layout may highlight and strengthen ideologies for the teacher and non-Chinese peers that Chinese international students 'do not take active part in class discussions because of their cultural disposition' (Kumaravadivelu, 2003: 711) and results in using their L1 instead of developing their L2—English. When asked why he stayed in this cocooned seating arrangement, Andy elaborated it was for a sense of comfort:

Excerpt 3 The Chinese students naturally huddled together

Now there are not [a lot of opportunities to meet non-Chinese students]. There are some in class, but we do not often communicate with each other. When students enter the classroom, we naturally ended up sitting separately, and then the Chinese students naturally huddled together. [...] But people will always be more close to those they feel more close to. You can feel this way when you see Chinese people, because you all share the same language. [...] Of course, I do want to practice my speaking skills [through the interaction with non-Chinese peers]. Just like I want to lose weight, but I just can't do it. (Andy, Interview 2)

Andy clearly stated that he wanted to improve his English through more interaction with presumably native English speakers. This seating

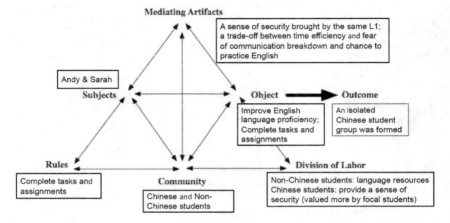

Figure 5.5 Classroom interaction activity model

arrangement, however, did not provide such opportunities. Instead, this arrangement was beneficial in creating a makeshift community that allowed Andy and his Chinese peers to translate English instruction (the main mediating artifact, see Figure 5.5) into Chinese in order to complete the tasks. In turn, this community allowed Andy to utilize his prior academic skills developed in China within the classroom. Moreover, the Chinese cluster within the classroom allowed Andy, who was still new to Western education expectations, to rely on his neighboring peers' resources (e.g. linguistic, material, academic skills) to mitigate the classroom expectations of learning Western-centric academic skills (Heng, 2018). The use of Andy's L1 with his peers to understand the content and the class discussion provides an insight as to how such makeshift communities allow international students such as Andy to overcome any amount of anxiety they may have before using L2 with the larger class (Kumaravadivelu, 2003). Nevertheless, this decision to sit at the edge of this cocoon community has both beneficial and detrimental outcomes concerning Andy's English development. Additionally, such makeshift communities also create a social distance between him and his non-Chinese classmates.

In Sarah's class, their teacher was aware of this cocoon community issue and took steps to offer more opportunities for students to speak English. Sarah described how the teacher achieved this purpose while sharing her feelings of concern:

Excerpt 4 It's still scary for me

The teacher would separate the Chinese students who always sit together, and he would group the students by assigning numbers to each student. In this case we would have some opportunities to have some American students in our group and we have to talk to them... it is a little bit scary, but I feel it might be helpful for myself. However, it's still scary for me. [...] I mainly study with my Chinese class-mates because we share the same language. If you are talking with an American classmate, it is a waste of time if he spends a lot of time explaining but probably, I still cannot understand it. It is not efficient. (Sarah, Interview 2)

From the excerpt, even though studying and living in an English-speaking environment, it appears that the opportunities that Sarah had to talk to non-Chinese were very limited, and she did not actually make full use of her already limited opportunities. Moreover, her emotional security, which is how one perceives their self-confidence and dignity (Sawir *et al.*, 2012; Tananuraksakul & Hall, 2011), was closely tied to her use of English within and outside the class. It is for this reason she may have had anxiety when the teacher enacted opportunities to interact with her non-Chinese peers.

Because of his lack of self-confidence in using English, Andy preferred to use his first language and previously acquired academic skills with his Chinese peers. These interactions, according to him, were conducive to his academic development. In contrast to his negative evaluation of the impact of his high school peers on his studies, the way in which Andy viewed his Chinese peers now as valuable academic and social resources further supports how moving spatially can alter the way in which individuals adapt their goals, use of mediating tools, values, and division of labor to fit the context and the activity (J. Liu, 2015). Sarah attributed her preference for her Chinese peers over her non-Chinese peers to her lack of confidence in her limited English proficiency; she found it inefficient to discuss academic work with her American classmates. While this understanding sheds light on the first and second research questions regarding their background experience, and the way they used their available resources within a classroom setting, we now turn to the second research question. The next section focuses on how Andy and Sarah used their available resources to cope and interact with the community outside the classroom.

Transcending the US and China's Borders through WeChat

From the previous section, we saw that while being socialized into a new culture and community that has its own rules, practices, division of labor, and mediating artifacts, Andy and Sarah integrated themselves into a cocoon community within the classroom that was emotionally secure. A question we had was how they integrated and navigated the community and these practices outside the classroom? Over the course of the semester, both participants engaged in using WeChat, China's most popular messaging app. From the survey results collected at the beginning of the study, we learnt that WeChat was the social media platform most frequently used by them, and the amount of time spent using it was considerable. A closer observation of their online social interactions is necessary for us to have an understanding of who they preferred to interact with, how these online interactions took place, and what impact their social media use may have had on their academic and social life. The excerpt below demonstrates how WeChat was used as a tool by Andy to build connections.

Excerpt 5 How can you know each other without being friends on WeChat?

[I use WeChat] to communicate with Chinese friends and family. The main point is to maintain my circle. [...] How can you know each other without being friends on WeChat? In general, I will friend people who are older than me and stayed here longer. They are more reliable, and they can bring me a sense of security because they have been here for at least one year. I can ask them questions if I have any. (Andy, Interview 2)

Excerpt 5 indicates the important role that social media played in Andy's life. According to him, social media mainly serves the function of building and maintaining relationships (c.f. De Costa *et al.*, 2016). Similarly, Sarah found communication in academic settings with her Chinese peers efficient and easier. The use of WeChat provided her with a means to access resources and potential social connections outside the classroom in order to navigate her classes and the academic community. In turn, this enabled her to navigate her way through challenges and difficulties in the new environment (Wang, 2016) by being part of a member in a closed group composed of her Chinese contemporaries at the same institution as her. Sarah further explained that as an active member in this group, she was able to request and exchange information and resources with other members of the group. Figure 5.6 shows a member-only post of a request of someone knowledgeable in using Adobe Illustrator.

Figure 5.6 provides a glimpse into the various kinds of information and help students could find on WeChat. As Sarah mentioned in follow-up interviews, students within this group would request and exchange a myriad of resources to tackle not only academic problems but also problems they faced while living in the United States, such as selling/buying secondhand furniture or sub-letting an apartment.

WeChat is a powerful and constant artifact that helped Andy and Sarah to navigate the various activities they found themselves within. Wang (2016) in particular has noted the importance of this online platform for assisting international students in leveraging their available resources or artifacts (e.g. car rides, English proficiency, knowledge regarding a particular course or subject) to acquire resources that allow them to navigate their particular activity inside and outside the academic

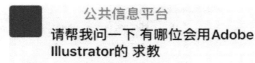

February 21, 2019 17:12

Figure 5.6 Asking for learning resources on WeChat[2] [Translation: Public information platform: Ask for someone who knows how to use Adobe Illustrator.]

community. Scholars (e.g. Li & Zhu, 2013) have also noted other affordances it can provide, such as allowing them to extend between and beyond the communicative space to mobilize their academic literacies and transform their understanding and knowledge while they are abroad (Blommaert & Horner, 2017; Wargo & De Costa, 2017). However, due to WeChat being a Chinese-user-dominant platform, Wang (2017) found the group acted like a cocoon community in which individuals like Andy and Sarah missed out on linguistic and social opportunities with their Western contemporaries (Li & Zhu, 2013).

Through the lens of activity theory, the two participants' choice to use only Chinese social media and interact mainly with other Chinese peers excluded them from the full range of resources available to them at a US university. Andy, although active in Chinese social media, did not display the same enthusiasm towards other platforms that are more likely to be used by native speakers of English. His main purpose by this practice was to maintain ties with China and to build a network of experienced peers with a similar background to his. In sharp contrast with his lack of motivation to interact with his non-Chinese peers, his prompt and active use of WeChat allowed him to expand his social network quickly, which was indispensable for his integration into the local community at the university in the US. This point was also affirmed by his rhetorical question, 'How can you know each other without being friends on WeChat?' Andy's inclination to 'friend' people who are older and more experienced signals how he mindfully built and used his connections to cope with problems and challenges he encountered.

Similarly, Sarah found WeChat to be important in her life. The WeChat information resources on the one hand allowed her to navigate various contexts within the US; on the other hand, WeChat afforded her

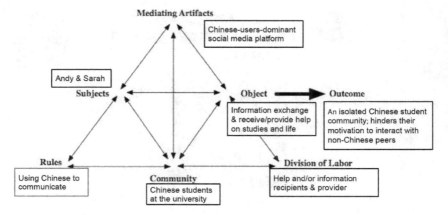

Figure 5.7 Social media use activity model

channels to expand her networks which, in turn, supported her integration into her Chinese social communities at the university. To some degree, the use of a Chinese-speaker-dominant social media platform (*Mediating Artifacts*; see Figure 5.7), which is governed by the rule of using Chinese to communicate (*Rules*; see Figure 5.7), limited both participants' access to interaction with non-Chinese peers. However, the gains yielded from WeChat use were highly valued by both Andy and Sarah (*Object*; see Figure 7). Unfortunately, this again may have hindered Andy and Sarah's motivation to step out of the local Chinese student community (*Outcome*; see Figure 5.7).

Implications and Conclusion

The results of the study shed light on important pedagogical implications for both pre-studies abroad institutions in China and universities in the US. As can be seen in this study, international students' navigation of linguistic and learning resources is directly related to their pre-study abroad experiences. Andy and Sarah made it clear that their high school education only focused on TOEFL test preparation and neglected other transferable skills that would be essential after arriving in the US. This arrangement affected Andy and Sarah in notable ways. The social challenges faced by Andy and Sarah partly resulted from the linguistic/language barrier (i.e. Andy's reliance on his L1 for interaction and Sarah's lack of confidence in her L2). Moreover, they both appeared to stay within an isolated Chinese community, regardless of whether they were inside or outside class, which to some extent ruled out the possibility for them to know people from different linguistic and cultural backgrounds. Such a social situation subsequently restricted their access to linguistic resources which they could have obtained from these people.

Additionally, WeChat was an essential tool since the platform allowed them to access a resource marketplace in which they could leverage and receive the necessary resources and tools to navigate the US academic and social community. However, this, in turn, constrained them to a cocoon community (Dervin & Korpela, 2013), resulting in their increased reliance on Chinese communication to seek help with their language and academic development. Nonetheless, the findings of this study suggest that although these international Chinese students seemed isolated from Western social and academic communities, they did actively integrate themselves, participate, navigate and manage to thrive in their Chinese-peer-dominant communities. As Heng has previously noted: '[d]ifferent is not deficient' (Heng, 2018: 22). While Andy and Sarah's pre-study abroad education had left them disadvantaged and under-prepared when studying in an English-speaking higher education context, they actively sought assistance from their Chinese peers inside and outside class to cope with challenges they encountered. The close examination of the activity system of Andy and Sarah revealed that their actions were mediated by a variety of factors (Kessler, 2020), many of which were *community-mediated* (influenced by their Chinese peers), *artifact-mediated* (e.g. bringing a feeling of belonging) and *rule-mediated* (e.g. use of Chinese to communicate on WeChat). Meanwhile, their strategies have been proven to be effective regarding the goals they wanted to achieve (e.g. to complete assignments, to exchange information).

In understanding their educational backgrounds in China and their experiences while attending university in the US, we suggest a greater need for awareness is needed regarding the challenges faced by these international students (see also Chapters 3 and 6, this volume). Additionally, we echo the recommendation of Li and Zhu (2013), who urge instructors to incorporate students' current resources and academic literacies in their curricula, especially during the first year when such students are studying outside their home country. This pedagogical practice is necessary to allow students to be emotionally secure (Tananuraksakul & Hall, 2011) and to enable them to integrate and interact with their classmates.

Notes

(1) This number does not include graduate students.
(2) The QR code has been altered to conceal our participant's anonymity. For information concerning ethical data collection from online sources, see Tao *et al.* (2017).

References

Akkerman, S.F. and Bakker, A. (2011) Boundary crossing and boundary objects. *Review of Educational Research* 81 (2), 132–169. https://doi.org/10.3012/0034654311404435.
Albusaidi, S. (2019) Using activity theory to explain how a student learns in an internalised classroom from a sociocultural perspective. *Journal of Language Teaching and Research* 10 (6), 1142–1149. https://doi.org/10.17507/jltr.1006.02.

Altbach, P.G. (2012) The globalization of college and university rankings. *Change: The Magazine of Higher Learning* 44 (1), 26–31.

Blommaert, J. and Horner, B. (2017) Mobility and academic literacies: An epistolary conversation. *London Review of Education* 15 (1), 2–20. https://doi.org/10.18546/LRE.15.1.02.

Bound, J., Braga, B., Khanna, G. and Turner, S. (2016) A passage to America: University funding and international students (Working Paper No. 229881). Cambridge, MA: National Bureau of Economic Research.

Carcary, M. (2009) The research audit trail: Enhancing trustworthiness in qualitative inquiry. *The Electronic Journal of Business Research Methods* 7 (1), 11–24.

De Costa, P.I., Tigchelaar, M. and Cui, Y. (2016) Reflexivity and transnational habitus: The case of a 'poor' affluent Chinese international student. *AILA Review* 29 (1), 173–198. https://doi.org/10.1075/aila.29.07dec.

Dervin, F. and Korpela, M. (2013) Introduction. In M. Korpela and F. Dervin (eds) *Cocoon Communities: Togetherness in the 21st Century* (pp. 1–13). Newcastle: Cambridge Scholars Publishing.

Dimmock, C. and Ong Soon Leong, J. (2010) Studying overseas: Mainland Chinese students in Singapore. *Compare: A Journal of Comparative and International Education* 40 (1), 25–42.

Duff, P.A. (2015) Transnationalism, multilingualism, and identity. *Annual Review of Applied Linguistics* 35, 57–80.

Engeström, Y. (1987) *Learning by Expanding: An Activity-theoretical Approach to Developmental Research*. Helsinki: Orienta-Konsultit. See http://lchc.ucsd.edu/MCA/Paper/Engestrom/Learning-by-Expanding.html. Accessed 11 November 2019.

Engeström, Y. (1999) Communication, discourse and activity. *The Communication Review* 3 (1–2), 165–185.

Engeström, Y. (2001) Expansive learning at work: Toward an activity theoretical reconceptualization. *Journal of Education and Work* 14 (1), 133–156.

Friedman, D. (2012) How to collect and analyze qualitative data. In A. Mackey and S.M. Gass (eds) *Research Methods in Second Language Acquisition: A Practical Guide* (pp. 180–200). London: Blackwell.

Heng, T.T. (2018) Different is not deficient: Contradicting stereotypes of Chinese international students in US higher education. *Studies in Higher Education* 43 (1), 22–36. https://doi.org/10.1080/03075079.2016.1152466.

Institute of International Education (2019) International students in the United States: 2019 fast facts [PDF file]. Retrieved 12 December 2019 from https://www.iie.org/Research-and-Insights/Open-Doors/Fact-Sheets-and-Infographics/Fast-Facts.

Kessler, M. (2020) Technology-mediated writing: Exploring incoming graduate students' L2 writing strategies with activity theory. *Computers and Composition* 55, 1025–1042.

Kozulin, A. (2018) Mediation and internalization: Conceptual analysis and practical applications. In J.P. Lantolf, M.E. Poehner and M. Swain (eds) *The Routledge Handbook of Sociocultural Theory and Second Language Development* (pp. 23–41). New York: Routledge.

Kumaravadivelu, B. (2003) Problematizing cultural stereotypes in TESOL. *TESOL Quarterly* 37 (4), 709–719.

Lantolf, J., Thorne, S.L. and Poehner, M. (2015) Sociocultural theory and second language development. In B. VanPatten and J. Williams (eds) *Theories in Second Language Acquisition* (pp. 207–226). New York: Routledge.

Leont'ev, A.N. (1978) *Activity, Consciousness, and Personality*. Englewood Cliffs, NJ: Prentice-Hall.

Li, W. and Zhu, H. (2013) Translanguaging identities and ideologies: Creating transnational space through flexible multilingual practices amongst Chinese university students in the UK. *Applied Linguistics* 34 (5), 516–535. https://doi.org/10.1093/applin/amt022.

Liu, D. (2016) Strategies to promote Chinese international students' school performance: Resolving the challenges in American higher education. *Asian-Pacific Journal of Second and Foreign Language Education* 1 (8), 1–16. https://doi.org/10.1186/s40862-016-0012-9.

Liu, J. (2015) Reading transition in Chinese international students: Through the lens of activity system theory. *Journal of English for Academic Purposes* 17, 1–11. https://doi.org/10.1016/j.jeap.2014.11.004.

Liu, S. (2018) Neoliberal global assemblages: The emergence of 'public' international high-school curriculum programs in China. *Curriculum Inquiry* 48 (2), 203–219. https://doi.org/10.1080/03626784.2018.1435977.

Saldaña, J. (2016) *The Coding Manual for Qualitative Researchers*. Thousand Oaks, CA: Sage.

Sato, T. and Hodge, S.R. (2009) Asian international doctoral students' experiences at two American universities: Assimilation, accommodation, and resistance. *Journal of Diversity in Higher Education* 2 (3), 136–148.

Sauro, S. (2014) Lesson form the fandom: Technology-mediated tasks for language learning. In M. González-Lloret and L. Ortega (eds) *Technology-mediated TBLT: Researching Technology and Tasks* (pp. 239–261). Philadelphia, PA: John Benjamins.

Sawir, E., Marginson, S., Forbes-Mewett, H., Nyland, C. and Ramia, G. (2012) International student security and English language proficiency. *Journal of Studies in International Education* 16 (5), 434–454. https://doi.org/10.1177%2F1028315311435418.

Straker, J. (2016) International student participation in higher education: Changing the focus from 'international students' to 'participation.' *Journal of Studies in International Education* 20 (4), 299–318.

Swain, M., Kinnear, P. and Steinman, L. (2015) *Sociocultural Theory in Second Language Education: An Introduction through Narratives* (2nd edn). Bristol: Multilingual Matters.

Swider, S. (2014) Reshaping China's urban citizenship: Street vendors, Chengguan and struggles over the right to the city. *Critical Sociology* 41 (4–5), 701–716. https://doi.org/10.1177/0969205145297676.

Tananuraksakul, N. and Hall, D. (2011) International students' emotional security and dignity in an Australian context: An aspect of psychological well-being. *Journal of Research in International Education* 10 (2), 189–200. https://doi.org/10.1177%2F1475240911410784.

Tao, J., Shao, Q. and Gao, X. (2017) Ethics-related practices in internet-based applied linguistics research. *Applied Linguistics Review* 8 (4), 321–335.

Vygotsky, L.S. (1978) *Mind in Society: The Development of Higher Psychological Processes*. Cambridge, MA: Harvard University Press.

Wang, X. (2016) Transnational Chinese students' literacy and networking practices. *Journal of Adolescent & Adult Literacy* 60 (6), 687–696. https://doi.org/10.1002/jaal.623.

Wargo, J.M. and De Costa, P.I. (2017) Tracing academic literacies across contemporary literacy sponsorscapes: Mobilities, ideologies, identities, and technologies. *London Review of Education* 15 (1), 101–114. https://doi.org/10.18546/LRE.15.1.09.

Yamagata-Lynch, L.C. (2010) *Activity Systems Analysis Methods: Understanding Complex Learning Environments*. New York: Springer.

Zhang, Y.L. (2016) International students in transition: Voices of Chinese doctoral students in a US research university. *Journal of International Students* 6 (1), 175–194.

Zhu, W. and Mitchell, D.A. (2012) Participating in peer response as activity: An examination of peer response stances from an activity theory perspective. *TESOL Quarterly* 46 (2), 362–386. https://doi.org/10.1002/tesq.22.

6 International Students' Writing Development from an Activity Theory Perspective

Myeongeun Son

Introduction

Many international students who attend US universities in pursuit of academic and social development are from diverse backgrounds (Anderson, 2015; Institute of International Education, 2019). Although their number has increased dramatically in recent years, not all students enjoy a successful transition to their new communities (e.g. De Costa *et al.*, 2016; Popadiuk & Arthur, 2004; Zhai, 2003). In particular, international students may encounter difficulties in interacting with people in the new community; in addition, they may have trouble adjusting to American academic, social and cultural differences.

In this regard, US universities generally support international students' transition to and development on campus by establishing an office for international students and mentoring programs between international and native students. The resources that universities offer include (1) a prerequisite writing course and (2) academic writing consultation in a writing center, both of which support the academic growth of international students (e.g. Blau *et al.*, 2002; Cheatle & Jarvie, Chapter 7, this volume; Moussu & David, 2015; Myers, 2003; Nakamaru, 2010; Okuda & Anderson, 2018; Powers, 1993; Rafoth, 2015). By taking such a prerequisite writing course, international students begin the necessary preparation for English academic writing skills before taking an introductory writing course with domestic students. A writing center can provide appropriate feedback on international students' academic writing and can facilitate students' understanding of diverse aspects in the new community. Since some international students usually have low English proficiency and limited experience with English academic writing, these forms of support can help them not only develop English proficiency but also become familiar with English academic writing.

Much research has been conducted on ways to support international students either through a prerequisite writing course or a writing center. For instance, Okuda and Anderson (2018) investigated Chinese graduate students' use of a writing center at a Canadian university. This case study examined Chinese graduate students' efforts to negotiate with tutors in the writing center to receive appropriate writing support that suited their specific needs. A writing center can help international students to improve their English academic writing in general; however, students who strategically ask tutors for particular feedback that they would like to receive may be able to use the services of the writing center most successfully.

However, few studies have investigated the interplay of the available resources, such as the prerequisite writing course and the writing center, and the multiple elements involved in the resources made available for international students' academic development and socialization. To address this gap, this study examined two international undergraduate students' academic development and socialization trajectories mediated by their participation in the FYW 100 writing course and by writing center consultations. Considering international students' multiple interactions while using the available resources at a US university, this study draws on activity theory as an interpretative framework and seeks to understand the students' academic development and socialization in sociocultural contexts (Lantolf & Thorne, 2006; Zhu & Mitchell, 2012).

Literature Review

Activity theory

Activity Theory (AT) is based in the Vygotskian sociocultural perspective (Vygotsky, 1978). This theory was first suggested by Leont'ev (1981) and later expanded by Engeström (1987, 1999, 2001). Engeström elaborated on the social dimensions of learning activities. His interpretation of activities demonstrated human activities as interacting with multiple elements, such as community, pertinent to social practices. He used a triangle to elaborate activity systems graphically. The upper triangle of Figure 6.1 shows Vygotsky's ideas of the subject (agent), object (goal), and mediating artifacts in Figure 6.1 (e.g. signs or tools). The subject is an individual who intends to achieve an object as they utilize mediating artifacts. Engeström expanded the dimensions of activity by stipulating that the system includes rules, communities and a division of labor, all of which constitute the social dimensions of activity as a unit of analysis. Cumming (2006) explained this activity system with an example of writing involving a student (subject) who tried to improve his writing

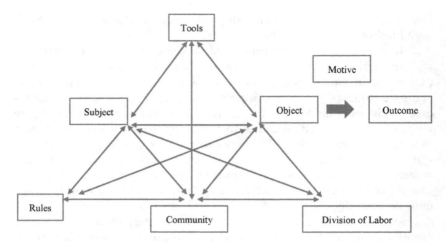

Figure 6.1 The activity system in activity theory

(object) in response to its discourse norms (rules) in the classroom context (communities), doing the writing task assigned by the teacher (division of labor) by using different source materials (mediating artifacts).

As Engeström (2001) considered the activity system to have potential for change, and to become interactive, he noted that contradictions may occur among the elements involved in the activity system. Further, he suggested that since the activity system is open and dynamic, it adopts new elements from the outside, which may introduce conflicts and subsequent contradictions within the various elements in the activity system. These contradictions subsequently generate conflict but are a crucial driving force of change and development. For instance, applying AT to their work, Nelson and Kim (2001) analyzed how L2 learners in first-year writing courses learn to write in English. During their writing courses, the students made efforts to resolve the contradictions between their understanding of online learning record assignment guidelines and implementing the portfolio; in pursuit of each of their goals to obtain a high grade they used different tools such as language, teachers, and other students' work. Fujioka (2014) also investigated the interactions between L2 students' and US native speakers involved in English writing assignments. She found that the interaction process was marked by tensions and contradictions because students wanted to respect the authority of their professors but complained about the demanding work. Despite the contradictions, the L2 students tried to prove academic competitiveness to their professors as they utilized the contradictions as their driving force in the final assignment.

AT has been applied to different areas of applied linguistics research to explain second language learners' behaviors, such as those relating to writing development (e.g. Yang *et al.*, 2004). Basturkmen and Lewis (2002), for example, examined how L2 students constructed activities and considered success in their writing course. By adopting a multiple case study design, the authors investigated three L2 students and interviewed two teachers regarding the AT perspective. Throughout a 12-week course, the students' perspectives toward success were different; in other words, their goals were diverse – from expressing their ideas in English to mastering conventions of English writing. The students were enrolled in the same course but their goals to develop their writing were different. Since the students' goals were different, teachers needed to provide feedback to students on aspects of writing that concerned them.

AT has also been useful in explaining writing development through academic socialization (e.g. Lei, 2008; Park & De Costa, 2015; Yang, 2006). Park and De Costa (2015), for example, examined the academic socialization of a graduate student from Nepal who enrolled in a TESOL master's program in the US. They looked at the student's academic writing process over a semester. The student realized the differences in the academic environment of her country versus that of the US and tried to resolve the contradiction caused by computer-mediated actions (e.g. finding sources from Google), because she was not used to using technological tools when completing her assignments. She also worked to improve her writing process in order to succeed in the academic community. More relevant to the current study, Yang (2006) explored the goals and activities of nine Chinese ESL students related to English academic writing improvement. He found that the Chinese ESL students learned the conventional acts of the discourse community and became functioning members of a particular academic discourse community in addition to activating their goals of learning English writing conventions. Thus, the L2 students became socialized academically, pursuing their goals of developing their writing skills.

Context

This case study, which investigated international students' L2 socialization, focused on the trajectories of two international students during one academic year (Fall 2017 through Spring 2018) at Great Lake University in the Midwestern US. These two participants enrolled in the same FYW 100 course. To complete this course, they were required to submit five essay assignments. Before submitting their final version of each essay, students are asked to complete small assignments, such as a writing cartoon and a skit with group members. They also have the opportunity to revise their writing drafts, based on feedback from peers, group members, instructors and tutors in the writing center.

Students are able to make an appointment with a tutor in the writing center at any stage in their writing process. At the writing center, students receive individual consultations with trained undergraduate and graduate staff members; these sessions last from 30 minutes to one hour.

Thus, international students are able to receive various types of support from the FYW 100 writing course and writing center consultation to develop their academic writing skills. Given the support offered by the US university, my study was guided by the following two research questions:

(1) How do international undergraduate students negotiate constraints and resources while engaging in writing assignments?
(2) How does the writing center scaffold the students' writing development in a prerequisite writing course?

Method

Participants

Two international undergraduate students participated in this study. Minji (a pseudonym) is from South Korea and she was a sophomore studying psychology; Carter (a pseudonym) is from Botswana, and he was a freshman studying chemical engineering. Minji is a native speaker of Korean who also speaks English and Chinese. Carter speaks Kalanga (his tribal language), Tswana (the official Bantu language in Botswana), English (the official language in Botswana) and Ndebele (his other tribal language). Minji came to the US as an exchange student when she was in her second year of high school; she graduated from the American high school. Carter graduated from an international private school in Botswana and entered the university with an ABC Credit Card Foundation (pseudonym) four-year scholarship. Because English is an official language in Botswana, he frequently used English at his high school.

Minji and Carter each had an intermediate level of English proficiency, based on their standardized test scores (i.e. Minji's TOEFL score was 74; Carter's IELTS score was 6.5). When taking the FYW 100 course, they were encouraged by their instructor to stop by the writing center whenever they would like to get feedback on their writing assignments throughout the year.

Data collection and analysis

Multiple data resources were collected in this study. These included classroom observations, writing center observations, observations of extracurricular activities (e.g. social clubs, social media and interactions with other international students), semi-structured interviews, literacy logs, questionnaires and artifacts (see Table 6.1).

First, the focal students completed a background questionnaire that included questions about their demographic information, previous experience with writing consultations at the writing center and in the writing course, and their use of social media. During the Fall semester, on two occasions, I observed the students in their writing course and at their writing center consultations. The focal participants' interactions

Table 6.1 Summary of data resources

Methods	Time period	Data
Questionnaire		Focal students' responses
Classroom observation	2 times in the semester	Audio-recorded interactions, audio-recorded whole classroom, field notes
Writing center observation	2 times in the semester	Audio-recorded interactions, field notes
Interview	2 times in the semester	Audio-recordings
Literacy log	One-week literacy log	Focal students' responses
Artifacts (e.g. writing assignments, social media)		Focal students' writing assignments, teacher and tutors' feedback

with their peers or groups in the classroom and with a tutor in the writing center were recorded, and field notes were taken.

The semi-structured interviews were conducted after observation of their classroom participation and writing center consultations and after they submitted their final writing assignments. Each time, the focal participants shared their latest experiences or thoughts about their writing class, writing center consultations, and writing assignments. The interviews usually lasted from 40 to 50 minutes and were recorded with an iPhone X. During the interviews, Minji used Korean, whereas Carter used English to communicate with me.

The focal students were also asked to complete an online survey that included open-ended questions regarding completion of their reading or writing assignments for one week. They could reflect on their work processes by answering these questions. Finally, at the end of each semester, I asked them to share their writing assignments and other relevant artifacts, including their text messages, for peer discussions and their social media postings.

Audio-recorded interviews were transcribed, and then all the data were organized based on recurring patterns. Following Corbin and Strauss's (2008) coding system, codes were assigned to these patterns. The data were examined through the lens of activity theory; in particular, following the previous research, I mainly focused on the rule, community, division of labor and tool elements (see Figure 6.2) in activity theory in my analysis.

Results and Discussion

Rules

In the case of my study participants, Minji and Carter, the syllabus and the objectives of the FYW 100 writing course, which are the rules in their activity system, interacted with multiple elements and facilitated the development of their academic writing skills. In particular, the FYW 100 writing course was offered to help international students prepare for academic writing and become familiar with a new society in the US university. In this course, the instructor explicitly stated the course objectives in the syllabus, such as 'enriching understanding of the types of literacy students will be engaged in as they move through the university' and 'gain a familiarity with the campus and the resources [the university] has to offer.' Based on the objectives, the instructor taught students what they should include in their writing and how to organize it; in other words, she focused on the content of their writing rather than pointing out grammatical errors. In this regard, she usually encouraged students to come up with and develop their ideas for academic writing.

> *Excerpt 1* Focal participants' comments on the instructor of
> prerequisite writing course
>
> **Minji:**   FYW 100 writing course instructor asked me to focus on
> content rather than grammar.
>
> **Carter:**   [the instructor] checked if my writing included the contents
> she just taught and if I could apply the contents to my writing
> correctly.

In the FYW 100 writing course designed under the syllabus, it was possible for Minji and Carter to understand the importance of content and structure in writing, which led to the development of their academic writing skills.

Community

Minji and Carter met various people in their new community. Interaction with these people, particularly with tutors in the writing center and peers in their writing course, mediated Minji and Carter's writing development and socialization.

Considering the importance of the content of their writings in their writing course, Minji and Carter wanted a tutor in the writing center to help them improve the organization of their work rather than having someone point out their grammatical errors.

> *Excerpt 2* Carter's actual needs of writing center consultation
>
> for me, I would say yes it's good for them to give you feedback based on grammar but the main thing when you look at a paper is the structure, the way your ideas are put together sequentially. ... if you're really on the right track to what your guidelines want you to do so instead of just giving you feedback about grammar. That's what I really want to get.

Because Minji and Carter agreed that non-native English speaking tutors in the writing center understood their actual needs in the consultations and their difficulties in using English, they were thus very satisfied with their writing center consultations. Minji thought that the non-native tutors were able to comprehend the intended meanings in her writing and to help her make revisions in order to better explain the meanings. She thought that the main focus of the consultations was on how to deliver her thoughts more clearly in academic writing,

Excerpt 3 Description of Minji's non-native tutor's consultation in writing center

... the tutor was so meticulous and he was so helpful. We talked about how to develop ideas and what to include in my writing. He always asked me what I want to explain and suggested some options to describe it clearly. He also checked my grammatical errors as well. The session was really helpful for me.

Likewise, Carter was also impressed by the efforts of the non-native tutors to understand his writings and this made him feel relieved. As a result of the tutors' encouragement and consideration, he was able to gather the courage to ask for assistance.

Excerpt 4 Description of Carter's non-native tutor's consultation in writing center

... [T]he most impressive part is her ability to keep me calm down... So [she kept saying] like 'I'm you', 'I'm in your position' and 'I'm helping you everything that you want, so don't be ashamed because of your grammar. We'll go through this'.

Minji and Carter filed a complaint, however, about the consultations of English native tutors because the latter were not usually patient in listening to their questions and they focused on the international students' grammatical errors, which was not in line with the actual objectives of the consultations. Because Minji and Carter felt uncomfortable due to their limited English proficiency and were not satisfied with their consultations with the native tutor, they gave up asking for additional help from the consultants. Tutoring by native tutors thus appears to conflict with not only the rules established by the syllabus and objectives of the FYW 100 writing course but also with international students' expectations. After several failures to obtain informative consultations for native tutors, Minji and Carter considered the interaction from native tutors disappointing and difficult, which made them avoid the consultations and hesitate in asking for help from native tutors. In other words, native tutors may hinder international students from developing the requisite writing skills and may hinder their ability to acculturate within a new community:

Excerpt 5 Minji's complaints about her native tutor's consultation in
           writing center

… English native tutors do not know why I make a mistake. L2 English
tutors try to find and assume why I make a mistake as they read the
overall context of my writing. The L2 tutors told me 'I know what you
mean, but you need to rephrase the sentence to deliver your message
clearly.' The English native tutors just check my grammar without
understanding my writing. They seem to have no idea what I would like
to explain in my writing.

Excerpt 6 Carter's disappointment about native tutor's consultation in
           writing center

.. I thought that she was a bit tense. So that's how I felt about her. You
know, sometime if someone is tense, you don't know …what you're
going to say. Yeah you know how she's been going to finish it so quickly.
[I don't] think it is comfortable.

Contrary to the international students who had participated in
previous research investigations (e.g. Harris & Silva, 1993; Leki, 1991;
Moussu & David, 2015; Myers, 2003; Nakamaru, 2010; Rafoth, 2015),
Minji and Carter wanted to resolve 'high-order concerns' (Moussu &
David, 2015), which are consistent with the general idea of a writing center.
International students' actual needs for writing center consultations
may not be simply to receive feedback on their grammatical errors
that previous research has addressed. Rather, it may be affected by the
objectives and/or directions of their course, as in this study. Thus, it is
important for the writing center consultants to consider various factors
that may interact with international students' use of consultation in
a writing center, so as to provide appropriate feedback aligned with
their actual needs. The writing center should conduct a needs analysis
for international students and train tutors accordingly to better provide
support to international students (see also Okuda & Anderson, 2018).

In addition to the writing center consultations, Minji and Carter
had opportunities to discuss some issues with their group members
and classroom peers, which helped them develop their ideas for their
writing. Although they were in the same classroom, Minji and Carter
had different points of view about group discussions and feedback from
group members. Minji had bad impressions about them. She thought that
students in her classroom pretended to be active in group discussions but,
in reality, they engaged in small talk by using their native languages and
provided less constructive feedback on her writings, with simple comments
such as 'great job' and 'good.' For instance, Minji filed a complaint about
Chinese students in her prerequisite writing course because they frequently
chatted with each other in Chinese and ignored other group members
during group discussion activities. Minji believed that group discussions
did not help improve her writing at all. Since she did not expect anything

from her group members, she frequently attended individual conference sessions with her instructor to get advice on her writings. In other words, she found an alternative way to get some constructive feedback.

Excerpt 7 Uselessness of Minji's group discussion in prerequisite writing course

Nobody says something. I sometimes do small talks with other students. When the instructor is coming close to us, we pretend to ask other students' thoughts. Group discussion takes about 5 minutes. No more than 10 minutes.

Excerpt 8 Minji's use of individual conference for writing assignments

I could meet my professor in the conference room. I brought this assignment prompt and talked with my professor in the conference room. I found the problems [in my writings] and could make sure what I need to focus on.

By contrast, Carter enjoyed group discussions in his classroom, and he thought that they were worthwhile in developing his writing. Specifically, he valued group discussions because he could listen to other students' different perspectives and ideas, which helped him brainstorm for his final writing assignments.

Excerpt 9 Carter's satisfaction of group discussion in prerequisite writing course

yes they're really helpful, because sometimes you might think that your idea is concrete but someone can might have a different look at what you wrote and help you... give you some more information to add on and develop that idea because there are many ways of life.

The rule and community parameters positively and negatively influenced Minji and Carter's writing development and socialization in their new academic and social environment. However, there were some contradictions between demands associated with enforcement of the rules and the expectations of the community in their respective activity systems. In particular, Minji and Carter wanted to strengthen the organization of the content of their writing, following the syllabus of their writing course and their instructor's encouragement. In spite of their expectations, the primary focus of the native tutors' consultations was to correct their grammatical errors; the consultant feedback thus did not match the guidelines of their writing assignment. In addition, Carter and Minji thought that native tutors were impatient when it came to listening to their difficulties and demands in the consultations. After these negative experiences, Minji and Carter made appointments with non-native tutors, who showed a willingness to communicate with them and improve their work.

In Minji's activity system, group discussions contradicted with the object and her ultimate outcome. Contrary to the original purpose and expectations of group discussions, interactions with group members did not have any positive effects on Minji's development; if anything, such interactive discussions may even have hampered her development. Thus, she tried to avoid the discussions and found an additional way to facilitate her own development as well as to resolve the contradiction.

Division of labor

As mentioned earlier, there were several stages that the students had to go through before submitting their final essays in the writing courses. One of the stages was group work in which group members were supposed to cooperate with each other to complete a task. These projects, however, affected Minji and Carter's writing development and socialization. For instance, before individual students wrote an essay about people's different disciplines and disciplinary practices and rules, they were randomly assigned to several groups to create a skit about group members' majors and relevant jobs and present it in front of the whole class. While discussing the topic of the presentation, Minji was frustrated with her group members. Three of the students were Chinese, and they kept using Chinese during the group discussion. Minji wanted to express her own opinion but she rarely participated in their conversation at all because of their use of Chinese. Although Minji was able to speak Chinese at a beginner level, her level of proficiency was not enough to discuss the class task with them; in addition, she did not want to use Chinese in the discussion, which was not ideal in the classroom. As a result, she was just given simple directions from the Chinese students and finished the task (a skit) without understanding what they talked about during the discussion. Minji felt marginalized and avoided group work with Chinese students after that. Later, her limited participation in the group work contributed to difficulties in her completing her final writing assignment. She should have included other people's experiences and thoughts about their majors in her writing, but she could not fully understand her group members' conversations and thus failed to reflect their input in her work (see Excerpt 10).

Excerpt 10 Part of Minji's group discussion with Chinese students in the writing classroom

Chinese S1:   [Chinese] I am asking her something about homosexuality.
Chinese S2:   [Chinese] You are writing a play about homosexuality. I'm the female actress. We two need to [know] how it feels to be a homosexual, their inner feelings, then, to act out those feelings.

Chinese S1:	[Chinese] When a homosexual person was facing a bunch of accusations, what should he/she do?
Chinese S2:	[Chinese] What he/she felt? What were his/her inner feelings, mental activities?
Chinese S1:	[Chinese] His/her inner feelings, what was he/she thinking?
Chinese S2:	[Chinese] Yeah.
Chinese S1:	[Chinese] Teacher, it's really difficult!
Chinese S2:	[Chinese] So I will write a play about homosexuality.
Chinese S1:	She is a psychologist. Maybe she has an office
Minji:	Yes, like conference office room.
Chinese S1:	We sit there, like me and [Chinese S2] one by one. You ask her 'What does a lesbian think about that?' And I may ask 'How may they express their feelings?'
Chinese S2:	I'm writing a book about a lesbian, but I have no idea. Could you tell me something about?

Minji's group discussion in Excerpt 10 illustrated yet another case of international students' marginalization and passive participation in their classroom. Previous research has demonstrated that international students' 'silence' may be led by their barrier of language, culture and gender (e.g. Flowerdew & Miller, 1995; Hilleson, 1996; Jones, 1999; Morita, 2004; Norton, 2000; Tsui, 1996). The distance between their own language, culture and perspectives of gender roles and those of their new environment has been focused primarily on investigating *when* international students' marginalization occurs; however, Minji's case suggests that the internal dynamics of international students may also affect their passive participation and failure to actively participate in the classroom. In other words, my findings revealed the consequences (i.e. the *what*) of such marginalization.

By contrast, Carter took pleasure in group work, not only because he had opportunities to interact with different people but also because group members encouraged him to develop his ideas or to complete his writing assignments (Excerpt 11). He considered their emotional support and help as important contributions to finishing his writing assignments. Carter used to carry out group activities with students from other African countries and from China who sat next to him. Compared to the Chinese students with whom Minji interacted, Carter's group members were eager not only to participate actively in the group discussion but also to develop their English proficiency and, therefore, were typically enthusiastic to discuss topics in English.

Excerpt 11   Carter's positive thoughts on group works in prerequisite writing course

through group work [I] meet different people every time... and that way yeah boost[s] your confidence now [I] feel like 'I can do that!' ...

it improves [my] confidence even though [I] know that I'm not good at it but [I'm] always willing to learn... Improves a lot.

Here [students] understand that English is not [my] first language yeah. If we're struggling, [they] always be there to help yeah.

The division of labor and object parameters resulted in contradictions in Minji's activity system, whereas they contributed to helping Carter realize the objectives and outcome in his activity system. Based on her experiences with other Chinese students, Minji believed that the group project in the FYW 100 writing course did not positively influence the completion of her writing assignments, so she tried to interact with other students from different (i.e. other than Chinese) backgrounds. On the other hand, Carter liked to participate in group work, and he believed that it helped him interact with various people and finish his assignments.

Tools

In order to overcome their limited English proficiency, Carter and Minji utilized diverse tools to communicate with other people in the new community. In her first draft, Minji failed to use appropriate English expressions in describing the artifact that represents Korean culture; this led to her instructor not understanding the essay. In the multimodal writing course, Minji was asked to create a video clip based on the essay. She thought that producing the clip offered her the chance to make the instructor understand her content; thus, Minji devoted herself to creating her content. As a result of this effort, Minji was successful in making a good impression on the instructor and receiving constructive feedback from the instructor with regard to her writing. Collectively, these events enabled her to earn a good grade.

Excerpt 12 Role of Minji's video clip for her instructor's understanding of her writing

After watching mine, she [the instructor] finally understood my story and told me 'your video clip is really helpful for me to understand your story, because I couldn't understand yours when I looked through your essay.'

Carter was impressed by his own improvements in English proficiency after entering the new community. He believed that the improvements would contribute to developing his writing skills. In other words, his improved English proficiency played a role as a tool that helped him achieve his ultimate goals of developing his English writing skills and socializing with other people at the university.

Excerpt 13 Carter's impression on his own improvement

Yes it's amazing because I've just been here for three months and yes few days back I had to like I have few essays I wrote in previous years so I had to I sit down and try to compare my writing down yeah so I was like oh yeah there's a lot of improvement here yeah you know I'm improving everyday... I'm improving everyday.

In sum, Minji and Carter engaged in various mediated activities while taking the FYW 100 writing course and receiving writing center consultations. Some mediated activities helped them achieve their ultimate outcomes of developing their writing and socializing within the university. However, contradictions were also found in some mediated activities, such as Minji's division-of-labor-mediated activities with Chinese students in the classroom. Figure 6.2 summarizes the mediated activities in Minji and Carter's activity system.

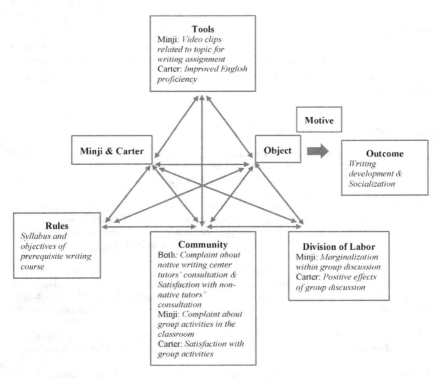

Figure 6.2 Minji and Carter's activity system for writing development and socialization

Conclusion

The aim of this study was to investigate international undergraduate students' L2 academic development and socialization through the lens of activity theory. In particular, this study explored how international undergraduate students (1) utilized a prerequisite writing course and writing center consultation, and (2) negotiated with other people and artifacts to develop their academic writing and socialization skills. Following the activity theory system, the study identified a variety of interactions for international undergraduate students that either positively or negatively affected their goal of L2 writing development and socialization.

The contradictions in my focal participants' respective activity systems have implications for better supporting international students. First, rather than the simple correction of grammatical errors, international students' needs for writing center consultation may need to be synchronized with the guidelines of their courses in order to maximize the value of their visits to the writing center. In this regard, the writing center needs to conduct needs analyses of international students and provide appropriate feedback accordingly. Second, the formation of in-class working groups of international students may prevent some international students from participating in the classroom activities. It may be important to understand the group dynamics among international students in order to help them become active learners in a new community.

References

Anderson, T. (2015) Seeking internationalization: The state of Canadian higher education. *Canadian Journal of Higher Education* 45 (3), 166–187.

Basturkmen, H. and Lewis, M. (2002) Learner perspectives of success in an EAP writing course. *Assessing Writing* 8 (1), 31–46.

Blau, S., Hall, J. and Sparks, S. (2002) Guilt-free tutoring: Rethinking how we tutor non-native-English-speaking students. *Writing Center Journal* 23 (1), 23–44.

Corbin, J. and Strauss, A. (2008) *Basics of Qualitative Research: Techniques and Procedures for Developing Grounded Theory* (3rd edn). Los Angeles, CA: Sage.

Cumming, A. (2006) Introduction, purpose, and conceptual foundations. In A. Cumming (ed.) *Goals for Academic Writing* (pp. 1–18). Amsterdam: John Benjamins.

De Costa, P.I., Tigchelaar, M. and Cui, Y. (2016) Reflexivity and transnational habitus: The case of a 'poor' affluent Chinese international student. *AILA Review* 29 (1), 173–198.

Engeström, Y. (1987) *Learning by Expanding: An Activity-theoretical Approach to Developmental Research*. Helsinki: Orienta-Konsultit.

Engeström, Y. (1999) Activity theory and individual social transformation. In Y. Engeström, R. Miettinen and R. Punamäki-Gitai (eds) *Perspectives on Activity Theory*. Cambridge: Cambridge University Press.

Engeström, Y. (2001) Expansive learning at work: Toward an activity theory reconceptualization. *Journal of Education and Work* 14 (1), 133–156.

Flowerdew, J. and Miller, L. (1995) On the notion of culture in L2 lectures. *TESOL Quarterly* 29 (2), 345–373.

Fujioka, M. (2014) L2 student–US professor interactions through disciplinary writing assignments: An activity theory perspective. *Journal of Second Language Writing* 25 (1), 40–58.

Harris, M. and Silva, T. (1993) Tutoring ESL students: Issues and options. *College Composition and Communication* 44 (4), 525–537.

Hilleson, M. (1996) 'I want to talk with them, but I don't want them to hear': An introspective study of second language anxiety in an English-medium school. In K.M. Bailey and D. Nunan (eds) *Voices from the Language Classroom: Qualitative Research in Second Language Acquisition* (pp. 248–275). Cambridge: Cambridge University Press.

Institute of International Education (2019) Enrollment trend. Retrieved 2 March 2020 from https://opendoorsdata.org/data/international-students/enrollment-trends.

Jones, J.F. (1999) From silence to talk: Cross-cultural ideas on students' participation in academic group discussion. *English for Specific Purposes* 18 (3), 243–259.

Lantolf, J.P. and Thorne, S.L. (2006) *Sociocultural Theory and the Genesis of Second Language Development*. Oxford: Oxford University Press.

Lei, X. (2008) Exploring a sociocultural approach to writing strategy research: Mediated actions in writing activities. *Journal of Second Language Writing* 17 (4), 217–236.

Leki, I. (1991) The preferences of ESL students for error-correction in college-level writing classes. *Foreign Language Annals* 24 (3), 203–208.

Leont'ev, A.N. (1981) The problem of activity in psychology. In J.V. Wertsch (ed.) *The Concept of Activity in Soviet Psychology* (pp. 37–71). Armonk, NY: M. E. Sharpe.

Morita, N. (2004) Negotiating participation and identity in second language academic communities. *TESOL Quarterly* 38 (4), 573–603.

Moussu, L. and David, N. (2015) Writing centers: Finding a place for ESL writers. In N. Evans, N. Anderson and W. Eggington (eds) *ESL Readers and Writers in Higher Education: Understanding Challenges, Providing Support* (pp. 49–63). New York: Routledge.

Myers, S.A. (2003) Reassessing the 'proofreading trap': ESL tutoring and writing instruction. *Writing Center Journal* 24 (1), 51–70.

Nakamaru, S. (2010) Lexical issues in writing center tutorials with international and US-educated multilingual writers. *Journal of Second Language Writing* 19 (2), 95–113.

Nelson, C.P. and Kim, M.K. (2001) Contradictions, appropriation, and transformation: An activity theory approach to L2 writing and classroom practices. *Texas Papers in Foreign Language Education* 6 (1), 37–62.

Norton, B. (2000) *Identity and Language Learning: Gender, Ethnicity, and Educational Change* (1st edn). London: Longman/Pearson Education.

Okuda, T. and Anderson, T. (2018) Second language graduate students' experiences at the writing center: A language socialization perspective. *TESOL Quarterly* 52 (2), 391–413.

Park, J.H. and De Costa, P. (2015) Reframing graduate student writing strategies from an activity theory perspective. *Language and Sociocultural Theory* 2 (1), 25–50.

Popadiuk, N. and Arthur, N. (2004) Counseling international students in Canadian schools. *International Journal for the Advancement of Counselling* 26 (2), 125–145.

Powers, J. (1993) Rethinking writing center conferencing strategies for the ESL writer. *Writing Center Journal* 13 (2), 39–47.

Rafoth, B. (2015) *Multilingual Writers and Writing Centers*. Logan, UT: Utah State University Press.

Tsui, A.B.M. (1996) Reticence and anxiety in second language learning. In K.M. Bailey and D. Nunan (eds) *Voices from the Language Classroom: Qualitative Research in Second Language Acquisition* (pp. 145–167). Cambridge: Cambridge University Press.

Vygotsky, L.S. (1978) *Mind in Society: The Development of Higher Psychological Processes*. Cambridge, MA: Harvard University Press.

Yang, L. (2006) Nine Chinese students writing in Canadian university courses. In A. Cummings (ed.) *Goals for Academic Writing: ESL Students and their Instructors* (pp. 73–89). Amsterdam: John Benjamins.

Yang, L., Baba, K. and Cumming, A. (2004) Activity systems for ESL writing improvement: Case studies of three Chinese and three Japanese adult learners of English. In D. Albrechtsen, K. Hasstrup and B. Henriksen (eds) *Angles on the English-speaking World* (pp. 13–33). Copenhagen: Museum Tusculanum Press.

Zhai, L. (2003) Studying international students: Adjustment issues and social support. *Journal of International Agricultural and Extension Education* 11 (1), 97–104.

Zhu, W. and Mitchell, D.A. (2012) Participation in peer response as activity: An examination of peer response stances from an activity theory perspective. *TESOL Quarterly* 46 (2), 362–386.

7 Responding to ELL Students Across Disciplines: Using Education Research to Inform Writing Center Practice

Joseph Cheatle and Scott Jarvie

Introduction

At institutions with significant populations of international and English Language Learning (ELL) students, writing centers are one of the best, if only, campus services that help with composition and language learning. However, institutions do not often provide adequate academic support for ELL students, who are frequently, but not always, international students (Nowacki, 2012). And there is rarely a sufficient support apparatus for these students to learn language (Nowacki, 2012). While some institutions may have English language centers and basic writing courses that are resources for ELL students' language and academic development, these are not universal and sometimes do not provide adequate services. Given the high-stakes pressure for ELL students to demonstrate proficiency in English (Thonus, 1993), ELL students often use writing center services disproportionately in comparison to their native English-speaking peers. Despite the fact that ELL students use writing center resources in high numbers, there has been no correspondingly expansive body of writing center literature focused on this population (Nowacki, 2012). While there are some key contributions to understanding the relationships between ELL students and writing centers, including, among others, Bruce and Rafoth's (2004) collection *ESL Writers: A Guide for Writing Center Tutors*, Abraham *et al.* (2021), Moussu (2013), Rafoth (2015) and Okuda and Anderson (2018), the need for additional literature, coupled with the importance of writing centers for ELL students and their high usage of those resources, points to the significance of researching and studying ELL students and writing centers.

In order to not reinvent the wheel, it can be productive for writing centers to look to other fields for guidance on ELL students. For our purposes here, we found the field of research on teacher education to be useful and generative, as scholars in that space have, for decades now, considered the ways to best attend to the needs of ELL students in teaching and learning. In that field, a body of work termed *linguistically responsive pedagogy* (LRP; e.g. Aguilera *et al.*, 2020; Lucas, 2010; Lucas *et al.*, 2008) seemed particularly promising as a frame for enriching the work of writing centers with ELL students. In our initial encounter with LRP literature, we found that there was already a significant overlap between that field and much of the work being done with ELL writers in writing centers. That is, many of the suggested practices of Lucas *et al.* (2008) associated with LRP are often already built into writing centers, serving as foundational principles and informing their interactions with multilingual clients. For example, writing centers typically strive to engage clients at a level just beyond their current writing proficiency – what in education literature is termed 'the zone of proximal development' (Vygotsky, 1978) – while also providing meaningful feedback for revision.

We also note LRP's finding that 'social interaction in which ELLs actively participate fosters the development of conversational and academic English (Gass, 1997; Vygotsky, 1978; Wong-Fillmore & Snow, 2002)' mirrors the dialogic structure of much writing center practice (Lucas *et al.*, 2008: 363), wherein clients are invited into conversation about their writing to facilitate its development. Moreover, Lucas *et al.* (2008) explain that research has found 'ELL students with strong native language skills are more likely to achieve parity with native-English-speaking peers than are those with weak native-language skills' (2008: 364), echoing writing centers' foundational understandings of students' native language as assets rather than hindrances to the development of their writing. If an ELL student has a strong native language proficiency, this serves as a resource for second language learning: 'language skills developed in one's first language—especially, literacy skills—transfer to a second language (Cummins, 2000)' (Lucas *et al.*, 2008: 364). This is especially true of academic language skills – the more proficient the student is with regard to their academic language skills in their native language, the easier it is to become proficient in the academic language of their second language. Finally, empirical research on the implementation of LRP has demonstrated that 'a safe, welcoming classroom environment with minimal anxiety about performing in a second language is essential for ELLs to learn' (Lucas *et al.*, 2008: 364), a finding that meshes well with the safe and inclusive structures long held to be essential for good writing center practice.

Across these findings then, we understand there to be substantial overlaps between the work of writing center consultants and linguistically responsive educators. Our goal in this chapter is to think about what LRP scholarship might offer writing center tutors working to better serve multilingual students. Because of the overlap we find between LRP literature and writing center research, we argue that writing centers can look to work on linguistically responsive pedagogies for constructing new writing center approaches for ELL students. We begin by examining the relationship between writing centers and ELL students in order to bring attention to the overlap between LRP and writing centers. We then provide an overview of linguistically responsive pedagogy. Lastly, we offer recommendations for how writing centers can translate LRP principles into writing center theory and practice.

Writing Centers

During the last 30 years, there has been a significant increase in international student enrollment at US higher education institutions (Nowacki, 2012; Okuda & Anderson, 2018), with Chinese students representing the largest percentage of international students over the past decade, according to the Institute of International Education (2018a, 2018b). Additionally, many of the international students are English Language Learner students. In the future, despite declining numbers, we expect international ELL students to represent a considerable segment of the higher education student body. At our former institution (Great Lake University, a large public institution), we experienced a similar trend in both international and ELL students. While not all international students are ELL students, and not all domestic students are native English speakers, the number of international students does give an approximation of enrolled ELL students. According to data from the writing center at Great Lake University, between Fall semester 2017 and Fall semester 2018, students who identified as ELL made up 36.49% of clients and made 50.76% of appointments. While making up only about 14% of the institution, ELL students used the center more than 50% of the time. Despite the high number of students from this specific demographic, the center did not place as much emphasis on them; rather, orientations and trainings were focused more on consulting in general. This is not unique: as we have shown previously, writing center studies as a field can better address this population that uses centers in extremely high numbers.

As we, and others, have experienced, ELL students present unique challenges for writing centers, such that the needs of ELL students can be at odds with what writing centers offer (Okuda & Anderson, 2018; Powers, 1993). This is particularly apparent around two foundational writing center philosophies: a global focus during consultations and indirect tutoring. As Linville (2004) and Okuda and Anderson (2018) point out, a collision of student and tutor goals is common because students are usually focused on the assignment at hand while tutors are focused on skills that can be applied to any assignment; the tension can be especially acute for ELL writers who are concerned about making *this* particular assignment sound like it has been written by a native English speaker. According to Moussu (2013), this leads to a situation where the writing center philosophy (a 'global' focus) can be frequently at odds with what ELL students want from consultations (a 'local' focus), including help with language, spelling and grammar.

Writing centers have long focused on non-directive/minimalist tutoring – as opposed to directive tutoring – as the primary means of consulting (Brooks, 1991). However, this approach does not necessarily work for ELL students who want more directive feedback, and then are disappointed when they don't receive it (Bitchener & Ferris, 2011; Diab, 2005; Ferris, 1995, 2002; Lee, 2005). Linville also highlights both these concerns in her work:

> When faced with editing an English as a second language (ESL) writer's paper, the tutor is often at a loss to determine how skillful an ESL student might realistically become in editing his own errors, knowing that he lacks the *native ear* for the language. Frustrated tutors are often tempted either to give the student too much help with errors or to give none at all, directing the student's attention to rhetorical issues instead. (Linville, 2004: 89)

The discrepancy between what ELL students need and what writing centers provide can even prompt tutors to question 'Is this my job?' (Gillespie, 2004) as they are asked to do things that are outside the 'typical' consultation. This discrepancy is particularly apparent when ELL students need more directive help in areas of language (spelling, grammar and syntax) that may increasingly place the tutor in the role of editor – something that is anathema to writing centers.

The discrepancy between what ELL students need and what writing centers can provide is most commonly manifested in issues of language, academic writing and tutor knowledge. Language functions as an overarching issue for ELL students: given the circumstance, the pressure to sound like a native English speaking student can be overwhelming. ELL students who use the center often do not have substantial backgrounds in writing and writing instruction in English (Powers, 1993); consequently, they often schedule an appointment for that very issue. Additionally, there is a lot of pressure on ELL students to be proficient in the English language – reading, writing and speaking. As Rafoth points out: 'United States colleges and universities operate in a culture that idealizes Standard American English' (Rafoth, 2015: 16).

This cultural idealization of Standard Academic English (SAE) leads to a situation in which ELL students believe that learning the language involves mastery of spelling and grammar, an idea which Moussu (2013) demonstrates as false. ELL students, especially international students, may also struggle with the conventions of academic writing. And many ELL writers are unaware of, or not familiar with, academic conventions in their discipline (Angelova & Riazantseva, 1999; Moussu, 2013). Therefore, in addition to language, academic writing is an important consideration for ELL students and writing centers. This results in a situation where ELL students are usually unaware of, or not familiar with, academic writing and conventions in their disciplines (Angelova & Riazantseva, 1999; Moussu, 2013).

Meanwhile, we ask that tutors be familiar with academic discourses (Thonus, 1993) and their 'variations by purpose and discipline; with errors and how to explain them; and with the struggles and rewards – both their own and others' – of learning and learning about languages' (Rafoth, 2015: 6). Even though we require tutors to be aware of a broad variety of academic discourse and conventions, tutors are often unprepared, and lack extensive training, to work with ELL students (Rafoth, 2015). This is a common theme among writing center practitioners and encompasses both language and writing issues. Because tutors come from a wide variety of disciplines, majors and backgrounds, they have a corresponding variety of experiences in working with ELL students. While most tutors are able to say that a sentence is not grammatically correct in SAE, they may not be able to explain why. For example, a tutor may be able to say that the subject and verb in a sentence need to agree, but they might not be able to explain why; tutors may also be able to say a sentence does not 'sound' correct to a native English speaker but be unable to diagram the components of the sentence. Because of the type of help needed, ELL students may require more time and specialized knowledge than the average tutor may possess (Canavan, 2015). And, as Rafoth (2015) notes, these issues are not confined to writing centers but also apply to colleges and universities that operate in a culture which idealizes SAE.

Linguistically Responsive Pedagogy

To realize this work of better serving ELL clients in writing centers, we turn to scholarship in the field of ELL[1] education. In particular, we have found research establishing linguistically responsive pedagogy (Aguilera et al., 2020; Gallagher & Haan, 2018; Lucas, 2010; Lucas & Villegas, 2013; Lucas et al., 2008; Met, 1999) useful as a framework for working with ELL students. As the student population in the US became increasingly demographically and linguistically diverse at the end of the 20th and beginning of the 21st century, the need arose for pedagogies to address new challenges of plurality in American schooling. Yet, as Lucas *et al.* note, most teachers working in the US today have little formal training for specifically teaching linguistically diverse students (Lucas *et al.*, 2008: 361). Scholars in ELL education envision LRP as a way of responding to those specific differences, addressing the particular needs and varied challenges of multilingual learners. As the name suggests, linguistically responsive pedagogy borrows from, and builds upon, the celebrated approach of 'culturally responsive pedagogy' (Au, 2009; Cazden & Leggett, 1981; Erickson & Mohatt, 1982; Ladson-Billings, 1994; Lee, 1998), which centers students' cultural practices, particularly those long marginalized in American schooling (e.g. communities of color) as well as responsive work from the field of ELL research (e.g. Cummins, 2000; Gibbons, 2002; Lenski *et al.*, 2006; Walqui, 2008). The approach theorizes what such a pedagogy would look like in classroom practice in contemporary pluralist classrooms, with the goal of building more meaningful and equitable pedagogy for students as well as diversifying the curriculum towards social justice.

LRP provides a framework for teaching students who speak languages other than English, providing research-backed conceptual matter and practical tools so that teachers can respond to students in ways that develop proficiency. Lucas *et al.* (2008) begin their own work by identifying foundational principles for working with ELL students:

(1) Conversational language proficiency is fundamentally different from academic language proficiency;
(2) Second language learners must have access to comprehensible input that is just beyond their current level of competence, they must have opportunities to produce output for meaningful purposes;
(3) Social interaction in which ELLs actively participate fosters the development of conversational and academic English;
(4) ELLs with strong native language skills are more likely to achieve parity with native-English-speaking peers than are those with weak native-language skills;
(5) A safe, welcoming classroom environment with minimal anxiety about performing in a second language is essential for ELLs to learn;
(6) Explicit attention to linguistic form and function is essential to second language learning.   (Lucas *et al.*, 2008: 363)

The goal of such principles is to inform scaffolded practices for ELLs to develop academic skills needed for classroom success. This means making the content of the curriculum accessible to ELL students and differentiating instruction such that teachers attend to ELL students' particular needs while building on the assets (both academic background and language proficiency) they bring to the classroom. For example, if teachers take seriously the well-established principle that 'Conversational language proficiency is fundamentally different from academic language proficiency', it follows that linguistically responsive pedagogical moves should be tailored to the varied proficiencies necessary for success with English in both conversational and academic contexts. In practice, this might mean spending time considering those latter contexts, and how academic uses of English – e.g. words commonly used on formal assessments, such as 'omit'; or the lexicon of particular academic genres, such as the research report – require specific curricular attention if they are to be taught well. If LRP can achieve the goal of better responding to the linguistic differences of ELL students through instruction then it, too, can be seen as part of the broader work of making curricula more responsive for all students.

Yet these foundational principles established by ELL research are still sufficiently abstract that translating them into actual classroom practice often proves difficult. LRP attempts to do just that, grounding teaching practice with ELLs in three specific areas of knowledge: '(1) familiarity with the students' linguistic and academic backgrounds; (2) an understanding of the language demands inherent in the learning tasks that students are expected to carry out in class; and (3) skills for using appropriate scaffolding so that ELLs can participate successfully in those tasks.' (Lucas *et al.*, 2008: 366). Especially welcome are the efforts of scholars to provide further concrete suggestions for envisioning effective teacher practices with ELL students.

In order to develop familiarity with students' linguistic and academic backgrounds, Lucas *et al.* suggest that a teacher 'directly ask a student to describe, orally or in writing, his or her previous experiences in school, or... ask the student's parents about those experiences' (Lucas *et al.*, 2008: 367). This move begins the work of engaging students' background history with language use, an approach that mirrors the established pedagogical practice of 'engaging prior knowledge' (Vygotsky, 1978). Such a move is important if LRP is to actually respond to students' linguistic diversity instead of providing generalized lessons that do not consider the particularities of students in the classroom, their varied histories and their experiences with language use.

The second theme, building an understanding of the particular linguistic demands of classroom activities, means identifying 'aspects of the language inherent in tasks that are likely to pose the greatest challenge to students' (Lucas *et al.*, 2008: 367). For example, they suggest teachers must consider and come to understand the complexities of syntax and semantics with respect to academic language use, as well as keep in mind the expectations of how that language will be used. In practice, this means a bit of forethought on the part of effective teachers of ELLs: Will students be listening to a lecture and taking notes? Or will they be collaborating with peers in small groups? Such questions point to the variation of particular linguistic demands placed on students in academic contexts.

Finally, appropriately scaffolding ELL content for success, the researchers argue, requires building upon both an understanding of students' backgrounds and the linguistic demands placed upon them in schools. Once teachers are familiar with the linguistic backgrounds of their students and the nature of the academic demands that will be placed upon ELL's language use, they can scaffold their lessons to be linguistically responsive. Lucas *et al.* (2008) offer a variety of strategies for such scaffolding, such as 'supplementing and modifying written text'; 'facilitating and encouraging use of students' native languages'; and 'engaging ELLs in purposeful activities in which they have many opportunities to interact with others and negotiate meaning' (Lucas *et al.*, 2008: 368–369). Using these research-backed practices, they argue, can help teachers develop more responsive pedagogies for addressing the needs of linguistically diverse students.

We argue, similarly, that there is much here that serves the work of writing center tutors, too. When tutors integrate such practices, across all three areas, into their work with ELL students, they can better address the increasing linguistic diversity of today's plural campuses, responding to students' varied languages more equitably and effectively to further their learning. Aguilera *et al.* find that 'pedagogical approaches that', like LRP, 'share a commitment to sustaining sociolinguistic diversity and promoting educational equity can be enacted across the lifespace to benefit all learners' (Aguilera *et al.*, 2020: 498). In what follows we offer specific recommendations, culled from the literature on LRP, that writing centers can take up in attempting to better serve ELL clients.

Recommendations

While there are some aspects of linguistically responsive pedagogy that are already built into writing centers, there are other aspects that can serve as recommendations. In Table 7.1 we provide a series of concrete suggestions from LRP that we applied to writing centers. We then provide more detailed explanations of each suggestion, including how each might apply to writing center consultation practices.

Tutors need to understand that conversational language proficiency is fundamentally different from academic language proficiency

Explanation: There are important differences, and distinctions, between conversational language and academic language proficiency. One may have conversational language proficiency while not having academic language proficiency; and this is true for both ELL students and native English speaking students. For example, a student may speak fluently about informal conversational subjects (like their

Table 7.1 Suggestions for teaching ELL learners and their writing center equivalents

Linguistically Responsive Pedagogy	Writing Centers
Teachers should understand that conversational language proficiency is fundamentally different from academic language proficiency (Cummins, 1981, 2000) and that it can take many more years for an ELL to become fluent in the latter than in the former (Cummins, 2008).	Tutors need to understand that conversational language proficiency is fundamentally different from academic language proficiency.
Teachers should pay explicit attention to linguistic form and function as it is essential to second language learning (Gass, 1997; Schleppegrell, 2004; Swain, 1995). This involves identifying the key vocabulary that students must understand to have access to curriculum content; understanding the semantic and syntactic complexity of the language used in written instructional materials; and knowing the ways in which students are expected to use language to complete each learning task.	Tutors should pay explicit attention to linguistic form and function as it is essential to second language learning.
Teachers should directly ask a student to describe, orally or in writing, his or her previous experiences in school, or a teacher can ask the student's parents about those experiences.	Tutors should directly ask a student to describe previous experiences in school, in order to gain a basic understanding of the student's previous linguistic and academic learning backgrounds.
Teachers should envision themselves learning some aspect of quantum theory in a language they do not understand. This will help them intuitively grasp the connection that exists between language and learning.	Tutors should envision themselves learning some difficult topic in a language they do not understand to help them intuitively grasp the connections between language and learning.
Teachers should use extra-linguistic supports. When the language of a lesson is too demanding for ELLs, extra-linguistic supports give them a medium other than language through which to access the content (Echevarria et al., 2000; Gibbons, 2002) i.e. visual tools.	Tutors should use extra-linguistic supports.
Teachers should supplement and modify written text. Several strategies can be used to reduce the burden on ELLs of having to process the oral language they hear in class while trying to make sense of new concepts. These include minimizing the use of idiomatic expressions (Hite & Evans, 2006; Yedlin, 2007); pausing more frequently and for longer periods than in usual speech (Verplaetse & Migliacci, 2008); providing outlines for lessons; repeating key ideas and building redundancy into teaching (Gibbons, 2002); and establishing classroom routines that enable ELLs to predict what is expected of them in different situations (Willett et al., 2007).	Tutors should supplement and modify written text.
Teachers should give clear and explicit instructions. It would be a mistake for teachers to introduce a task and assume that all students, especially ELLs, will know how to carry it out.	Tutors should give clear and explicit instructions.
Teachers should facilitate and encourage the use of students' native languages. The use of students' native languages can scaffold their learning in English.	Tutors should facilitate and encourage the use of students' native languages.

personal experiences or what they did over the weekend) but they may not understand the language of academia (like 'hypothesis', 'thesis', 'topic sentence' and 'transition'). While the meaning of conversational language can be derived from cues in the setting (Lucas *et al.*, 2008), academic language, which relies less on personal and shared experience, is more impersonal, technical and abstract (Gibbons, 2002).

Writing Centers: As Matsuda and Cox (2004) note, ELL writers are often in the process of developing an 'intuitive' understanding of the English language. And Linville (2004) focuses on six types of errors that tutors and ELL writers can focus on during consultations. However, for writing centers, the distinction between language acquisition and academic language means that we cannot assume an ELL student's proficiency in academic language on the basis of their speaking skills. Rafoth (2015) recognizes that academic language is unique; tutors must recognize that achieving academic language proficiency takes a much longer time than language acquisition. Furthermore, academic language poses unique challenges for ELL students due to the specialized vocabulary and particular language forms (Lucas *et al.*, 2008; Okuda & Anderson, 2018; Schleppegrell, 2004). For example, ELL students in physics must know the components of a lab report, proposal, and article conventions; tutors should be trained to broadly know about, and understand, the conventions of the field as well as the components of composition. By recognizing the differences between conversational language and academic language, tutors will be better prepared to help ELL students navigate their coursework.

Tutors should pay explicit attention to linguistic form and function, as it is essential to second language learning

Explanation: As Lucas *et al.* (2008) show, the idea that exposure to a language is sufficient to learn a new language is being challenged by those, like Harper and de Jong (2004), who argue that exposure to English is not sufficient. Recently, scholars like Gass (1997), Schleppegrell (2004) and Swain (1995) have renewed the focus of language learners on the formal elements of the language rather than just exposure. Form, in this case, refers to the features and rules of the language; form includes the internal grammatical structure of words and phrases as well as the words themselves. Lucas *et al.* are not advocating the generalized learning of form: rather, because language learning fulfills certain functions, they instead advocate what they term 'purposeful learning' (Lucas *et al.*, 2008: 365), where specific academic disciplines provide boundaries for the special linguistic forms that students need to learn.

Writing Centers: Lucas *et al.* (2008) are *not* suggesting that teachers become experts on language; rather, they are arguing that teachers 'can learn to identify and articulate the special characteristics of the language of their disciplines and make these explicit to their ELLs' (Lucas *et al.*, 2008: 365). For writing centers, that means tutors need to have a basic knowledge of the forms of English and, as we argued above, of the academic language used in a variety of disciplines. Because writing centers do not usually emphasize the local (spelling, grammar and syntax) as much as the global (thesis, organization, supporting evidence), this would mark an important shift. Training for tutors, then, would include conventions of usage, syntax, organization, and conventions of punctuation (among other things); tutors should be trained in linguistics throughout their time in the center, including language rules and forms. Additionally, tutors should be knowledgeable about the linguistic forms and functions of common academic disciplines in the center.

Tutors should directly ask a student to describe previous experiences in school

Explanation: ELL students are not monolithic and come from diverse backgrounds (both domestically and internationally; for more examples, see the chapters by Zhang, Son, and Ma and Green-Eneix, in this volume); they also have a broad array of experiences before arriving in English speaking academic institutions. Some ELL students enter institutions highly proficient in academic literacy, while others may enter with low academic literacy; some ELL students may be US-born while others may be international students; some may have gone to academically rigorous high schools while others may not; some may understand their subject matter while others may not; some may have a strong understanding of language while others may not – all of these require very different approaches. Lucas *et al.* (2008) advocate that we should learn about each student's linguistic and academic experiences in their primary language because this can be transferred to a second language. For example, a student with high proficiency and academic experience in their own language will need a different approach from a student whose proficiency and academic experience in their own language is low. Without knowing the background of the ELL student, it is difficult to know what type of help they may need.

Writing Centers: Writing center tutors can sometimes skip asking about the previous experiences of ELL students in favor of jumping right into the consultation. Instead, drawing on Lucas *et al.* (2008), tutors should ask students to describe their academic and linguistic experiences. Similarly, Okuda and Anderson (2018) highlight the importance of listening during a consultation. This can be very beneficial to the success of consultations with ELL students. For example, if a tutor knows that a student does not have academic literacy in their primary language, the tutor can spend time explaining academic concepts. And if a student indicates that they have a high academic literacy (which may differ across cultures) in their own language, then the tutor can focus on the client's linguistic competence in English. In this way, the tutor can better serve a student's unique academic and literacy needs.

> *Tutors should envision themselves learning some difficult topic in a language they do not understand to help them intuitively grasp the connections between language and learning*

Explanation: For many people, language functions as an afterthought – something to look through rather than at (de Jong & Harper, 2005). Lucas *et al.* (2008) argue that looking at language can allow us to see how academic learning is inseparable from language. Learning, then, is often dependent on language proficiency; as language capacity for ELL students increases, so too does learning. The point of asking native English speakers to envision themselves learning some difficult topic in a language they do not understand is to develop empathy for ELL students while also highlighting the importance of language to learning. By turning a critical eye to language, particularly academic language, we can better identify vocabulary and linguistic forms that ELL students need to know.

Writing Centers: Tutors should envision learning a difficult topic in a language they do not understand. For example, they could imagine that they are trying to learn about driverless cars or 3D printing in another language. This is particularly helpful if they have some competency in that language. As tutors try to explore complicated subject matter in another language, this process can help them consider the connections between language learning and academic language. Furthermore, tutors can learn to approach language with the intention of 'looking at the language of academic learning rather than simply seeing through it' (Lucas *et al.*, 2008: 368). This approach encourages tutors to slow down and consider the components of language necessary to learning rather than learning uncritically.

Tutors should use extra-linguistic supports

Explanation: Lucas *et al.* (2008) recommend the use of extra-linguistic supports when language demands become too much for ELLs in a lesson. When teachers provide scaffolds in a medium other than language, ELL students have opportunities to help access content and learn successfully. In effective ELL instruction, extra-linguistic supports might include, for example, visuals such as pictures, illustrations, maps, or graphic organizers which communicate and arrange information primarily visually (Lucas *et al.*, 2008: 368). These suggestions are in line with a larger turn within literacy studies towards multimodality, which theorizes new and multiliteracies (e.g. Early *et al.*, 2015; New London Group, 1996; Serafini & Gee, 2017; Vasudevan *et al.*, 2010) in keeping with a broader view of literacy, incorporating not just the linguistic but also the extra-linguistic as a reaction to the changing social environment of contemporary schooling and its increased cultural and linguistic diversity. Multiliteracy work argues that 'bringing multiple digital and non-digital modalities into the classroom that allow students to use their knowledge and experience from their homes and communities holds possibilities for new understandings of authoring texts and participation in school' (Vasudevan *et al.*, 2010: 465), possibilities that 'connect school learning to students' interests, knowledge, and experiences from outside of school' (2010: 444). By providing students with extra-linguistic ways of working with language learning, teachers can attend to the expanding realities of language use and needs in today's increasingly diverse ELL classrooms.

Writing Centers: As noted above, the context in which multiliteracies emerged – that is, in response to increasing contemporary plurality in today's diverse educational spaces – is, of course, also the context in which university writing centers operate today. Accordingly, if we are to meet the needs of ELL students in writing center consultations, then we would do well to consider how we might leverage the extra-linguistic in support of our work as tutors. For example, an ELL student struggling to conceptualize the trajectory of their argument in written language might create a map instead, visually organizing the sequence of, and relationship between, the premises. Bruce (2004) recommends something similar for ELL writers – that they should map their plan for the consultation as a way of visualizing their plan of action. Or, when working with a client on a close reading of a novel like Toni Morrison's *Beloved*, a timeline of the plot and the novel's major events can prove useful to conceptualizing a complicated text; furthermore, this extra-linguistic support can then help with a written analysis of the text. There are, of course, many other examples we could give, considering how extra-linguistic media – such as pictures, videos, Venn diagrams, non-verbal audio, etc. – could be leveraged to serve this work. The point is that if we draw from established research on working with ELLs on their writing, then extra-linguistic supports will likely prove useful in providing those clients with traction in completing the task.

Tutors should supplement and modify written text

Explanation: In addition to utilizing extra-linguistic supports, ELL research has found adding language to written text can be generative in support of ELL students' learning. Brown (2007) found that providing ELLs with written study guides that include vocabulary, questions and outlines, to be effective in helping with ELL reading instruction. Similarly, Hite and Evans (2006) studied the efficacy of rewritten adaptations of texts for pedagogical purposes, finding them useful for making a text more accessible to ELL students who found the original difficult. Meanwhile, research also suggests that teachers add margin notes to textbooks so that ELLs can better understand the text's content (Verplaetse & Migliacci, 2008). Across the strategies, it is clear that supplementing and modifying classroom text can be an effective strategy for supporting ELL's learning.

Writing Centers: Writing center tutors could easily adopt similar strategies in their work with ELL students. As Rafoth (2015) points out, tutors should ask clients for their writing prompt or, if that is not available, a plan for getting the prompt from their instructor or even creating one together. Often, however, clients will bring with them the prompt and directions for a particular written assignment; tutors could make the prompt more accessible by writing out definitions to key terms and providing explanations of unclear directions. And, as the tutor progresses towards the writing proper, tutors can help ELL clients conduct clarifying research and identify useful background information to support the argument. Tutors might also provide written templates, i.e. 'sentence starters', as a way of supplementing the formulation of statements in academic writing. Linville (2004) makes a similar argument about the benefits of creating word-form grammar resource sheets for writing centers working with ELL students. Writing centers might further create and provide ELL clients with study guides for specific academic disciplines. Such additional text provides context, in the literal sense: language with which ELL clients can further the composition they are in the process of creating.

Tutors should give clear and explicit instructions

Explanation: Of particular importance in research on ELL learning is the need for teachers to give clear and explicit instructions, directly communicating the demands of the lesson and their expectations of students (Gibbons, 2002). While this has long been a tenet of effective teaching practice generally, research has demonstrated that ELLs especially benefit from this approach (Lucas, 2010). Practices such as providing instructions in both written and oral form, requiring students to take notes, and requesting that they repeat instructions back to the teacher, have been found significantly helpful for supporting ELL learning. (Lucas *et al.*, 2008: 369).

Writing Centers: In their work with clients, writing centers should similarly emphasize the practice of providing instructions in support of ELL student writing. In some ways this requires a paradigm shift from the way many writing centers operate: rather than taking a dialogic approach which emphasizes asking questions of clients to facilitate their learning and writing development, Lucas *et al*. (2008) and Okuda and Anderson's (2018) work find that a more directive approach proves effective with ELLs. Accordingly, writing centers should consider the efficacy of their dialogic approach and consider how moments of clear and direct instruction may prove useful in working with ELL clients. For example, if an ELL student is unclear about an instructor's assignment prompt, it may be more beneficial to tell them what the prompt is asking for rather than asking questions about their interpretation of the prompt. In this way, the tutor can act as a translator who then gives explicit instructions for what to work on for the ELL writer. Additionally, Staben and Nordhaus (2004) encourage tutors working with ELL writers to be direct (giving students information they do not have) while not being directive (telling writers what they have to do with that information for a specific assignment). While asserting the need for clarity in providing instructions may seem basic – even obvious – it is clear from the literature on LRP and best practice with ELL students that attending to the particular conversations between tutors and clients is essential in supporting ELL writers.

Tutors should facilitate and encourage the use of students' native languages

Explanation: Finally, Lucas *et al*. (2008) assert the need for teachers to facilitate and encourage the use of students' native languages in their work with ELLs. The difficulty with this approach, of course, is that teachers may not themselves be familiar or comfortable with students' native languages. To that end, research has found the use of bilingual peer teacher–translators (Hite & Evans, 2006; Walqui, 2008) helpful for bridging the gap between teacher and ELL student while allowing for the latter to use their native language. The role of the peer–teacher translator is to 'translate and explain content' (Lucas *et al*., 2008: 369) to ELLs; this intervention can prove crucial, as it is often the only way for nascent/novice ELLs to access that content. Those researchers also suggest encouraging ELLs to write their first drafts in their native languages before subsequently translating the writing into English during the revision phase.

Writing Centers: In working with ELL clients, writing center tutors could themselves facilitate and encourage the use of clients' native languages. Staben and Nordhaus (2004) argue that an effective strategy is for ELL clients to compose in their first language and translate into English – or even write in a mixture of both languages. While ambitious and perhaps difficult to scale, the recruitment and hiring of bilingual tutors would be one way to ensure that students' native languages could be a part of the consultation. We run into the problem, too, of matching bilingual tutors with ELL clients who share a common language. However, there may still be value in matching bilingual tutors with clients regardless of whether they share a common first language, as the tutor will understand more about the translingual processes of language learning and will be able to draw upon their bilingual language learning experiences. Abraham *et al.* (2021) found that translanguaging, the use of different languages together, creates a space where bilingual learners are free to practice their languages while resisting monolingual discourses. On a smaller scale, the incorporation of materials in ELL's native languages, e.g. translations of paper prompts and assignments, would be one way to encourage generative engagement from ELL clients in support of their writing in English. Tutors could also ask ELL clients to draft their papers first in their native language, or perhaps only portions of the work, or outline the work, as a way of helping ELLs think about their writing first in their native language. What is common to all these approaches is that writing centers should invite, rather than problematize, the use of languages other than English as they work with ELL clients.

Conclusion

Writing centers are ideal places for taking up the practices of linguistically responsive pedagogy because writing centers are a campus-wide resource. Centers not only serve students: they also serve all disciplines and majors. And writing centers are better for their interdisciplinary focus; as Lee *et al.* (2014) note, interdisciplinary collaboration mirrors the collaborative nature of one-on-one consultations that are the foundation of writing center work. In addition to having a broad mandate, writing centers often recruit and employ tutors from a wide variety of disciplines (Scanlon, 1986). In fact, as interdisciplinary hubs, writing centers are essential to promoting writing, and the learning of writing, in all disciplines. These collaborations, and interdisciplinary focus, make writing centers stronger and better positioned to support student learning.

Broadly, this work speaks to the value of interdisciplinarity, as we are ourselves scholars from the fields of writing center studies and English education, respectively. More particularly, our collaboration points to the generative value of interdisciplinary work between scholars of education and researchers studying writing centers. Going forward, we hope others will undertake similar collaborations, considering how speaking across fields and working beyond established paradigms can enrich thought and invigorate research within those distinct fields.

While this work focuses primarily on writing centers, it has also been valuable for considering the field of teacher education. The particular nature of a writing center consultation, typically one-to-one attention to a single piece of composition, provides an opportunity to be responsive to the individual student and their diverse set of experiences, backgrounds and needs – something not always available in the classroom. The problem of how to attend to individual difference while also teaching an entire class has long been a challenge to educators and has been much discussed in education research, most recently in response to calls for more effectively differentiated approaches to special education and for more just approaches to racial and cultural diversity in schools. (This, against a backdrop of cost-cutting education reform bent on packing more students into fewer classrooms.)

Thinking about education practice in conversation with writing center work, then, offers a different way to consider what are central problems in both writing center studies and teacher education. Put differently, we would note that in an important sense what writing centers do is teach writing, and thus it makes sense – as this study suggests – to look to scholarship on teaching as we consider how best to teach writing center clients.

This study makes clear that, given the opportunities and challenges presented by increasing diversity – linguistic and otherwise – in today's institutions of higher education, it is crucial that writing centers attend to established research on effective practices with diverse students. To that end, our work here demonstrates how writing centers might effectively leverage the findings of ELL research to support tutor work with ELL students. Linguistically responsive pedagogy, we suggest, may be particularly useful in this endeavor, as it provides an evidence-based framework for responding to students' linguistically diverse backgrounds without marginalizing or ignoring them. This is a promising approach, we feel, and one that future research on writing center practice would do well to take up and explore further. Moreover, we understand this chapter as the beginning of a larger interdisciplinary conversation: clearly more empirical work is needed to see how and in what ways LRP might be useful in writing center practice.

Note

(1) A plethora of terms has emerged for describing students with varying linguistic backgrounds: English Language Learning (ELL), English as a Foreign Language (EFL), English as a Second Language (ESL), Multilingual, Second Language Learning and Emergent Bilingual, among others. These terms of course express particular nuances and shifting field priorities over the years. Here we use 'ELL' in keeping with the practices of scholars theorizing linguistically responsive pedagogy.

References

Abraham, S., Kedley, K., Madjiguene, F., Sharada, K. and Tulino, D. (2021) Creating a translanguaging space in a bilingual community-based writing program. *International Multilingual Research Journal* 15 (3), 211–234.

Aguilera, E., Greenstein, I. and Shannon, L.A. (2020) Linguistically-responsive literacy pedagogies across primary and secondary classrooms. In G. Neokleous, A. Krulatz and R. Farrelly (eds) *Handbook of Research on Cultivating Literacy in Diverse and Multilingual Classrooms* (pp. 496–515). Hershey, PA: IGI Global.

Angelova, M. and Riazantseva, A. (1999) 'If you don't tell me, how can I know?' A case study of four international students learning to write the US way. *Written Communication* 16 (4), 491–525.

Au, K. (2009) Isn't culturally responsive instruction just good teaching? *Social Education* 73 (4), 179–183.

Bitchener, J. and Ferris, D.R. (2011) *Written Corrective Feedback in Second Language Acquisition and Writing*. New York: Routledge.

Brooks, J. (1991) Minimalist tutoring: Making students do all the work. *Writing Lab Newsletter* 15 (6), 1–4.

Brown, C.L. (2007) Strategies for making social studies texts more comprehensible for English language learners. *The Social Studies* 98 (5), 185–188.

Bruce, S. (2004) Getting started. In S. Bruce and B. Rafoth (eds) *ESL Writers: A Guide for Writing Center Tutors* (pp. 30–38). Portsmouth, NH: Boynton/Cook.

Bruce, S. and Rafoth, B. (eds) (2004) *ESL Writers: A Guide for Writing Center Tutors*. Portsmouth, NH: Boynton/Cook.

Canavan, A. (2015) They speak my language here: An ELL-specific tutoring pilot project in a midwestern regional university. *Writing Lab Newsletter* 39 (9–10), 1–5.

Cazden, C. and Leggett, E. (1981) Culturally responsive education: Recommendations for achieving Lau remedies II. In H.T. Trueba, G.P. Guthrie and K. Au (eds) *Culture and the Bilingual Classroom: Studies in Classroom Ethnography* (pp. 69–86). Rowley, MA: Newbury House.

Cummins, J. (1981) The role of primary language development in promoting educational success for language minority students. In California State Department of Education, *Schooling and Language Minority Students: A Theoretical Framework* (pp. 3–49). Sacramento, CA: CA Department of Education.

Cummins, J. (2000) *Language, Power and Pedagogy: Bilingual Children in the Crossfire*. Clevedon: Multilingual Matters.

Cummins, J. (2008) BICS and CALP: Empirical and theoretical status of the distinction. In B. Street and N.H. Hornberger (eds) *Encyclopedia of Language and Education. Volume 2: Literacy* (2nd edn, pp. 71–83). New York, NY: Springer.

de Jong, E.J. and Harper, C.A. (2005) Preparing mainstream teachers for English language learners: Is being a good teacher good enough? *Teacher Education Quarterly* 32 (2), 101–124.

Diab, R.L. (2005) Teachers' and students' beliefs about responding to ESL writing: A case Study. *TESL Canada Journal* 23 (1), 28–43.

Early, M., Kendrick, M. and Potts, D. (2015) Multimodality: Out from the margins of English language teaching. *TESOL Quarterly* 49 (3), 447–460.

Echevarria, J., Vogt, M. and Short, D.J. (2000) *Making Content Comprehensible for English Language Learners: The SIOP Model*. Boston, MA: Allyn & Bacon.

Erickson, F. and Mohatt, C. (1982) Cultural organization and participation structures in two classrooms of Indian students. In G. Spindler (ed.) *Doing the Ethnography of Schooling* (pp. 131–174). New York: Holt, Rinehart & Winston.

Ferris, D.R. (1995) Student reactions to teacher response in multiple-draft composition classrooms. *TESOL Quarterly* 29, 33–53.

Ferris, D.R. (2002) *Treatment of Error in Second Language Student Writing*. Ann Arbor, MI: University of Michigan Press.

Gallagher, C. and Haan, J. (2018) University faculty beliefs about emergent multilinguals and linguistically responsive instruction. *TESOL Quarterly* 52 (2), 304–330.

Gass, S.M. (1997) *Input, Interaction, and the Second Language Learner*. Mahwah, NJ: Lawrence Erlbaum.

Gibbons, P. (2002) *Scaffolding Language, Scaffolding Learning: Teaching Second Language Learners in the Mainstream Classroom*. Portsmouth, NH: Heinemann.

Gillespie, P. (2004) Is this my job? In S. Bruce and B. Rafoth (eds) *ESL Writers: A Guide for Writing Center Tutors* (pp. 117–126). Portsmouth, NH: Boynton/Cook.

Harper, C. and de Jong, E.D. (2004) Misconceptions about teaching English language learners. *Journal of Adolescent and Adult Literacy* 48 (2), 152–162.

Hite, C.E. and Evans, L.S. (2006) Mainstream first-grade teachers' understanding of strategies for accommodating the needs of English language learners. *Teacher Education Quarterly* 33 (2), 89–110.

Institute of International Education (2018a) International student enrollment trends, 1948/49–2017/18. *Open Doors Report on International Education Exchange*.

Institute of International Education (2018b) Top 25 places of origin of international students, 2012/13–2017/18. *Open Doors Report on International Education Exchange*.

Ladson-Billings, G. (1994) *The Dreamkeepers*. San Francisco, CA: Jossey-Bass.

Lee, C.D. (1998) Culturally responsive pedagogy and performance-based assessment. *Journal of Negro Education* 67 (3), 268–279.

Lee, I. (2005) Error correction in the L2 writing classroom: What do students think? *TESL Canada Journal* 22 (2), 1–16.

Lee, J.C., Caronia, N. and Beltran, D.Q. (2014) Interdisciplinary writing center collaborations. *Academic Exchange Quarterly* 18 (4), 1–6.

Lenski, S.D., Ehlers-Zavala, F., Daniel, M.C. and Sun-Irminger, X. (2006) Assessing English language learners in mainstream classrooms. *The Reading Teacher* 60 (1), 24–34.

Linville, C. (2004) Editing line by line. In S. Bruce and B. Rafoth (eds) *ESL Writers: A Guide for Writing Center Tutors* (pp. 84–93). Portsmouth, NH: Boynton/Cook.

Lucas, T. (ed.) (2010) *Teacher Preparation for Linguistically Diverse Classrooms: A Resource of Teacher Educators*. New York: Routledge.

Lucas, T. and Villegas, A.M. (2013) Preparing linguistically responsive teachers: Laying the foundation in preservice teacher education. *Theory Into Practice* 52 (2), 98–109.

Lucas, T., Villegas, A.M. and Freedson-Gonzalez, M. (2008) Linguistically responsive teacher education: Preparing classroom teachers to teach English Language Learners. *Journal of Teacher Education* 59 (4), 361–373.

Matsuda, P.K. and Cox, M. (2004) Reading an ESL writer's text. In S. Bruce and B. Rafoth (eds) *ESL Writers: A Guide for Writing Center Tutors* (pp. 39–47). Portsmouth, NH: Boynton/Cook.

Met, M. (1999) *Content-based Instruction: Defining Terms, Making Decisions*. NFLC Reports. Washington, DC: The National Foreign Language Center.

Moussu, L. (2013) Let's talk! ESL students' needs and writing centre philosophy. *TESL Canada Journal* 30 (2), 55–68.

New London Group (1996) A pedagogy of multiliteracies: Designing social futures. *Harvard Educational Review* 66 (1), 60–92.

Nowacki, J.C. (2012) An ongoing ESL training program in the writing center. *Praxis: A Writing Center Journal* 9 (2), 1–4.

Okuda, T. and Anderson, T. (2018) Second language graduate students' experiences at the writing center: A language socialization perspective. *TESOL Quarterly* 52 (2), 391–413.

Powers, J. (1993) Rethinking writing center conferencing strategies for the ESL writer. *The Writing Center Journal* 13 (2), 39–47.

Rafoth, B. (2015) *Multilingual Writers and Writing Centers*. Logan, UT: Utah State University Press.

Scanlon, L.C. (1986) Recruiting and training tutors for cross-disciplinary writing programs. *The Writing Center Journal* 6 (2), 37–41.

Schleppegrell, M.J. (2004) *The Language of Schooling: A Functional Linguistics Perspective*. Mahwah, NJ: Lawrence Erlbaum.

Serafini, F. and Gee, E. (2017) *Remixing Multiliteracies: Theory and Practice from New London to New Times*. New York: Teachers College Press.

Staben, J. and Nordhaus, K.D. (2004) Looking at the whole text. In S. Bruce and B. Rafoth (eds) *ESL Writers: A Guide for Writing Center Tutors* (pp. 71–83). Portsmouth, NH: Boynton/Cook.

Swain, M. (1995) Three functions of output in second language learning. In G. Cook and B. Seidlhofer (eds) *Principle and Practice in Applied Linguistics: Studies in Honour of H.G. Widdowson* (pp. 125–144). Oxford: Oxford University Press.

Thonus, T. (1993) Tutors as teachers: Assisting ESL/EFL students in the writing center. *The Writing Center Journal* 13 (2), 13–26.

Vasudevan, L., Schultz, K. and Bateman, J. (2010) Rethinking composing in a digital age: Authoring literate identities through multimodal storytelling. *Written Communication* 27 (4), 442–468.

Verplaetse, L.S. and Migliacci, N. (2008) Making mainstream content comprehensible through sheltered instruction. In L.S. Verplaetse and N. Migliacci (eds) *Inclusive Pedagogy for English Language Learners: A Handbook of Research-informed Practices* (pp. 127–165). New York: Lawrence Erlbaum.

Vygotsky, L. (1978) *Mind in Society*. Cambridge: Cambridge University Press.

Walqui, A. (2008) The development of teacher expertise to work with adolescent English learners: A model and a few priorities. In L.S. Verplaetse and N. Migliacci (eds) *Inclusive Pedagogy for English Language Learners: A Handbook of Research-informed Practices* (pp. 103–125). New York: Lawrence Erlbaum.

Willett, J., Harman, R., Hogan, A., Lozano, M.E. and Rubeck, J. (2007) Transforming standard practice to serve the social and academic learning of English language learners. In L.S. Verplaetse and N. Migliacci (eds) *Inclusive Pedagogy for English Language Learners: A Handbook of Research-informed Practices* (pp. 33–53). New York: Lawrence Erlbaum.

Wong-Fillmore, L. and Snow, C.E. (2002) What teachers need to know about language. In C.T. Adger, C.E. Snow and D. Christian (eds) *What Teachers Need to Know about Language* (1st edn, pp. 7–54). Washington, DC/McHenry, IL: Center for Applied Linguistics and Delta Systems, Inc.

Yedlin, J. (2007) Pedagogical thinking and teacher talk in a first-grade ELL classroom. In L.S. Verplaetse and N. Migliacci (eds) *Inclusive Pedagogy for English Language Learners: A Handbook of Research-informed Practices* (pp. 55–77). New York: Lawrence Erlbaum.

Part 3: Theoretical and Pedagogical Orientations

8 Shifting from Linguistic to Spatial Repertoires: Extending and Enacting Translingual Perspectives in Our Research and Teaching

Steven Fraiberg

In the area of writing studies, there has been a turn towards a translingual approach (Canagarajah, 2013; Horner *et al.*, 2011) that locates the teaching and study of writing in the context of other languages and globalization. This has entailed a pedagogical shift from a deficit perspective towards asset-based approaches, in which students' home languages and literacies are seen as assets or resources for teaching and learning (see Wang, Chapter 9, this volume, who discusses in great depth writing assignments that are informed by an asset-based pedagogical framework). In parallel with these changes, a theoretical shift has occurred. Broadly, the shift from the prefix multi-(lingual) to trans-(lingual) signifies a break from static and bounded models of language. This framework organizes language and literacy into isolated units or archipelagos: a one-to-one mapping of language, culture, community and the nation-state. However, as the onset of globalization has challenged territorial borders and boundaries so, too, have the discrete borders of language and literacy been destabilized. In response, writing scholars have shifted towards a conception of language and literacy as dynamic, relational, networked, hybrid, contested and co-constituted in the context of everyday practice. In this chapter, I wish to examine this interplay. More specifically, I wish to bring together a number of emergent threads of scholarship and examine what this transdisciplinary approach implies for our theoretical and methodological frameworks.

Broadly, to accomplish these aims I bring together scholarship in literacy, disciplinary enculturation, transnationalism and spatial theory. This framework is identified as a mobile literacies approach (Blommaert, 2013; Fraiberg *et al.*, 2017; Lorimer Leonard, 2013; Nordquist, 2017; Pennycook, 2012; Wargo & De Costa, 2017), which centers on how literacy mediates the movement of actors, identities and practices across space and time. Core to this focus is attention to the politics of mobility (Cresswell, 2010): who/what moves, when they move, how fast, how far, and to what effect. These uneven and differential effects entail what Tsing (2006) refers to as 'friction' or unequal encounters across difference. Useful for conceptualizing this process is what Massey (1999) identifies as power geometries: the alignments and positioning of participants, the coordination of activity, and the fluid, fuzzy pathways through which literacies, actors and objects circulate. Opening up power relations for scrutiny, this framework links local literacies to networks of power and the material and political effects of these relationships.

Dovetailing with this mobile literacies approach is a rich body of scholarship across a number of areas. This includes a long strand of scholarship in literacy studies and academic socialization (Casanave, 2002; Ivanič, 1998; McCarthy, 1987; Russell & Yañez, 2003; Sternglass, 1997; Zamel & Spack, 2004). This scholarship is focused largely on the ways that students learn to invent the university (Bartholomae, 1986): i.e. ways students acquire academic, disciplinary and literate identities as they learn to adopt ways of speaking, being and knowing. Moreover, recent scholarship has challenged models of academic enculturation (Prior, 1998; Roozen & Erickson, 2017) grounded in structuralist assumptions that focus on container metaphors of 'going into' disciplines. This paradigm shifts away from a classroom-as-container metaphor that conceptualizes educational spaces as bounded and discrete (Leander *et al.*, 2010). Alternatively, this networked approach uncovers complex ways in which higher educational institutions (HEIs) are increasingly entangled in wider transnational social spaces.

In parallel, transnational studies has proposed a shift away from container models of the nation-state and what is referred to as 'methodological nationalism' (Wimmer & Glick Schiller, 2002). This transnational optic indexes how transnational actors frequently live out their lives across borders as they cultivate multilayered and multi-sited identifications across local, regional and national spaces (Lam & Warriner, 2012; Vertovec, 2004). Key to this research is attention to the interplay between the local and distant, with participants engaged in a process of layered simultaneity (Blommaert, 2005), as transnational actors draw on multiple resources from home and host cultures. It is through this uneven and messy process that they construct polycultural identities and traverse multiple life worlds. Part and parcel of this relational interplay, transnationalism suggests not only movement across the social and geographic landscape but also the changing nature of the landscape itself (Ong, 1999). This includes the higher educational landscape as colleges and universities are increasingly entangled in a transnational social field (Brooks & Waters, 2011; Rizvi, 2009; Sidhu, 2006; Singh *et al.*, 2007; Waters, 2012; You, 2018).

Finally, to capture the embodied and material nature of this deeply contested process, scholarship has begun to foreground spatial theory (Latour, 2005; Leander & Sheehy, 2004; Lefebvre, 1991; Massey, 2005; Soja, 1996). This scholarship broadly attends to the intersections of material and imagined spaces and the ways they shape and are shaped in the context of everyday practices. In a shift from neutral understandings of context, space is not a backdrop or stage against which activity takes place: instead, it is conceptualized as dynamic, changing, sedimented with ideologies and co-constituted by the participants. Core to this move is a breakdown of human and non-human actors as the two together form what Latour (1999) refers to as a 'third agent.' Central to the analysis is always the question: Who or what is carrying out the action? The answer is always at least two actors. Relevant to inquiry in educational spaces, Latour (2005) offers the scene of a university lecture hall that was planned 15 years ago and 200km away by an architect who drew up the blueprints. These plans provide a wider blueprint or social script shaping how loud the lecturer will need to speak, the arrangement of a number of students in well-ordered tiers and the teacher located behind the podium. These structures both shape and are shaped by everyday interactions, so it is no longer only the teacher giving the lecture, but the teacher–lecture hall–university delivering it. In this fashion, the focus is on questions asking who/what is doing the acting (translating) and who/what is being acted on (translated).

In sum, this mobile literacies framework attends to the ways that transnational actors move in and across social worlds as they draw on a heterogeneous repertoire of resources distributed across near and far-flung spaces and historical moments. It is through attention to these moments of uptake that actors develop literate identities, dispositions and practices as they gradually become sedimented and stabilized over time.

Key Theoretical and Methodological Shifts: Generating a New Set of Terms

In this section, I wish to further unpack these processes. To accomplish this aim, I identify a key set of terms for orienting to this conceptual framework with the goal of generating a heuristic or theoretical and methodological lens for scholarly research and teaching. I then ground the discussion in a case study of a transnational student at Great Lake University, a major Midwestern university. In doing this work, I suggest how a mobile literacies framework extends current

Table 8.1 Key theoretical shifts

Limited Scope	Broader Scope
Translingual	Transliteracy
Linguistic Repertoires	Spatial Repertoires
Literacy Sponsors	Literacy Sponsorscapes
Code Meshing	Meshworking
Activity System	Mobility System

translingual approaches in research and teaching. Broadly, this section proposes a number of key shifts (see Table 8.1).

Transliteracy

First is a shift from translingualism to transliteracy (Hull & Stornaiuolo, 2010; You, 2016). The turn from a narrower focus on translingualism is part of a call for a more expansive orientation with attention to all the semiotic modes: i.e. a conceptualization of language as one resource in a wider rhetorical repertoire, including text, talk, image, sound, objects and gesture. Gesturing towards a broader and more holistic approach, the term has been increasingly taken up in literacy studies 'to signal the availability of a variety of modes, platforms, and tools for meaning making' (Hull & Stornaiuolo, 2010: 87). This approach is further coupled with attention to transnational literacies and cosmopolitan practices (De Costa, 2014, 2016; Fraiberg, 2017; Hull & Stornaiuolo, 2010; You, 2016). This focus is grounded in the notion that movement across language, modes, cultures and geographies can foster a bifocal perspective, transnational habitus, translingual disposition (Lee & Jenks, 2016) or cosmopolitan outlook. The aim is to produce global citizen–scholars able to navigate cultural, civic, ethical borders.

Spatial repertoires

Closely related to this move is a shift from linguistic repertoires to multimodal and spatial ones (Canagarajah, 2018; Fraiberg, 2010, 2017; Pennycook & Otsuji, 2014). This focus foregrounds literacy as an embodied practice while attending to ways that actors mobilize a repertoire of signs, symbols, actors and objects as they navigate social, semiotic and geographic landscapes. As part of a spatialized approach, this analytic lens situates literacy practices in the context of material ecologies of 'language, space, objects, and activities' (Pennycook & Otsuji, 2014: 167). These social and material spaces are sedimented with ideologies and orientations that mediate their uptake as part of an ongoing struggle.

Literacy sponsorscape

Useful for understanding more fully the ways that this process affords and constrains the development of literate practices and dispositions is an extension of the concept of literacy sponsor. Traditionally, Brandt's (1998) notion of literacy sponsor has been used as an analytic for tracing social mobility as actors develop literacies and accrue cultural capital across space and time. A literacy sponsor is defined as 'any agents local or distant, concrete or abstract, who enable, support, teach, model, as well as recruit, regulate, suppress, or withhold literacy—and gain advantage of it in some way' (1998: 167). Broadening this analytic lens, Wargo and De Costa (2017) propose the term literacy sponsorscape to more fully situate it in the context of globalization. This concept links Brandt's literacy sponsorship to Appadurai's definition of globalization: a 'complex, overlapping disjunctive order' characterized by multidimensional flows or 'scapes' (Appadurai, 1990: 296). Bringing together these strands of scholarship provides a means of tracing ways that literacy is bound up in the fluid, messy and distributed trajectories of actors and objects.

Meshworking

Pointing to fluid, relational, rhizomatic conceptions of space and place, Ingold (2009) uses the concept of a meshwork. This conceptual metaphor is taken up to characterize the various trails or pathways along which one's life is lived as part of an ongoing process of becoming. This tapestry of activity includes histories, stories and trajectories that are always emergent, unfinished and on the move (Klenk, 2018). It is through weaving, or knotting, together these varied threads of activity (a process referred to as wayfinding) that identities, mobilities and geographies are co-constituted over time. Extending this concept, I propose a shift from a focus on code meshing (Canagarajah, 2006) to *meshworking*, or the tying and untying of an array of texts, tools and objects distributed across space and time. Code meshing is traditionally used to describe ways to incorporate one's home's language into the dominant discourse in order to disrupt unquestioned language and cultural ideologies, assumptions and worldviews. The shift to *meshworking* is aligned with a more encompassing approach that points to material ways in which actors can jointly take up a range of texts, tools and objects as a means to 'write back' to the dominant discourse.

Mobility system

To finally attend to the power dynamics mediating this process, I shift from a focus on activity system to mobility system (Fraiberg *et al.*, 2017; Nordquist, 2017; Urry, 2007). Traditionally scholarship in cultural–historical activity theory (CHAT) tends to situate everyday literacy practices in what is referred to as an activity system (for a more detailed discussion of activity theory, see Chapters 5 and 6 of this volume, by Ma & Green-Eneix and Son, respectively). Moving towards a less bounded approach (Prior, 1998) that foregrounds actors and literacies on the move, I propose a shift to what is referred to as a mobility system. This fluid, fuzzy network – or meshwork – mediates social and geographic trajectories across borders. In this fashion, higher educational institutions (HEIs) are imagined as physically and symbolically transporting students, teachers, administrators, textbooks, policies and pedagogies. Operating as a mobility system, HEIs afford movement of some actors while constraining the mobilities of others, as part of an ongoing struggle with actors shaping and shaped by these systems. Urry (2007) compares the emergent and dynamic nature of mobility systems to walking through a maze whose walls rearrange themselves as one travels. Methodologically, applying this perspective to transnational student mobility forces one to attend to the various and material resources that afford and constrain 'how they [students] come to travel, how they travel, how often, and to what effect' (Brooks & Waters, 2011: 130). Consequently, the mapping of literate trajectories necessitates the tracing of 'trajectories of participation' (Dreier, 1999) across scenes of literacy, as actors draw on a diverse array of heterogeneous resources. This is the rationale for the unit of analysis as mediated action (Wertsch, 1991), serving to link situated practices to wider transnational social spaces.

The Case of a First-year Transnational Student

To unpack these effects, I draw on a case study of a transnational university student, Bruno, from the central region of Bolivia. As a trilingual (or translingual) speaker who has resided in various parts of Bolivia, Brazil and the United States, his translingual trajectory serves as a telling case. The central question is focused on how this first-year student's movement in and across social, semiotic and geographic landscapes fosters a meta-awareness or sense of attunement (Lorimer Leonard, 2014) to the rhetorical nature of language and literacy. The case further sheds light on the ways these traversals were bound up in the cultivation of a disposition towards language and literacy in which translingual actors perceive the world from multiple and varied perspectives. In the transnational literature, this disposition is defined as a transnational habitus (De Costa et al., 2016; Meinhof, 2009) or bifocal perspective (Vertovec, 2004): actors learning to perceive the world through the lens of home and host cultures. As such, the case contributes to the translingual and transnational literature on the ways social literacies are complexly bound up in the cultivation of global citizen–scholars (De Costa, 2014, 2016; Fraiberg, 2017; Hull & Stornaiuolo, 2010;

You, 2016) able to rhetorically and flexibly navigate an array of social, cultural, digital and transnational landscapes.

I first encountered this seriously minded first-year student in a basic writing course at a major Midwestern university. As a bridge writing course (i.e. FYW 100), this classroom is traditionally populated by a diverse range of international and domestic students, including students from China, India, Korea, Africa, South America and urban and rural parts of the United States. To leverage the students' linguistic and cultural diversity, I adopted a translingual framework in designing the curriculum. A central tenet of a translingual curriculum is making difference a centerpoint of the course. To that end, assignments, activities and pedagogies were geared towards inquiry into language and cross-cultural difference.

As part of a longitudinal study on translingual literacies, the analysis is based on a semester-long study of the course. Taking up the stance of a teacher–researcher, I collected data through classroom recordings of student activity, the collection of student drafts and notes (jottings), written self-reflections and a three-hour elicited interview with the focal participant. In the interview, Bruno narrated his literate trajectory; provided samples of in-class and out-of-class literacies; and discussed his rhetorical decisions and everyday literacy practices. This recorded interview was transcribed and coded as part of a grounded theoretical approach (Charmaz, 2014). Triangulating the data, one emergent theme with theoretical sensitivity and reach centered on his attunement (Lorimer Leonard, 2014) to the rhetorical nature of language. This disposition was fostered by his various social, linguistic and geographic border crossings. Moreover, his movement across multiple semiotic modes – centered on a deep interest in visual media and drawing – further instilled in him a meta-awareness of affordances and constraints associated with multimodal forms of composing. Turning to the ways in which he composed his life story, I specifically limit the discussion here to a number of key examples. Central to his story is how an uneven, messy assemblage of texts, tools, actors, objects and media formed part of a complex sponsorscape (Wargo & De Costa, 2017) mediating the development of his literate identity and practices.

To provide a broad-brushed background, Bruno was born in central Bolivia in Cochabamba. The city is located in a valley in the Andes mountain range as the fourth largest city in Bolivia. Residents in the area are commonly referred to as a Cochalas or Cochabambinos. More broadly, the term *Colla* has become widely used throughout the country (Fabricant, 2009; Lopez Pila, 2014; Swinehart, 2012) to refer to them and other indigenous people from Bolivia's highlands. Historically, the term dates back to the *Colla* kingdom of the Aymara nation that was conquered in the 15th century by the Inca empire. In the context of the current historical moment, it has transformed into a key social marker bound up in identity politics within the country, as further discussed below. However, at the age of eight, Bruno found himself entangled in other identity politics: having to master a new language and fit into a new culture in a family move to Rio de Janeiro, Brazil, for his father's work. Later, as a teenager at the age of 14, he returned to Bolivia to the city of Santa Cruz before traveling the US for his studies as an international student. In this manner, his literate trajectory is one that crossed languages (English, Portuguese, Spanish), countries (Bolivia, Brazil, United States), regions (Cochabamba, Santa Cruz), and, as I will discuss, modalities. Turning to Bruno's story, I focus on three major assignments from a first-year writing course that serve as rich points (Agar, 1994) to bring together these interlocking threads of activity.

Example 1: Remixing Language, Literacy and Identity through Visual Media

I first turn to a remix assignment that involved repurposing an autobiographical literacy narrative into a graphic story or comic that Bruno entitled 'Born to Adapt.' The assignment required the students to remix or adapt a literacy narrative into a comic while applying design principles articulated by comic book theorist Scott McCloud. The assignment was grounded in the notion that engaging students in transmodal (or multimodal) tasks would help to heighten their generic awareness and rhetorical sensitivity to the affordances and constraints of all the semiotic modes, including writing. In fact, already a practiced artist and comic book aficionado, he was in many respects highly oriented to these issues.

As suggested previously, the background for his autoethnographic account is situated within the identity politics of the region. The social geography of Bolivia is generally characterized by divisions between highland and lowland cultures. While multiple racial–social groups are scattered throughout the areas, broadly these regional differences have at their base 'two main identity concepts which point to a historic situation dating back to before country formation in 1825 – that of being *Camba* (lowland) and *Colla* (highland)' (Lopez Pila, 2014: 435). Historically, conflicts between the groups have stemmed from cultural and ethnic differences. Undergirding these tensions are structural inequities linked to social class and political economy. Though both terms have historically indigenous roots, the term *Colla* has come to signify an ethnically indigenous highlander. Closely identified with the MAS (Movement for Socialism) party and former populist president, Evo Morales, this socioracial group is further associated with peasant laborers in support of nationalizing the economy. In contradistinction, *Camba* has come to denote a privileged capitalist elite with European origins who launched a nationalist separatist movement in reaction to the *Collas*' socialist agenda.

Though hardly aligned with every aspect of this sweeping narrative (solidly located in the middle class), Bruno began his story (Figure 8.1) by identifying himself with the highland region as a 'stereotypical Coya [Colla].' Drawing on this social identity marker, he describes *Collas* as working class people who lack a sense of agency and typically 'don't have a voice.' In key respects, the narrative is built around his struggle to find his voice quite literally as he struggles to adapt to a new country and language in his move from the Bolivian highlands to the Brazilian

Figure 8.1 'Born to Adapt' comic (images relates to numbers 1–7 of the Appendix)

coastline (see Appendix for full text). In telling this story, Bruno mobilized a multimodal and spatial repertoire embedded in a semiotic system:

> Semiotic systems are human cultural and historical creations that are designed to engage and manipulate people in certain ways. They attempt through their content and social practices to recruit people to think, act, interact, value, and feel in certain specific ways. In this sense they attempt to get people to learn to take on certain sorts of new identities, to become, for a time and place, certain types of people. In fact, society as a whole is simply a web of these many different sorts of identities and their characteristic associated activities and practices. (Gee, 2004: 43–44)

In this fashion, Bruno was weaving and woven into these complex semiotic webs (meshworks). Drawing on a culturally situated design grammar, he meshed together an array of signs and symbols. That included the representation of himself with a knitted woolen hat that typifies the working class *Collas* of the region. Repeated throughout the first two-and-a-half pages, the iconic dress points to ways in which it functioned as part of a performable repertoire (Agha, 2003) or identity kit (Gee, 2004). He also wove, or meshed, together an ensemble of other signs and symbols: a scene of himself in a box to signify his shyness or reserved nature (a stereotypical *Colla* trait); an outline or silhouette of workers in a field, to symbolize the working class; a cross or 'x' over his mouth to indicate that the *Colla* were without a political voice (erased or rendered invisible and without agency); an image of himself from behind, looking out over the water towards the cityscape of Rio de Janeiro in the distance to imagine the next phase of his life. Together, this spatial repertoire was bound up in the construction of a global social imaginary.

The first major turning point in the story is the move to Brazil. This is indicated with a lightning bolt to signal the jolt or sudden split between his old and new lives: the line divides half an image of Bolivia, and half an image of Brazil (Figure 8.2). The incorporation of this visual framing device in fact is common in the genre of the superhero comics and graphic novels, which Bruno regularly consumed. In this fashion, he was reweaving, remixing and remediating a visual vocabulary linked both to his national culture as well as global popular culture – as he 'meshed' together these strands of activity. Core to developing this ability was copying artistic images. In doing this work, Bruno displayed fine-grained attention to detail in his artistic drawings in a sketchbook that he used to carry with him. He further carried with him the semiotic repertoires and design practices he had developed through this sketch work into other areas of his life.

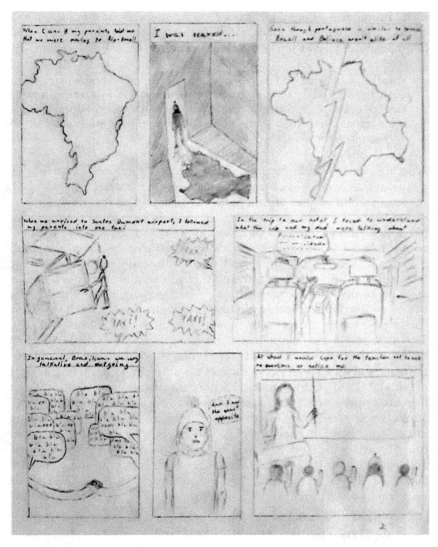

Figure 8.2 'Born to Adapt' comic: Move to Brazil (images relate to numbers 8–15 of the Appendix)

This is evidenced in the second part of the story centered on his effort to adapt or adjust to what felt like a 'different world' in Santa Cruz with new forms of dress, attitudes, food and social norms. Disoriented and socially isolated in the new school system, he realized that, to be accepted, he would need to adapt or change, as he gradually started to observe and internalize how other kids talked and acted. He wrote: 'I became so good at *copying* that I could speak with their accent.' As such, Bruno was becoming attuned to the process of *uptake* in and across various semiotic modes: talking, dress, gestures and even drawing (aforementioned). Moving beyond rote imitation, he was developing:

> knowledge of what to take up, how, and when: when and why to use a genre, how to select an appropriate genre in relation to another, how to execute uptakes strategically and when to resist expected uptakes, how some genres explicitly cite other genres in their uptake while some do so only implicitly, and so on. (Bawarshi, 2006: 653)

Working across multiple modalities, Bruno developed a sense of rhetorical attunement to all available means of persuasion.

As a second major turning point in the story, his transformation is marked by a new drawing or representation of himself as the narrator. No longer drawn with the woolen hat, instead he is now sketched with a relaxed smile in new articles of casual clothing with a football t-shirt and shorts. The dress and open stance aligned him with the more informal Brazilian culture and their passion for the sport. In this fashion, Bruno was learning to play with language and culture as he began to inhabit a new identity and enter the field: i.e. a system of social positions structured by power relationships (Bourdieu, 1977). This shift was deeply embodied as he quite literally joined the football field/pitch in pick-up games. Through this process he was learning to navigate and appropriate new ways of speaking and interacting as part of an embodied performance. His practice of close observation to fit in echoes other immigrant stories of newcomers (Hoffman, 1989) who adopt a role similar to an ethnographer doing fieldwork or engaging in the practice of participant observation. Through occupying a dual role of participant and observer, he was attuning himself to linguistic and rhetorical differences. He was developing a bifocal perspective (Vertovec, 2004) as he learned to see the world through the lens of home and host cultures.

Example 2: Decolonizing Linguistic Ideologies

In the next example, I turn to an activity in which students were asked to locate key terms from their cultures and define them for outsiders. This idea is grounded in the notion that each culture has key words, concepts, root metaphors and symbols that are central to understanding the underlying values, assumptions and worldviews. Broadly, this idea is further connected to the notion that language itself travels beyond the dictionary with its histories, uses, orientations and meanings only fully understood in the context of everyday lived experiences. In examining this process, I pick up the story as Bruno returned home from Brazil to Bolivia at the age of 14. However, instead of returning to his hometown of Cochabamba, he moved with his family to Santa Cruz. To expand the discussion, Santa Cruz is an economic hub and home to a capitalist elite who have led a national separatist movement with historical roots that precede the founding of the country in 1824. A product of neocolonial legacies and a free-market agenda, the *Camba*s' opposition to the *Collas* is linked to a struggle over the economic order, structural inequalities, territorial power, racial hierarchies, spatial hegemonies and historical privilege. In the most basic terms, the two groups are in binary opposition: the civilized, European lowlander (*Camba*) in opposition to the uncivilized, indigenous highlander (*Colla*). It is in the context of these tensions that Bruno returned to his home country.

Describing the strangeness of a place that he expected to find deeply familiar, he reflected:

> And then I'm coming back to what I supposed I knew. And I supposed that it was familiar to me. And now, wow, there's like a lot of other stuff. You know?

If he had continued the second chapter of his graphic novella about his return home, he speculates that he would have begun with a question mark to symbolize his sense of confusion. It was during his return at the age of 14 that he began to question his own culture and what he thought he had naturally understood. Socially labeled as 'other' in his nation of origin or as a *Colla*, this was the first time he had encountered the racialized term. Previously he had always simply considered himself to be a Cochabambino as he aligned himself with the traditional term people in his city used to identify themselves. In this new region of the country, these unequal encounters across difference (Tsing, 2006) caused him to attune to a new social geography.

It is at this historical moment that he came across the term 'yappa.' Presenting it as an example of a key cultural term, the indigenous Quechan word itself literally means 'more please' or 'bonus' and was often used by patrons (*Cambas*) when purchasing goods from sellers in the open market (*Collas*).

> So basically, the way you would use this word is like you go to the fair or market and you want like, I don't know, a kilo of meat and you say yappa, which means the bonus. And the meat seller will give you a kilo and 200 grams basically.

In everyday exchanges, *Cambas* used this word to get extra portions and servings from sellers. This assumption was grounded in the idea that when they purchased goods from highlanders they were entitled to a bonus. As such, the word indexed a sense of entitlement or privilege among the *Camba* population. Having lived in both Cochabamba and Santa Cruz, Bruno reflected:

> ...the only place I heard this word being used was in Santa Cruz, which is kind of interesting. Because why a *Camba* would use a word from a Native American, not American, but a native language, right. I think it is because that sort of contrast, that the *Colla* is the exploited and the *Camba*... thinks he's better. Therefore he wants more.

In this fashion, Bruno became deeply attuned to the ways that linguistic repertoires and language ideologies were deeply embedded in social orders. His unequal encounters across difference further instilled a felt sense of ways that languages and cultural practices not only varied across nation-states but also within their sharply contested borders. Assuming his move to Santa Cruz would feel completely natural, he reflected: 'I thought it was... going to be just like Cochabamba, but it wasn't. And I gradually was learning more about the place.' The norms of this place were strikingly different: strange accents, new slang, different ways of socializing and interacting, a warmer climate and a more heated political climate. In relation to this final area, he reflected on his initial surprise in bumping up against these unexpected issues: 'So when I get back from, when I leave Brazil, I now have to encounter another culture which is the *Cambas*... I'm just learning more stuff about the, my country, that I didn't imagine existed.' As this particular case makes evident, even understanding a single term necessitated a complex engagement with Bolivia's multilayered history and social geography. It further points to the ways in which Bruno became attuned to the ideological and colonizing aspects of language and literacy.

Adjusting to his new social geography, Bruno went through a process of enculturation similar to his experience in Brazil. He had to learn how to present himself, but this time in six months he had picked up the social slang and accents.

> Yeah, so what happened then, I sort of *copied* [emphasis added] what I did in Brazil. I started to listen carefully to what the *Camba*s said and how they acted, and everything, and so I did sort of personalize my personality, to theirs. And that process was way faster than it was in Brazil. And, yeah, then I made friends like easier, and we started hanging out. It was a process way faster, than it was in Brazil.

Adapting to a different dialect, he learned to speak it without a highland accent and to pass as a *Camba*. The goal was to be unmarked in the dominant culture. He said, 'Yeah. I learned how to speak like a *Camba*, and, even my mom was surprised – so I sound differently when I talk to my mom, than I talk to my friends.' In this way, he was learning to code mesh, or meshwork, as he navigated back and forth between the cultures.

Example 3: Politics of Literacy across Transnational Social Worlds

I turn finally to Bruno's third major assignment: analyzing a cultural artifact, practice or community. Closely aligned with the translingual curriculum, the aim was to encourage students to denaturalize or de-familiarize their everyday linguistic and cultural surroundings. In this assignment, Bruno focused on a key political controversy surrounding an unprecedented fourth election of President Evo Morales. Closely identified with the *Cambas*, Morales had risen to power in 2005 on a populist platform aimed at giving the poor indigenous of Bolivia a stronger political voice. But the longest serving president in Bolivian history was testing the boundaries of the country's constitution in an effort to run for another term. The country had narrowly rejected increasing the term limit in a national referendum on 21 February 2015, which would have legitimized another run. However, a ruling by an Evo-appointed court overrode the results, in a decision that stated not allowing him to run for office again would constitute a human rights violation.

This background serves as the context for a paper by Bruno that analyzed a series of memes from a movement called 21F-Boliva Dijo Lo (Bolivia Says No). The name was shorthand for the date of the referendum along with the groundswell of people who had come out against the court decision. Mass protests emerged, with activists and everyday citizenry asserting that it was a court overreach and abuse of power. As part of Bruno's analysis of this grassroots movement, he included a meme (Figure 8.3) of the vice president and president with text underneath each political figure: '90*3=180' and 'N+O=SI [Yes].' The underlying critique was that the political logic of the party in power did not add up. Indexed in the analysis was Bruno's own

Figure 8.3 Political meme from 21F protest movement

political stance or position. On the side of the opposition to the president, he was also simultaneously sympathetic to many of the *Colla* supporters. Indeed, despite these differences and his middle-class identity, he was often inescapably labeled as such in Santa Cruz. Entangled in this class and ethnic conflict, he occupied multilayered and conflicting positions as he traversed the cultural, political, semiotic and regional landscape.

This was part of a complex, messy process that continued with his travels to the United States, first as a high school exchange student and later as an international student at a major Midwestern university. Complicating these tangled intersections was another strand of activity linked to the global spread of English. It was during his years in Brazil and later in Santa Cruz that he took supplementary English classes. His father had enrolled him in after-school courses in anticipation of the future. Bruno explained about his father: 'He was thinking about my future, like English is the universal language, per say. Like everyone speaks it and it opens you a lot of doors.' This social imaginary mediated his father's subsequent decision to send him to Kalamazoo, Michigan, as an exchange student for his senior year of high school.

Surprisingly, the transition went more smoothly than past moves, at least in part due to his new-found maturity along with the translingual disposition (Lee & Jenks, 2016) that he had cultivated through engaging with difference. Rather than encountering a difficult period of adjustment as in the past, his status as an international student in the Midwestern school proved to be asset. Serving as a form of social capital, many locals took an interest in him personally because of his international experience and sought to learn about his life in Bolivia. The interactions point to how difference was constructed unevenly and unequally across contexts in unexpected and messy ways. Whereas in the US his outsider status worked to his advantage, in Brazil, as well as the Bolivian lowlands, it limited his mobility and operated as a constraint.

In turn, Bruno had the opportunity to engage with some of the cultural differences he was encountering in the United States. Arriving on the heels of Donald Trump's 2016 presidential win, what particularly stood out was the peculiar nature of American politics. As political theater, it was best characterized by a term he picked up on YouTube called *kayfabe*. The term is a reference to the world of professional wrestling and the portrayal of the staged events and bouts as if they were true or real. The concept was one that he felt applied to American political life. Much of the drama had a staged quality. For example, he believed that Donald Trump and Hillary Clinton's anger towards one another was largely an act. He also believed that the participants (e.g. voters, politicians, political pundits) were generally in on this secret but nevertheless continued to play along as if it was real. As opposed to the political satire in his own country aimed at unmasking social realities, American culture seemed to be engaged in sustaining a fiction. The popular culture term *kayfabe* is one that he had learned from a YouTube channel, *Wisecrack*, as a site focused on edgy media analyses. Forming part of a literacy sponsorscape (Wargo & De Costa, 2017), the concept served to inform his own comparative analysis of language and society. As part of a relational interplay, it became layered into his literate life. More broadly it was through this ongoing, emergent, multidirectional process that he moved across the digital, social, semiotic and geographic landscape.

Conclusion

As this case makes evident, Bruno was entangled in a wider network, or meshwork, of activity that he continually negotiated. This entailed an ongoing, jointly mediated process as he wove and was woven into semiotic systems distributed across near and distant spaces. Broadly, we might understand these texts, tools, actors and objects as comprising a meshwork, or mobility system, constraining and affording his mobilities, identities and practices. In this fashion, these multilayered strands of activity served as a literacy sponsorscape distributed across transnational social fields. It is through moving in and across these fields – as he continually mobilized spatial and multimodal repertoires – that he developed a bifocal (or multifocal) perspective (Vertovec, 2004) or transnational habitus (Meinhoff, 2009). This process was ongoing, on-the-fly, emergent and unfinished, with Bruno's literate identity in motion as part of an ongoing state of becoming. It is to these multilingual (or translingual) and multimodal (or transmodal) processes that we must attend as literacies, identities and mobilities are increasingly bound up in 21st-century globalization.

References

Agar, M. (1994) *Language Shock*. New York: Quill/William Morrow.
Agha, A. (2003) The social life of cultural value. *Language & Communication* 23 (3–4), 231–273.
Appadurai, A. (1990) Disjuncture and difference in the global cultural economy. *Theory Culture & Society* 7 (2–3), 295–310.
Bartholomae, D. (1986) Inventing the university. *Journal of Basic Writing* 5 (1), 4–23.
Bawarshi, A. (2006) Response: Taking up language differences in composition. *College English* 68 (6), 652–656.
Blommaert, J. (2005) *Discourse: A Critical Introduction*. Cambridge: Cambridge University Press.
Blommaert, J. (2013) *The Sociolinguistics of Globalization*. Cambridge: Cambridge University Press.
Bourdieu, P. (1977) *Outline of a Theory of Practice*. Cambridge: Cambridge University Press.

Brandt, D. (1998) Sponsors of literacy. *College Composition and Communication* 49 (2), 165–185.

Brooks, R. and Waters, J.L. (2011) *Student Mobilities, Migration and the Internationalization of Higher Education*. London: Palgrave Macmillan.

Canagarajah, A.S. (2006) The place of world Englishes in composition: Pluralization continued. *College Composition and Communication* 57 (4), 586–619.

Canagarajah, S. (2013) *Translingual Practice: Global Englishes and Cosmopolitan Relations*. New York: Routledge.

Canagarajah, S. (2018) Translingual practice as spatial repertoires: Expanding the paradigm beyond structuralist orientations. *Applied Linguistics* 39 (1), 31–54.

Casanave, C.P. (2002) *Writing Games: Multicultural Case Studies of Academic Literacy Practices in Higher Education*. New York: Routledge

Charmaz, K. (2014) *Constructing Grounded Theory*. Thousand Oaks, CA: Sage.

Cresswell, T. (2010) Towards a politics of mobility. *Environment and Planning D: Society and Space* 28 (1), 17–31.

De Costa, P.I. (2014) Cosmopolitanism and English as a lingua franca: Learning English in a Singapore school. *Research in the Teaching of English* 49, 9–30.

De Costa, P.I. (2016) Constructing the global citizen: An ELF perspective. *Journal of Asian Pacific Communication* 26 (2), 238–259.

De Costa, P.I., Tigchelaar, M. and Cui, Y. (2016) Reflexivity, emotions and transnational habitus: The case of a 'poor' cosmopolitan Chinese international student. *AILA Review* 29, 173–198.

Dreier, O. (1999) Personal trajectories of participation across contexts of social practice. Outlines. *Critical Practice Studies* 1 (1), 5–32.

Fabricant, N. (2009) Performative politics: The *Camba* countermovement in eastern Bolivia. *American Ethnologist* 36 (4), 768–783.

Fraiberg, S. (2010) Composition 2.0: Toward a multilingual and multimodal framework. *College Composition and Communication* 62 (1), 100–126.

Fraiberg, S. (2017) Pretty bullets: Tracing transmedia/translingual literacies of an Israeli soldier across regimes of practice. *College Composition and Communication* 69 (1), 87–117.

Fraiberg, S., Wang, X. and You, X. (2017) *Inventing the World Grant University: Chinese International Students' Mobilities, Literacies, and Identities*. Logan, UT: Utah State University Press.

Gee, J. (2004) *What Video Games Have to Teach Us about Learning and Literacy*. Basingstoke: Palgrave Macmillan.

Hoffman, E. (1989) *Lost in Translation: A Life in a New Language*. London: Penguin Books.

Horner, B., Lu, M.Z., Royster, J.J. and Trimbur, J. (2011) Language difference in writing: Toward a translingual approach. *College English* 73 (3), 303–321.

Hull, G.A. and Stornaiuolo, A. (2010) Literate arts in a global world: Reframing social networking as cosmopolitan practice. *Journal of Adolescent & Adult Literacy* 54 (2), 85.

Ingold, T. (2009) Against space: Place, movement, knowledge. In P. Kirby (ed.) *Boundless Worlds: An Anthropological Approach to Movement* (pp. 29–42). New York: Berghahn Books.

Ivanič, R. (1998) *Writing and Identity: The Discoursal Construction of Identity in Academic Writing*. Amsterdam: John Benjamins.

Klenk, N. (2018) From network to meshwork: Becoming attuned to difference in transdisciplinary environmental research encounters. *Environmental Science & Policy* 89, 315–321.

Lam, W.S.E. and Warriner, D.S. (2012) Transnationalism and literacy: Investigating the mobility of people, languages, texts, and practices in contexts of migration. *Reading Research Quarterly* 47 (2), 191–215.

Latour, B. (1999) *Pandora's Hope: Essays on the Reality of Science Studies*. Cambridge, MA: Harvard University Press.

Latour, B. (2005) *Reassembling the Social: An Introduction to Actor-network Theory*. Oxford: Oxford University Press.

Leander, K.M. and Sheehy, M. (2004) *Spatializing Literacy Research and Practice*. Bern: Peter Lang.

Leander, K.M., Phillips, N.C. and Taylor, K.H. (2010) The changing social spaces of learning: Mapping new mobilities. *Review of Research in Education* 34 (1), 329–394.

Lee, J.W. and Jenks, C. (2016) Doing translingual dispositions. *College Composition and Communication* 68 (2), 317–344.

Lefebvre, H. (1991) *The Production of Space*. Oxford: Blackwell.

Lopez Pila, E. (2014) 'We don't lie and cheat like the *Collas* do.' Highland–lowland regionalist tensions and indigenous identity politics in Amazonian Bolivia. *Critique of Anthropology* 34 (4), 429–449.

Lorimar Leonard, R. (2013) Traveling literacies: Multilingual writing on the move. *Research in the Teaching of English* 48 (1), 13–39.

Lorimar Leonard, R. (2014) Multilingual writing as rhetorical attunement. *College English* 76 (3), 227–247.

Massey, D. (1999) Imagining globalization: Power-geometries of time-space. In A. Brah, M.J. Hickman and M.M. an Ghaill (eds) *Global Futures: Migration, Environment and Globalization* (pp. 27–44). London: Palgrave Macmillan.

Massey, D. (2005) *For Space*. London: Sage.

McCarthy, L.P. (1987) A stranger in strange lands: A college student writing across the curriculum. *Research in the Teaching of English* 21 (3), 233–265.

Meinhof, U.H. (2009) Transnational flows, networks and 'transcultural capital': Reflections on researching migrant networks through linguistic ethnography. In J. Collins, M. Baynham and S. Slembrouck (eds) *Globalization and Languages in Contact: Scale, Migration, and Communicative Practices* (pp. 148–169). London: Continuum.

Nordquist, B. (2017) *Literacy and Mobility: Complexity, Uncertainty and Agency at the Nexus of High School and College*. Abingdon: Taylor & Francis.

Ong, A. (1999) *Flexible Citizenship: The Cultural Logics of Transnationality*. Durham, NC: Duke University Press.

Pennycook, A. (2012) *Language and Mobility: Unexpected Places*. Bristol: Multilingual Matters.

Pennycook, A. and Otsuji, E. (2014) Metrolingual multitasking and spatial repertoires: 'Pizza mo two minutes coming'. *Journal of Sociolinguistics* 18 (2), 161–184.

Prior, P.A. (1998) *Writing/disciplinarity: A Sociohistoric Account of Literate Activity in the Academy*. Abingdon: Routledge.

Rizvi, F. (2009) Global mobility and the challenges of educational research and policy. *Yearbook of the National Society for the Study of Education* 108 (2), 268–289.

Roozen, K.R. and Erickson, J. (2017) *Expanding Literate Landscapes: Persons, Practices, and Sociohistoric Perspectives of Disciplinary Development*. Logan, UT: Computers and Composition Digital Press/Utah State University Press.

Russell, D.R. and Yañez, A. (2003) 'Big picture people rarely become historians': Genre systems and the contradictions of general education. In C. Bazerman and D.R. Russell (eds) *Writing Selves, Writing Societies: Research from Activity Perspectives* (pp. 331–362). WAC Clearinghouse.

Sternglass, M.S. (1997) *Time to Know Them: A Longitudinal Study of Writing and Learning at the College Level*. Abingdon: Routledge.

Sidhu, R.K. (2006) *Universities and Globalization: To Market, to Market*. Abingdon: Routledge.

Singh, M., Rizvi, F. and Shrestha, M. (2007) Student mobility and the spatial production of cosmopolitan identities. In K. Gulson and C. Symes (eds) *Spatial Theories of Education: Policy and Geography Matters* (pp. 195–214). Abingdon: Routledge.

Soja, E.W. (1996) *Thirdspace: Journeys to Los Angeles and Other Real-and-Imagined Places*. Oxford: Blackwell.

Sternglass, M.S. (1997) *Time to Know Them: A Longitudinal Study of Writing and Learning at the College Level*. Abingdon: Routledge.

Swinehart, K.F. (2012) The enregisterment of *Colla* in a Bolivian (*Camba*) comedy. *Social Text* 30 (4), 81–102.

Tsing, A.L. (2006) *Friction: An Ethnography of Global Connection*. Princeton, NJ: Princeton University Press.

Urry, J. (2007) *Mobilities: New Perspectives on Transport and Society*. Abingdon: Routledge.

Vertovec, S. (2004) *Transnationalism*. Abingdon: Routledge.

Wargo, J.M. and De Costa, P.I. (2017) Tracing academic literacies across contemporary literacy sponsorscapes: Mobilities, ideologies, identities, and technologies. *London Review of Education* 15 (1), 101–114.

Waters, J.L. (2012) Geographies of international education: Mobilities and the reproduction of social (dis)advantage. *Geography Compass* 6 (3), 123–136.

Wertsch, J.V. (1991) *Voices of the Mind: Sociocultural Approach to Mediated Action*. Cambridge, MA: Harvard University Press.

Wimmer, A. and Glick Schiller, N. (2002) Methodological nationalism and beyond: Nation-state building, migration and the social sciences. *Global Networks* 2 (4), 301–334.

You, X. (2016) *Cosmopolitan English and Transliteracy*. Carbondale, IL: Southern Illinois University Press.

You, X. (ed.) (2018) *Transnational Writing Education: Theory, History, and Practice*. Abingdon: Routledge.

Zamel, V. and Spack, R. (eds) (2004) *Crossing the Curriculum: Multilingual Learners in College Classrooms*. Abingdon: Routledge.

Appendix: Text for 'Born to Adapt' Comic

(1) Change is something that has captured my attention ever since I was little, it was as intriguing but yet terrifying.

(2) as a kid I used to be very shy and introvert…

(3) I was an stereotypical "coya"

(4) Coyas are often described as the working class

(5) the ones who don't have a voice

(6) the ones who rather look down and accept the things how they are

(7) Back then little I knew that my personality would be challenged over and over as I grew older

(8) When I was 8 my parents told me that we were moving to Rio de Janeiro – Brazil

(9) I was scared

(10) even though Portuguese is similar to Spanish, Brazil and Bolivia aren't alike at all

(11) when we arrived to Santos Dumont airport, I followed my parents into one taxi

(12) in the trip to our hotel, I tried to the cab and my dad were talking about/talk

(13) in general Brazilians are very talkative and outgoing

(14) and I was the exact opposite

(15) at school I would hope for the teacher not to ask me questions or notice me
(16) I'd rather be facing my desk
(17) Unfortunately my classmates wouldn't associate themselves with someone that shy
(18) I realized if I wanted to be accepted I needed to change
(19) so I slowly started to observe the other kids
(20) How they talked
(21) What words they used/talk
(22) I became so good copying them that I could speak with their accent
(23) And for my fortune it was easier to meet new people/ "toca ae"
(24) However there were other aspects about Brazilian culture I didn't know about
(25) In class there was a kid that needed special care/who wants to take Rodrigo to the bathroom?
(26) Him and I became friends after meeting for the first time
(27) But suddenly I had no time for myself
(28) The others were very supportive but never wanted to carry him
(29) Not until my mom find out I was pushing a kid around by myself I stopped.
(30) She made me understand how other have responsibility over him as well
(31) I am positive that there is other aspects of Brazilian culture I haven't discovered, but a part of their culture will be always with me

9 Writing about Where We Are from: Writing Across Languages, Genres and Spaces

Xiqiao Wang

Introduction

The Department of Writing, Rhetoric and American Cultures (hereafter referred to as WRAC), the home department of the first-year writing program, is an important academic unit that is key to introducing undergraduate students to academic discourse and disciplinary writing practices at Great Lake University (GLU). In particular, the bridge writing course (i.e. FYW 100), entitled Preparation for College Writing, which welcomed more than 900 multilingual, heritage, and first-generation students at the time of the study, was a key site where significant research efforts and pedagogical innovation had taken place to explore multilingual writer's literacy practices and to develop best teaching practices to support such students' literacy learning (Fraiberg et al., 2017; Kiernan et al., 2016; Wang, 2020).

Since 2014, a team of teacher scholars has worked collaboratively to develop a pedagogical framework that now centers students' semiotic repertoires, cultural knowledge and reflective practices through sustained efforts in developing and refining theory-informed teaching practices and assignments. Such pedagogical innovation not only responds to the local and institutional exigency arising from the growing number of diverse learners enrolling in first-year writing courses, but also addresses a pedagogical gap in the field of composition studies – a lack of asset-based pedagogy that adequately enacts theoretical advancements in translingual scholarship. The unique positioning of the course, with its large population of international students, as well as the pedagogical innovation and curricular changes which now position students' semiotic repertoires and cultural differences as sites of inquiry, subjects of analysis and assets for learning, has lent itself as a key research site for year-long project as researchers regularly conducted classroom observation, identified and recruited participants, and traced students' complex experiences with multiple academic units and resource centers. Indeed, as suggested in Chapter 3 (Zhang) and Chapter 4 (Wang & Straayer), the basic writing class allowed for a space to explore how international students were socialized into academic discourse at the university, how they learned to navigate competing expectations for literacy learning across stakeholders and developed strategies and practices to navigate a host of academic, social and disciplinary challenges. Also evidenced in Chapter 6 (Son) and Chapter 8 (Fraiberg) respectively, the asset-based pedagogical framework, which began to explore ways of honoring and leveraging students' language and cultural differences, has provided opportunities to observe students' practices and strategies as they mobilize a dynamic semiotic repertoire to negotiate meanings across languages, modes, relationships networks, digital platforms and spaces.

In this chapter, I provide an account of the pedagogical framework that informed the revised curriculum, which operated with a series of writing assignments that invited students' reflections on their literacy experiences dispersed across time–space relationships, encouraged translingual and transcultural conversations, and motivated students' efforts to access learning resources on and off campus. In so doing, this chapter provides an account of the pedagogical intentions, structures and objectives of assignments, which could usefully contextualize ethnographic descriptions of classroom events, student artifacts and literacy practices documented across chapters in this volume.

Enacting Translingual Pedagogy

The field of composition studies has begun to explore how multilingual students draw on rich semiotic and linguistic resources to engage in translingual practices, with negotiation of difference at the core of such language work (Canagarajah, 2006; Lorimer Leonard, 2014; Lu & Horner, 2013; Wang, 2020). But theoretical recognition of and empirical investigation into translingualism have yet to fully explore concrete teaching strategies to facilitate students' inquiry into language differences or offer ways to help students develop an attitude of openness towards such differences. In this chapter, I offer examples of writing assignments that enact translingual principles by centering students' languages/cultures and encouraging students' multimodal representations of and inquiry into their language differences and practices. In so doing, I discuss how such assignments create a space for teachers and students alike to describe, analyze and strategize ways of negotiating language differences.

With the increasing linguistic and cultural heterogeneity of students enrolled in US institutions of education, how to better support such students' literacy learning through strategic leverage of their rhetorical repertoire has become a critical question for literacy teachers across all levels. The translingual turn in composition broadly seeks to highlight the practice-based, adaptive, emergent and mutually constitutive nature of languages (Canagarajah, 2013; Lu & Horner, 2013). In particular, Lu and Horner (2013) challenge a monolingual view of languages, such as English, Chinese or French, as 'discrete, preexisting, and enumerable entities' bound to geographical territories, nation-states or speech communities (Lu & Horner, 2013: 587). While a static view of language provides the ideological foundation for privileging standard English as the dominant dialect, translingualism approaches language as inherently dynamic, evolving and varied. Recognizing languages, including standard English, as historical codifications that change through dynamic processes of use, translingualism focuses on the innovative ways in which language users shape language to specific ends. Such a perspective not only recognizes the increasing linguistic heterogeneity as the norm, but also values the rhetorical and linguistic resources that non-dominant students bring to their writing. Accordingly, language differences, manifested as accented Englishes in the basic writing classroom, are not interpreted as deviations but as valuable resources that writers work with and against.

Translingualism provides a way to access and develop multilingual writers' language performance through local, situated practices of communication, which involves dynamic negotiation of fluid languages and cultures. Such acts of linguistic, cultural and disciplinary border-crossing involve the ongoing fine-tuning of students' disposition towards language negotiation. Horner *et al.* (2011: 311) distinguish translingual disposition from knowledge of multiple languages, highlighting an open and inquiry-driven attitude toward language differences. Similarly, Canagarajah emphasizes the importance of writers' meta-awareness of the 'possibilities and constraints of competing traditions of writing' as central to writers' abilities to carve out a space for themselves within conflicting discourses (Canagarajah, 2006: 602). As such, writers develop 'rhetorical sensibility' toward the inherent instability and contingency of languages (Guerra, 2016). In important ways, the emphasis on translingual disposition recognizes that all students, multilingual and monolingual alike, already mobilize multilingual resources and deploy translingual practices to write themselves and their life worlds into meaning. Continuous fine-tuning of such dispositions of openness and negotiation is critical to successful performance of translingual practices.

Similar to the less-bounded conceptions of language, proponents of multimodality have argued that students need to develop a full mastery of the rhetorical and semiotic resources at their disposal to address the 'wickedly complex communicative tasks' in an increasingly globalized and digital world (Selfe, 2009: 645). Shipka emphasizes the importance of using multimodal genres to help students understand that meaning can be rendered in multiple ways in response to variant contingencies

(Shipka, 2013). Such a view is coherent with translingual theorists' arguments that all meaning-making acts involve 'traffic in meaning,' where one negotiates 'ideas, concepts, symbols, [and] discourses' (Pennycook, 2008: 33) across languages and modes (Horner & Tetreault, 2016: 19). Scholars have also urged us to go beyond the symbolic dimension to include affective, bodily and material connections that shape writing (Gonzalez, 2018; Jordan, 2015). As such, a translingual and multimodal lens encourages us to view writing as socially situated, emergent and negotiated rather than as a static, rule-driven phenomenon. A translingual, multimodal view thus considers meaning-making as involving layers of translation across codes, modes, languages and cultures.

While research guided by translingualism has thus far approached the issue of negotiation through researchers' inductive reading of students' writing samples for textual evidence of code-meshing, which involves the merging of 'diverse language resources with the dominant genre conventions to construct hybrid texts for voice' (Canagarajah, 2013: 40), there has been less effort in documenting and analyzing students' inquiry into their own meaning- and error-making experiences. Indeed, the subtle and invisible acts of composing across differences often evade our attention because they function as such a routine part of our language work that they often recede into the background of our consciousness. If untapped, such cultural and linguistic knowledge that shapes multilingual writer's language practices may very well remain invisible and never turn into transferrable meta-knowledge of writing (DePalma & Ringer, 2011; Lorimer Leonard & Nowacek, 2016). It is with such concerns that scholars have argued that the focus on visible examples of code-meshing risks flattening the nuanced ways in which writers from distinct backgrounds engage with language differences, thereby overshadowing the subtle examples of language negotiation (Gilyard, 2016; Matsuda, 2014). Inherent to such conversations has been an increasing attention to translingual dispositions and translingual practices as interconnected aspects of the translingual phenomenon, with *inquiry-driven dispositions* guiding strategic practices and with ongoing practices providing opportunities to enrich such dispositions.

While echoing translingual scholars' arguments that all acts of linguistic performance are essentially translingual (Horner *et al.*, 2011), I offer writing assignments such as *Translation Narrative*, *Writing Theory Cartoon* and *I Am from Poetry* as pedagogical tools to help multilingual students analyze their struggles and triumphs when working through linguistic, cultural and rhetorical differences. The design of such assignments is grounded in an increasing body of scholarship that maintains that a translingual approach brings ideological discussions to the teaching of writing and enriches such teaching by way of encouraging meaning negotiation across genres and modalities (Canagarajah, 2006; Creese & Blackledge, 2010; Hornberger & Link, 2012; Lorimer

Leonard, 2014; Sun & Lan, 2020). Scholars have described translingual dispositions as consisting of an attitude of openness towards language differences and understanding all language acts as ongoing processes of negotiating linguistic, rhetorical and cultural differences. Accordingly, assignments that leverage multiple languages and modes of inquiry and representation are particularly useful in supporting students' discovery and theorization of the negotiated nature of their own meaning-making. Drawing on examples of student work and reflection, I discuss how such assignments encourage an attitude of openness towards language differences by:

- Enabling students' development of metalinguistic understanding of language as historically conditioned linguistic, cultural and ideological structures.
- Inviting students' exploration of their literacy practices and rhetorical repertoire as resources that could be mobilized and reconfigured across contexts.
- Facilitating the development of a meta-vocabulary to describe, theorize and strategize language negotiation.

The pedagogical innovation described here therefore adds to current conversations in translingualism in several ways. First, it shifts our emphasis from the production of code-meshed texts towards students' theorization of complex language negotiation that happens in all communicative acts, even those that seemingly adhere to and replicate standard conventions. Second, it positions multilingual writers' linguistic, cultural and rhetorical knowledge as resources for learning and their linguistic performance as a site of innovation and inquiry. Centering on students' experiences and languages not only facilitates the development of rhetorical awareness/understanding of how situations constantly influence linguistic performance, but also positions such students as agents whose inquiry into their linguistic, cultural and disciplinary border-crossing produces rhetorical strategies central to learning to write across contexts. Lastly, productive exploration of multimodal representation provides writers with multiple pathways towards meaning-making as negotiated across codes, modes and languages. Together, such assignments give writing teachers a glimpse into students' translingual lives.

The Context of Pedagogical Innovation

The pedagogical move to incorporate translingual inquiry in the first-year writing classroom described here is a local and institutional response to population shifts. The curricular redesign described in this chapter occurs in a bridge writing course (i.e. FYW 100) entitled *Preparation for College Writing*, which serves largely first-generation and international students, the majority of whom are Chinese, with others from such countries as South Korea, Saudi Arabia and Thailand. In response to this shifting demographic, a team of teacher researchers has engaged in a program-wide, collaborative re-invention of the curriculum and pedagogy for FYW 100, which now feature a series of assignments that reflect principles of translingual pedagogy. The re-invented curriculum foregrounds students' linguistic, rhetorical and cultural resources as assets through a series of assignments and curricular events, such as *Translation Narrative*, *Writing Theory Cartoon* and *I Am from Poetry*. In what follows, I provide a brief description for the procedures involved in implementing each assignment and offer examples of student artifacts to discuss the pedagogical facility of such a curriculum in enabling translingual negotiation. Doing so allows me to illustrate how such assignments support students' tuning of translingual disposition and practice, which allows them to access and evaluate a dynamic, evolving repertoire of literacy practices, campus resources and peer networks central to their academic socialization.

Translation narrative

The implementation of the *Translation Narrative*, the very first assignment in a series of pedagogical innovations, reflects the goal of our research-informed teaching practices, which surfaces students' home languages and cultures as well as reflective practice. Despite the diverse linguistic backgrounds, pedagogical orientations and teaching approaches among the core faculty involved, there are a number of commonalities in each iteration of this writing task.

Procedure

The assignment can be divided into three stages: a group translation, a comparative reflection, and translation narrative. Stage one is a collaborative translation: students work in groups of 3–4 based on home language and choose a text that is written in this language. Excerpts of texts are identified, distributed and translated into English. Members in the group then translate the excerpts individually before sharing their individual translation with the group. Stage two of this assignment, the comparative reflection, is a collaborative process, where students share their translated texts, compare differences and similarities in translation, and reflect on personal experiences, feelings and choices during the translation process. The third stage of this assignment is the translation narrative, which incorporates all previous steps and encourages students to create a final personal narrative, where they consider their translation process, strategies and practices. In what follows, I offer examples from one student's translation narrative to discuss the pedagogical affordances of the assignment, including understanding language as cultural and linguistic structures, language differences as resources for learning, and writing as mobile literacy practice.

Translation narrative assignment

When students translated an idiom, a song or a cultural tale, students often worked to achieve balance between representing the intention of the original text and adjusting textual and linguistic features in anticipation of audience expectations. Multilingual writers learned to negotiate meaning to make it accessible to their readers even if their translations were often not perfect semantic equivalents of the original. Jessica, a Chinese international student, chose to entitle her translation reflection paper 'How to Translate a Story to Foreign People' and wrote of the difficulty of translating as a profoundly rhetorical practice:

> When Chinese writers describe how sad they are when we lose something valuable, we write about standing in front of a loquat tree, staring at it and immersed in your memories. This was a successful [strategy] to catch the reader's attention in Chinese, but it would never work here.

This reflection emerges from her translation of an excerpt from an essay written in classical Chinese, '有枇杷树，吾妻死之年所手植也，今已亭亭如盖矣,' which captured a moment when Su Shi, a renowned Chinese classical essayist, stood in solitude in front of a luscious loquat tree planted in in his backyard, which reminded him of his beloved deceased wife. Jessica translated the sentence into English: '[There] was [this] loquat tree, [which I] planted by hand [when] my wife died. [It is] now flourishing as an *umbrella*.' Individual translation and comparison of translations with members in her group invited her to consider productive means to negotiate syntactic, semantic and rhetorical structures when moving meaning across languages.

Individual and group reflection invited the student to recognize the importance of attending to languages as rule-driven, linguistic structures. For one thing, she paid attention to the lack of relative pronouns in Chinese to drive cohesion at the clause level. However, she also noted the presence of modal particles, a category missing in English. On this, she notes:

> In order to make sense to my English readers, I will added some English words that it actually not exist in original story. For example, the sentence I mentioned in above doesn't have connection words in its Chinese version, but it has lots of special Chinese words to end sentences with. I had to add connection words and delete special words.

Evidenced here is the affordance of the assignment to provide a space to develop metalinguistic understanding of languages as rule-governed systems. Such metalinguistic awareness, manifested in an understanding of the need to adjust syntax structure, is mirrored in a research study using design research methods conducted by Jiménez *et al.* (2015), where middle school students learned to collaboratively translate excerpts from grade-appropriate literature in Spanish. Jiménez *et al.* not only observe how translation activities encourage students to 'draw on their cultural and linguistic knowledge to derive meaning' (2015: 249), but position translation as a metalinguistic activity involving systematic comparison of, reflection on, and manipulation of multiple languages (2015: 251). Foregrounding translation as a resource for learning, the assignment also leads to discussions of how semantic choices are derived in socioculturally ascribed ways. Here, the same student discusses her translation of '盖' (Gai, cover of pot or ceremonial umbrella) into 'umbrella.' She suggests:

> 盖 in classical Chinese has different meanings. It could be the cover of the tea pot or the beautiful decorative umbrellas used by emperors. To make my story more attractive and readable, I used more familiar words. Umbrella lets the reader feel more familiar.

Such semantic choices reflect the students' effort to appeal to American readers, who are perceived to be unfamiliar with the Chinese cultural rituals of tea-drinking or imperial ceremony. The need to adapt to her American audience was explained in her reflections, where she complicated, named and elucidated her efforts to unpack cultural ways of being, acting and relating. Additionally, students learn to recognize language practice as informed by rhetorical traditions and strategies. In particular, the student recognizes the inadequacy of literal translation, which fails to capture the subtle expression of the poet's feelings of sorrow. She reflects:

> To make my readers understand, I can't say he was staring at a loquat tree. I added a sentence to explain that he was thinking of his wife and how long she has died. The tree represented his sadness.

Such reflection focuses on unpacking culturally specific aesthetics, rhetorical styles and ideological features of languages as operative within community, disciplinary and national contexts. The author's use of the loquat tree embodies a sophisticated use of a rhetorical strategy known as 'combine emotion with scenery' (寓情于景), which is often used by classical authors to articulate their emotions and aspirations. The tree embodies affectionate memories of a loved one, which contrasts with the feeling of loss to highlight the gravity of sorrow. Inferring that her American audience might not be aware of cultural frames and tropes familiar to a Chinese reader, the student approached the affective meaning of the text by surfacing it in a straightforward manner. This move partially resulted from ongoing conversations with a diverse audience, which brought into convergence multiple interpretations and rhetorical strategies. Through sustained individual and collective exploration, students recognize the importance of decoding the 'hidden meanings' of examples, canonical texts and cultural tropes in consideration of their audience's needs and expectations. Doing so invited the student to temporarily suspend established, familiar assumptions about her language and culture, while learning to consider her language/culture in the context of another, thereby developing transcultural awareness.

Writing theory cartoon

Writing theory cartoons have been used to help writers access a range of rhetorical options at their disposal, negotiate conventions and rules, and understand such choices as tied to identities, values and interests (Prior & Shipka, 2003). Student-generated cartoons could be interpreted as visual metaphors of the thought processes and emotions of writers and therefore could be used to elicit accounts of the material, cognitive and affective dimensions of their writing process (Prior & Shipka, 2003: 181). Such attention to writing as embodied practice is coherent with translingual scholars' concern to understand writing as unfolding through the intersecting forces of histories, social worlds and affective contingencies. It is in this spirit that I adapt the writing theory cartoon into a pedagogical tool, which encourages multilingual writers to explore the affordances of multiple modes to discover, formulate and represent meaning regarding their translingual practices.

Procedure

The assignment involves a sequence of drafting, revision and reflective activities that typically unfolds across six regular class meetings. The recursive process creates a space to sustain and deepen conversations around translingual practices, introduce grammars of visual composition, and leverage students' informal literacies. The assignment begins with *sampling multicultural texts,* which makes use of student-identified texts from their home cultures. Students then *construct writing theory metaphors* to further theorize languages as linguistic, cultural and rhetorical structures and represent students' beliefs, attitudes and theories about writing. Building on such metaphors, students used an online drawing tool (flockdraw.com) to *draft writing theory cartoons,* which is an opportunity to experiment with visual representations of abstract ideas and visceral feelings through experimentation with colors, shapes and visual symbols. Coupling course reading of 'grammar of visual design' (Kress & van Leeuwen, 1996) and class discussion of exemplary student work, students *construct grammars of multimodal composition*, with attention given to what, how and why symbols, shapes, colors and spaces are arranged to articulate certain meanings. In a recursive process of review and revision, students are given multiple opportunities to play with personal theories of translingual practice and explore multiple modes of representation.

Supporting language negotiation

The assignment affords collective development of rhetorical understanding of writing as tied to cultural, rhetorical and disciplinary traditions. Many students approach the writing theory cartoon as an opportunity to examine their own struggles with writing across languages. In Figure 9.1, I offer an example of such rhetorical inquiry from one

English: I used lines with different colors to stimulate the structure of the paper which I can use my home language. The thickest and vertical line not only represents the theme, but also means construction of the paper. the reason why I used many different colors cross the vertical line because they seem like diverse writing skills, vocabulary and grammar in my home language.	English: I think this visual design can totally express the structure of my English paper, which is weak, incomplete and insipid. Comparing to the first one, when I use my home language, there are 'theme' and consecutive 'strung' the paper. However, this one doesn't have the 'backbone' same as my English paper often dim the theme of it. The Black zigzag design means I wish I can use diverse writing skills, vocabularies and grammars when i writing and English paper, but it's unpractical till now.
Chinese: 图中黑色的竖线代表一篇文章的 "主心骨"和逻辑顺序，循序渐进并且串连起文章其他元素。彩色的线代表多种多样的文章修饰，写作手法等等用于文章润色的方法。 (Researcher translation: The black vertical line represents the 'backbone' or the logical order of an essay, which strings together all the elements in a progressive way. Colorful lines represent a wide range of rhetorical devices and writing techniques, which can embellish the essay.)	Chinese: 这幅图片和中文设计的最大不同就是图中缺少一条主线，就像英语写作的时候，感觉怎么写都写不到点上去，经常会模糊焦点找不到中心。同样的z字型设计但是使用黑色表达是有种心有余而力不足的感觉，英语学了那么多年学了很多语法和用法，但是真正拼在一起的时候会使用不当没有什么给文章添彩的效果。(Researcher translation: The main difference between this image and the one on Chinese is the lack of a main thesis. It is like when I write an essay in English, the focus is often blurry and I can't find the main idea. The 'z' design remains the same, but I use black to represent a feeling of frustration. I have spent years studying English grammar and usage, but I often misuse them when attempting to piece them together in my essay, which works against the purpose of adding to the appeal of my essay.)

Figure 9.1 Xiaoqi's writing theory cartoon and bilingual explanation

Chinese international student, a sophomore economics major from China, who used the assignment to reflect on the difficulty of transferring writing-related knowledge and skills across languages. Before the writing cartoon theory assignment, Xiaoqi had just completed a Learning Memoire assignment, which invited her deployment of a range of creative writing techniques in telling a personal story. Xiaoqi struggled with the assignment's expectation to 'show rather than tell,' noting in particular the challenge to use colorful language, to express feelings and to replicate/translate dialogues that took place in Chinese into English. In this process, Xiaoqi became more cognizant of the limitation of her strategy to translate Chinese idioms directly into English, which often led to much loss of meaning. Negotiating different conventions of cross-cultural storytelling, Xiaoqi directed her attention to global issues of insight, organization and style.

Xiaoqi's cartoon makes clear the challenge to deliver a unifying 'main idea' clearly and coherently in her second language. Observing language as a vessel for thought, Xiaoqi commented on how ideas that would otherwise appear crystal clear remained fuzzy when presented in English. Additionally, she was frustrated by her inability to articulate a 'main thread' that could be used to organize details into a coherent whole.

Her cartoons made use of a basic design, using a thick line to represent the main idea (backbone of an essay) and zigzagged lines to represent writing techniques and rhetorical devices that supposedly embellish the writing. The choice of colors, with the former using a thick black line to represent a well-articulated main idea, and colorful zigzags projecting a variety of writing techniques at one's disposal – the latter, representing English writing – showed the absence of a main thread and the constraints of linguistic and rhetorical resources, including limited vocabulary, and rhetorical devices that did not translate. Xiaoqi's understanding of writing as rhetorically motivated and multi-dimensional arose from a systematic comparison of and reflection on the two languages she constantly manipulates for communicative and expressive purposes, especially in the context of academic writing.

The assignment, in strategically targeting students' experiences juggling such differences, helps Xiaoqi attribute her struggles to the difficulties in negotiating the dynamic use of linguistic and rhetorical strategies across languages and modes, a view raised in Pennycook (2008), who sees English as a language always in translation. Xiaoqi's cartoon reflects her consideration of different ways in which rhetorical devices, grammar and lexicon are formulated to allow the passing (to and from) of social, cultural and historical meanings and how such linguistic conventions need to be reconfigured. Even though Xiaoqi's reflection at the moment seems to focus on the difficulty of transferring writing-related strategies and knowledge acquired in Chinese into English writing, such consideration also encourages her to consider her multiple languages as equally important components of a holistic linguistic repertoire, which not only positions her writing expertise in her home language as a tool to formulate ideas and manage global structures, but to carefully negotiate tensions that necessarily arise from such attempted transfers. In important ways, the assignment encourages an analysis that uncovers writing as rhetorically, historically and culturally informed.

Xiaoqi's reflection challenges a monolingual view that positions her lack of vocabulary and accuracy as deficits, as she simultaneously recognizes her writing expertise in her home language and begins to attribute her struggle to the lack of exposure to authentic texts and practice in English writing. As she critiqued, her English learning tended to focus on the instruction of isolated grammatical constructs and rules, which led to her difficulty in applying such principles effectively in writing. Recognizing her 'problem' as the products of language acts sanctioned in pedagogical spaces of English instruction in China, Xiaoqi could then perform the difficult task of determining 'what kinds of difference to make through [her] writing, how, and why' (Lu & Horner, 2013: 585). This understanding in turn helped Xiaoqi strategize her learning to facilitate such linguistic crossing (e.g. formulate the main idea in Chinese and then translate, transfer writing techniques from Chinese to English). As such, the assignment allowed Xiaoqi to take up an issue from a difficult writing assignment and turn it into an opportunity to deepen her understanding of language differences as partially derived from linguistic differences and educational backgrounds.

I Am from Poetry

I Am from Poetry is an assignment offered to facilitate students' understanding of linguistic, cultural and disciplinary crossing as co-constituted processes. The assignment was designed in response to calls to position translingual practices as enabling 'students to construct and constantly modify their sociocultural identities and values, as they respond to their historical and present conditions critically and creatively' (García & Li, 2014: 62). Undergirding the assignment was an interest in understanding transnational students' language practices and literacy identities as negotiated across time–space relationships through the mediation of assemblages of artifacts, persons, practices and texts (Leander & Rowe, 2006; Wang, 2020). With the attention to literacy as simultaneously fluid, frictive and fixed mobile practices that are differently valued (Lorimer Leonard, 2017), instructors could use *I Am from Poetry* to engage students in reflections on their literacy and identities as negotiated across time–space relationships operating with different value systems. According to Stewart and Hansen-Thomas (2016), *I Am from Poetry* writing sanctions a space for the purposeful examination of transnational experiences, to engage in translanguaging by integrating phrases from multiple languages into the poem, and to access a range of cultural and linguistic resources to express creativity and criticality. It is in this spirit that I adapt the writing theory cartoon into a pedagogical tool, which encourages multilingual writers to understand their literacy repertoire and identity as shaped by and shaping their social worlds.

Procedure

This poetry assignment consists of *whole class reading of multi-cultural texts, journal writing around cultural themes, class construction of artifactual literacies* and the *creation of a multimodal poetry writing project*. Each element was chosen purposefully to connect to students' transnational lives and allowed multiple opportunities for translingual performance. At the outset, the class read biographical poetry about the (transnational) life of Supreme Court Justice Sonia Sotomayor, and autobiographical accounts by multicultural authors (Amy Tan's *Mother Tongue*, Judith Ortiz Cofer's *The Myth of Latin Woman*), with the conversation focused on understanding culture as a fluid composite of components and experiences. Using photos from their personal albums, students explore visceral experiences with their home communities. Students are then invited to select artifacts representative of their literacy and cultural practices, which gives rise to growing theorization of their movements across languages and cultures as sites for inquiry into differences. Working from the original *I Am from Poem* template (Lyon, 1993), students then integrate such artifactual and visual information into a multimodal poem, with key concepts illustrated with photos. In what follows, I draw on Hui's poem to discuss the assignment as an opportunity to negotiate and rewrite culturally inscribed gender scripts.

Literacy mobility

I am from Walled Village
Everyone living there shares my last name
I am from the bubbles in the bathtub
Transparent, fluttering, they were touched and broken
I am from kapok
Glaring brightly red in the sun
I am from weekend hiking trips and the loud voice of my grandmother
Constantly reminding me to be strong and tough as any other boy
I am from bickering this minute and singing songs next
From "A degree is your only way out" and "Go back for ancestral worship this and every year"
I am from the Lantern festival on the sixth day of lunar new year
The deafening explosion of fireworks and cheers celebrating the new lives of boys, not girls;

I am from Hakkas migrating and settling in Huizhou, Guangdong Province
Sliced cold chicken, stuffed bean curd on the dinner tables of family reunion;
From the stories of two rural youngsters fighting for a better life away from their village
The arduous farm work my grandmother shouldered to raise her children
On the wall of our living room is the wedding photo of my parents
Reminding me that happiness is hard to achieve.

In poems like this, young women surface experiences of social and geographic mobility as intricately entangled with literacy learning and identity. Hui's poem provides an increasingly sharpened commentary on culturally inscribed gender scripts that shape her literacy and professional trajectory in powerful ways. Especially poignant here is her identification as a young professional with deep roots in Hakka cultural and ethnic traditions.

Her use the 'Walled Village' as a cultural artifact points to her awareness of historical mobilities that inform her identity. Hakka, or 客家, literally translated as 'guest families,' and less literally as newcomers and settlers, are Han Chinese with ancestral homes in chiefly northern parts of China, who, in a series of migrations, moved and settled in their present areas in Southern China and various countries throughout the world. Such migration brought the Hakkas into conflict with locals, who had developed distinctive cultural identities and languages. Figure 9.2 shows

Figure 9.2 Walled Village

the Walled Village, a communal living structure that is easily defensible and emerged as a result of Hakkas fending off attacks from hostile locals and animals. Even today, members of the younger generation, such as Hui, experience the tight communal ties to Hakka culture in both material and symbolic forms, particularly as gender preference as a means to maintaining the tribal bloodline. In addition to urging her to visit the village 'where everyone living there shares [her] last name' and 'go back for ancestral worship this and every year,' her family has always made their gender preference clear to Hui. In her memory, at bath time, her grandma would often share her regrets about her only grandchild being a girl. To Hui, these reminders have always carried unbearable emotional weight that breaks her transparent and fluttering dreams upon touching.

As a young college student who hopes to pursue a career in English and cultural studies, Hui grows increasingly critical of a culture that suppresses young women's pursuit of academic and professional aspirations. For instance, her reflection has drastically shifted her view towards a festive occasion that she used to enjoy – the Hakka Lantern festival, which takes place on the sixth day of the Chinese lunar new year, when the entire village gathered to celebrate the births of boys in the village. A cultural practice unique to this occasion is the lighting of customized festive 'lanterns,' accompanied by a village-wide parade that ends at the household with the arrival of a boy. 灯 'lantern' is the homonym of '丁,' a cultural term to describe a male offspring that carries on the familial blood line. Whereas the birth of boys was considered an event worthy of recognition and celebration, the birth of girls was often deemed insignificant or shameful: the same shame, which used to torture the young Hui, who learned from early on that her only way to be as 'strong and tough as any other boy' is through working hard.

Hui's literacy and professional trajectories are profoundly shaped by such inscribed gender scripts with deep roots in historical mobility. For one thing, she has always been driven to achieve academic excellence because of constant reminders that she was able to receive a good education because she was treated as a boy and the only heir to the family bloodline. As the first in her family to attend college, Hui's academic achievement has earned her family the kind of recognition that other families have earned through the birth of male offspring. The familial pressure to prove it worthy in the communal structure has translated into strong motivation for Hui.

Meanwhile, historical mobility creates social scripts that constrain Hui's further professional development. For one thing, Hui was expected to fulfill her filial duty by caring for her aging parents as her parents had cared for her grandmother. In considering her professional trajectory, Hui felt bound to the geographic region of her birth, partially arising from her parents' request for her to stay close. She was not to seek a job in metropolitan cities such as Shanghai and Beijing, where opportunities are bountiful in her professional area. Second, Hui's family is insistent on her marrying a Hakka man from the close proximity of her village, which further limits her geographic and professional mobility.

Literacy scholars have long argued for the importance of examining symbolic tools present in scenes of literacy learning, such as narratives, phrases, and tropes embodying the practices, values and identities of a *figured world* (Wertsch, 1998). These artifacts, historically developed across spaces and times, embody valuable cultural resources and travel afar to frame young people's enactment, representation and expression of identities. As we observe here, the poetry writing assignment brings our attention to narratives and artifacts that powerfully shape students' beliefs, attitudes and approaches to literacy practices and identities. Hui herself was surprised by the various forms of intersecting mobilities that infiltrate her trajectory, including the historical mobility of the Hakka people, the mobility of her parents, who moved to Huizhou as a result of their own academic mobility, and the prospect of her parents' (im)mobility as a result of her need to simultaneously seek professional growth and to fulfill filial duties. Coming to terms with such existent and prospective mobilities compelled Hui to consider the decisions she makes about her academic and professional goals.

This assignment facilitates students' development of a holistic understanding of literacies developed across a life span as connected and inter-aminating. On the one hand, students like Hui begin to observe literacy as inflected with mobile potentials – the movements of her and her family provides increasing access to literacy resources and materials, which allows her to move across linguistic and disciplinary borders with flexibility and dexterity. Her poetry creates an opportunity to observe 'ways meaning bubbles up in interactions among people, texts, and thing' and 'the emergent, felt, mobile dimensions of literacy practice' (Stornaiuolo & LeBlanc, 2016: 77). Her poetry, as well as the literacy narratives encoded in it, calls attention to moments of fixity in her literacy practices, suggesting that mobile practices cannot be fully understood without consideration of boundary-enforcing forces that restrict and regulate mobility. Indeed, culturally inscribed gender scripts can be considered a central feature of mobility, which is inflected with inequality, struggles and suppression (Lorimer Leonard, 2017).

Conclusion

These assignments recognize students' multilingual and multimodal resources as a holistic repertoire. Through the process of negotiating language differences and engaging in translanguaging, students develop metalinguistic understandings, meta-awareness and meta-vocabulary towards productive negotiation across differences. The assignments respond to a disciplinary move towards positioning multilingual writers' rhetorical repertoire and lived experiences as sites for inquiry. Such assignments, striving for an asset-based approach to teaching, not only treat students as experts of their own languages and cultures, inquiry into which leads to metalinguistic understanding of diverse cultural and linguistic systems as dynamically related and negotiated, but also encourage students to learn about and to analyze their language, cultural and rhetorical traditions as embodying different social, cultural, economic and political realities. As the examples have shown, such a process encourages students to make sense of linguistic, cultural and rhetorical differences as normal, fluid and negotiated.

Students' development of translingual dispositions is grounded in collaborative creation of a meta-vocabulary to name translingual practices they already perform. For many, the difficulty of finding the right word in English mirrors the frustration they encounter in negotiating small mundane details, including ordering food from the cafeteria, seeking help from a professor, or having a conversation with an American roommate. Analyzing these daily struggles creates an occasion to sharpen strategies that facilitate students' socialization into the social, cultural, academic and language practices of the university. For students such as Jessica, Xiaoqi and Hui, reflections on their translingual practices help them articulate and sharpen strategies that guide their choices and actions in academic and social situations. The validity of such theories aside, such meta-awareness and meta-vocabulary allow for the transfer of writing knowledge and strategy into unfamiliar situations.

The inclusion of translingual themes, through purposeful centering of students' languages and cultures as objects of inquiry, invites students to recognize and negotiate the vast range of literate experiences they mobilize from one place in the world to another. Multilingual writers learn to configure and reconfigure rhetorical resources and strategies at their disposal in response to rhetorical situations that demand informed explanation of one's social and cultural experiences to diverse audiences (peers, faculty across disciplines). Placing multiple languages in juxtaposition to each other, multilingual writers learn to challenge binaries that separate languages as sealed and isolated entities, while developing metalinguistic understandings of language as linguistic, cultural and ideological structures that can be negotiated and recast. In the case of Jessica, recognizing language differences as derived from linguistic features enables her to develop meta-awareness of language differences, name her successes and challenges, and strategize her negotiative moves. For Xiaoqi, thinking about English compels him to examine his home language, which often leads to the recognition of languages as historically fluctuating and language differences as a norm within and across languages. For Hui, problematizing her literacy and academic learning as partially produced by historical trajectories of mobility helps her to see herself as an agentive user of an integrated linguistic repertoire. As such, these assignments not only render visible some of the linguistic and cultural struggles that often remain invisible or peripheral in writing classrooms, but they also encourage students' negotiation of such struggles.

In so doing, students also begin to see language differences as the norm, meaning as fulfilled through negotiated linguistic and semiotic acts, and themselves as agents who make adaptive and creative uses of a rich rhetorical repertoire that embodies shifting social, cultural and historical meanings. While the cases presented here illustrate the broader patterns of how students navigate the translingual curriculum, they have not captured the full range of student learning. For instance, students draw on a far broader range of metaphors informed by different facets of their cultural lives to discuss language differences (religion, food culture, politics) than this study has the space to discuss. It is in this access to a range of experiences that we find the pedagogical appeal of the assignments – they encourage multilingual writers to draw on familiar rhetorical and cultural resources to make sense of unfamiliar aspects of their social and linguistic reality, a task that chapters throughout the book show to be particularly challenging for international students.

References

Canagarajah, S.A. (2006) Toward a writing pedagogy of shuttling between languages: Learning from multilingual writers. *College English* 68 (5), 589–604. https://ncte.org/resources/journals/college-english/.

Canagarajah, S.A. (2013) Negotiating translingual literacy: An enactment. *Research in the Teaching of English* 48 (1), 40–67. https://ncte.org/resources/journals/research-in-the-teaching-of-english.

Creese, A. and Blackledge, A. (2010) Translanguaging in the bilingual classroom: A pedagogy for learning and teaching. *Modern Language Journal* 94 (1), 103–115. https://doi.org/10.1111/j.1540-4781.2009.00986.x.

DePalma, M. and Ringer, J.M. (2011) Toward a theory of adaptive transfer: Expanding disciplinary discussions of 'transfer' in second-language writing and composition studies. *Journal of Second Language Writing* 20 (2), 134–147. https://doi.org/10.1016/j.jslw.2011.02.003.

Fraiberg, S., Wang, X. and You, X. (2017) *Inventing the World Grant University: Chinese International Students' Mobilities, Literacies and Identities*. Logan, UT: Utah State University Press.

García, O. and Li, W. (2014) *Translanguaging: Language, Bilingualism and Education*. Basingstoke: Palgrave MacMillan.

Gilyard, K. (2016) The rhetoric of translingualism. *College English* 78 (3), 284–289. https://ncte.org/resources/journals/college-english/.

Gonzales, L. (2018) *Sites of Translation: What Multilinguals Can Teach Us About Digital Writing and Rhetoric*. Ann Arbor, MI: University of Michigan Press.

Guerra, J.C. (2016) Cultivating a rhetorical sensibility in the translingual writing classroom. *College English* 78 (3), 228–33. https://ncte.org/resources/journals/college-english/.

Hornberger, N. and Link, H. (2012) Translanguaging in today's classrooms: A biliteracy lens. *Theory into Practice* 51 (4), 239–247. https://doi.org/10.1080/00405841.2012.726051.

Horner, B. and Tetreault, L. (2016) Translation as (global) writing. *Composition Studies* 44 (1), 13–30. https://compstudiesjournal.com/.

Horner, B., Lu, M., Royster, J.J. and Trimbur, J. (2011) Opinions: Language difference in writing: Toward a translingual approach. *College English* 73 (3), 303–321. https://ncte.org/resources/journals/college-english/.

Jiménez, R.T., David, S., Fagan, K., Risko, V.J., Pacheco, M., Pray, L. and Gonzales, M. (2015) Using translation to drive conceptual development for students becoming literate in English as an additional language. *Research in the Teaching of English* 49 (3), 248–272. https://ncte.org/resources/journals/research-in-the-teaching-of-english.

Jordan, J. (2015) Material translingual ecologies. *College English* 77 (4), 364–382. https://ncte.org/resources/journals/college-english/.

Kiernan, J., Meier, J. and Wang, X. (2016) Negotiating languages and cultures: Enacting translingualism through a translation assignment. *Composition Studies* 44 (1), 89–107.

Kress, G. and van Leeuwen, T. (1996) *Reading Images: The Grammar of Visual Design.* London: Routledge.

Leander, K. and Rowe, D. (2006) Mapping literacy spaces in motion: A rhizomatic analysis of a classroom literacy performance. *Reading Research Quarterly* 41 (4), 428–460. https://doi.org/10.1598/rrq.41.4.2.

Lorimer Leonard, R. (2014) Multilingual writing as rhetorical attunement. *College English* 76 (3), 227–247. https://ncte.org/resources/journals/college-english/.

Lorimer Leonard, R. (2017) *Writing on the Move: Migrant Women and the Value of Literacy.* Pittsburgh, PA: University of Pittsburgh Press.

Lorimer Leonard, R. and Nowacek, R. (2016) Transfer and translingualism. *College English* 78 (3), 258–264. https://ncte.org/resources/journals/college-english/.

Lu, M.Z. and Horner, B. (2013) Translingual literacy, language difference, and matters of agency. *College English* 75 (6), 582–607. https://ncte.org/resources/journals/college-english/.

Lyon, G.E. (1993) *Where I'm From.* http://www.georgeellalyon.com/where.html.

Matsuda, P.K. (2014) The lure of translingual writing. *PMLA* 129 (3), 478–483. https://www.mla.org/Publications/Journals/PMLA.

Pennycook, A. (2008) English as a language always in translation. *European Journal of English Studies* 12 (1), 33–47. https://doi.org/10.1080/13825570801900521.

Prior, P. and Shipka, J. (2003) Chronotopic lamination: Tracing the contours of literate activity. In C. Bazerman and D. Russell (eds) *Writing Selves, Writing Societies: Research from Activity Perspectives* (pp. 180–238). WAC Clearinghouse.

Selfe, C.L. (2009) The movement of air, the breath of meaning: Aurality and multimodal composing. *College Composition and Communication* 60 (4), 616–663. https://cccc.ncte.org/cccc/ccc.

Shipka, J. (2013) Including, but not limited to the digital: Composing multimodal texts. In T. Bowen and C. Whithaus (eds) *Multimodal Literacies and Emerging Genres* (pp. 73–90). Pittsburgh, PA: University of Pittsburgh Press.

Stewart, M. and Hansen-Thomas, H. (2016) Sanctioning a space for translanguaging in the secondary English classroom: A case of a transnational youth. *Research in the Teaching of English* 50 (4), 450–472. https://ncte.org/resources/journals/research-in-the-teaching-of-english.

Stornaiuolo, A. and LeBlanc, R.J. (2016) Scaling as a literacy activity: Mobility and educational inequality in an age of global connectivity. *Research in the Teaching of English* 50 (3), 263–287. https://ncte.org/resources/journals/research-in-the-teaching-of-english.

Sun, Y. and Lan, G. (2020) Enactment of a translingual approach to writing. *TESOL Quarterly.* https://doi.org/10.1002/tesq.609.

Wang, X. (2020) Becoming multilingual writers through translation. *Research in the Teaching of English* 54 (3), 206–230. https://ncte.org/resources/journals/research-in-the-teaching-of-english.

Wertsch, J. (1998) *Mind as Action.* Oxford: Oxford University Press.

Afterword

Wenhao Diao

More than 1 million international students studied in US institutions of higher education in the academic year of 2017–2018 (Institute of International Education, 2019). Even without national statistics, the demographic changes of college students can be felt across individual university campuses, and these trends have transformed the linguistic landscape of many college towns where these campuses are located. I had the pleasure of visiting 'Great Lake University,' pseudonym for the focal institution throughout this volume. During my trip I noticed many restaurants intended to serve primarily international student populations, with names and menus written mostly in other languages (e.g. Chinese). When I visited a Korean restaurant near the campus, I spotted a wall of post-it notes in various languages by its students there (Figure A.1).

Figure A.1 Multilingual notes on the wall of a restaurant near Great Lake University

This volume is thus a timely collection of essays that examine how international students learn to adjust to their academic life in the US by focusing on their engagement in academic English writing. While each individual chapter is a stand-alone study by itself, together they form a cohesive volume comprising diverse cases and perspectives all related to one writing center, one set of interrelated writing courses (FYW100 and FYW101) and at one institution – Great Lake University.

In my final remarks, I would like to comment on the rare and welcome themes that I have noticed while reading this volume. Before I start, however, I would like to describe my own positionality while offering these comments. I was an international student from mainland China in the US, though my own research focuses on L2 learning and socialization processes mostly among American students studying abroad elsewhere. For well over a decade now, the study abroad scholarship in applied linguistics has highlighted the interplay between identity, socialization and language learning. Many of us now sense a need to shift more toward a translingual approach that can capture the multilingual realities, students' transnational movements, as well as the ideologies around different languages that they often encounter while moving across national borders (Diao & Trentman, 2021; Park & Bae, 2009). For international students pursuing higher education in the US, learning to write academically is integral to being and becoming in their new academic settings; simultaneously it is also symbolic of their transnational and social mobility (e.g. Canagarajah, 2013). Yet, despite these connections, there has not been much overlap between the study abroad literature and the scholarship on L2 writing in applied linguistics. Therefore, I comment on this volume not only as an applied linguist who was formerly an international student in the US but also as someone who believes we should have more multilingual literacy socialization research to bring the study abroad and L2 writing scholarships closer together.

Transdisciplinarity and Translingualism in L2 Writing Pedagogy

Perhaps the most apparent feature of the current volume is how it cuts across different disciplinary traditions and encompasses multiple perspectives and experiences, all while examining how international students engage in academic discourse socialization processes at one institution, Great Lake University. The contributing authors include tenured professors, writing center staff, as well as novice researchers who were still graduate students at the time of the project. As several authors throughout the volume made it explicit that they viewed themselves as having the dual role of teacher–scholar, the collaboration across teaching, researching and learning is made the center of the volume.

The collaborative theme is also apparent in the transdisciplinary design of the research project that shaped the volume. As documented in the chapters by Cheatle and Jarvie (Chapter 7) and Wang (Chapter 9), this volume was based on an innovative pedagogical intervention that incorporated insights from SLA, writing and rhetoric, as well as education at Great Lake University. Specifically, Cheatle and Jarvie's chapter details the incorporation of L2 learning and teaching research into the writing center practices at Great Lake University, so that the writing center could better respond to its changing student demographics. Wang's chapter, on the other hand, provides us with information regarding the translingual pedagogical intervention used in her FYW 100 course that also constituted a part of the project. Despite the multilingual realities among both students and teachers in US institutions of higher education and the translingual practices in which they participate, a monolingual English-centric approach has often been the norm in postsecondary writing classrooms across the US (Tardy, 2011). A multilingual writer herself, Wang illustrates how an innovative translingual literacy approach that involves literary works from different cultures, poetry and translations, and explicit discussions of identity and transnationality can be incorporated in first-year writing instruction for international students.

Meanwhile, the chapter by Lee and Li (Chapter 2) provides a very different perspective from the research team. As graduate students at the time, Lee and Li document how their own academic identities were shaped and developed through participation in the project as research assistants and also international students themselves. The chapter is an autoethnography of their own socialization and identity development process throughout the project, and it allows us to see the evolution of the project that came to shape this volume – from its initial conception, to its implementation, and to its data analysis and presentations. Although there have been attempts to implement translingual literacy in writing courses (e.g. Canagarajah, 2013; Tardy, 2011), this volume is a rare example of collaborative research and teaching that involved not only instructors and program administrators but also graduate students who would become writing instructors elsewhere after they completed their degrees.

These three chapters provide implications for teaching not only undergraduate students in beginning writing classes but also graduate students who are learning to become researchers and scholars in the field. Furthermore, these three chapters also help readers contextualize the case stories reported in other chapters of the volume. Even though the information included in these three chapters is typically background stories that often do not become published – at least not in such great detail – the incorporation of them here provides critical contextual information of the project and allows readers to make sense of the findings reported in the remaining chapters, to which I will turn now.

Situatedness and Transnationality in L2 Academic Socialization

Six chapters of this volume are case studies of individual students and their experiences with L2 writing at Great Lake University. While these six chapters share a qualitative core, they draw from different theories to capture the diverse processes that international students experienced while learning to write academically. These theories include activity theory, language socialization, as well as literacy mobility in transnational context.

Two chapters in this volume adopted activity theory as their framework (Son, Chapter 6; Ma & Green-Eneix, Chapter 5). Influenced by Vygotsky's (1978) theorization that cognition is a mental process of understanding social reality through mediated actions with tools, activity theory (e.g. Engeström, 1987) situates learning in a sociocultural process that encompasses not only the individual learner but also organization of the community, distribution of labor, tool use, etc. Using this theoretical lens and combining it with ethnographic case study methods, these two chapters provide detailed analyses of how individual international students form social relationships and communities and negotiate within their writing classrooms, the writing center and other settings beyond those two sites, and the findings demonstrate how students' engagement (or the lack thereof) in academic writing is both a consequence and a part of their negotiation of their roles in these communities. For example, Son's chapter illustrates how Minji and Carter experienced L2 academic socialization differently despite being in a very similar environment with similar rules, and it was due to factors such as their use of different tools, their divergent assignments in the distribution of labor, and their own interpretations of the community.

Another recurring theory in this volume is language socialization. As a theory of learning initially used to examine child development, language socialization has its origin in the field of anthropology and postulates that language learning is a part of the process of becoming a member of a cultural community (e.g. Ochs & Schieffelin, 2001). Because L2 learners have typically already established membership in various communities prior to their arrival to the new language, L2 socialization has its own particularities with more explicit themes such as agency and resistance (Duff, 2012). Indeed, Zhang's chapter in this volume (Chapter 3) illustrates how international students' engagement in academic discourse is a part of their agentive participation in their new communities. The focal case of Charles shows both patterns of participation and resistance. Even though Great Lake University enrolled many students from mainland China, Charles agentively chose to play basketball with American students and avoided his co-nationals in his social life. Charles also resisted the writing center, where he felt he was positioned as an ESL learner, and he preferred the writing class in which he could receive feedback on the content of his writings rather than how his English use deviates from native norms. Lee and Li's chapter (Chapter 2) is another study examining the language socialization process but from the perspective of novice researchers and international graduate students. As aforementioned, this chapter is an autoethnography documenting the academic socialization processes of two members of this research project. Autoethnographies are uncommon in applied linguistics, and this chapter is quite unique as it documents how graduate students learn ways of being and becoming through socialization with both more experienced and other peer team members of this research project.

The remaining two chapters (Straayer-Gannon & Wang, Chapter 4; Fraiberg, Chapter 8) investigated international students' experience through the theoretical lens of literacy and transnational (im)mobility. Transnationalism has become a topic of interest in disciplines across the social sciences, and particularly in migration studies. The concept of transnationalism refers to the process of 'how migrants construct and reconstitute their lives as simultaneously embedded in more than one society' (Caglar, 2001: 607). Applied linguists are urging us to consider transnationalism in our research, because both language learners and the languages that they speak and learn are no longer connected to one locality but instead to several places in different parts of the world (Duff, 2015). For (educational) migrants such as international students, linguistic and literacy practices constitute 'forms of capital production' that index different values in different communities based on both local and translocal rules of recognition and conversion, and therefore through these literacy practices migrants 'are variously able to attain particular positions' within and across localities and communities (Lam & Warriner, 2012: 192). The striking stories of Albina (Straayer-Gannon & Wang) and Bruno (Fraiberg) in this volume demonstrate how international students may draw from literacy resources in their lived transnational experience to negotiate their social positions. A student born and raised in Ghana, Albina was initially socialized into a set of gender norms at home and in her Ghanaian communities that delegitimized her agency prior to her study abroad trips. While she was able to move beyond the gender conventions with the financial help of an NGO, she also used English writing to reflect upon and critique these gender norms. In the writing class, she would pay attention to alternative gender traditions in class discussions about cultural differences. Moreover, Albina's story also highlights the significance of human agency in navigating through transnational academic discourses, even when the institutionalized gender norms in her upbringing denied her of agency. Although her mentor assigned by the NGO was overwhelmed because of the sheer number of girls she had to mentor, Albina agentively took the initiative to connect to the mentor through writing and constructed a meaningful relationship. Her agency to connect with mentors enabled her to navigate through her transnational experiences from Ghana to South Africa, and then to the US, and finally to her imagined future self as a mentor for other girls in her home country of Ghana.

Bruno's story, on the other hand, highlights the politics around ethnoracial identities in Latin America. Born in Bolivia, where ethnoracial inequalities are prevalent and can determine social statuses (Telles *et al.*, 2015), Bruno moved with his family from a Bolivian *colla* region to Brazil and later back to Bolivia but to its urban center of Santa Cruz. While in Santa Cruz, he claimed a *camba* identity and adopted *camba* ways of speaking to gain social mobility. To him, the politics between *colla* and *camba* continued to be relevant and meaningful even after he arrived at Great Lake University in Midwestern US, where presumably not many would be familiar with such identity politics in Bolivia. Bruno's story illustrates exactly how language use and literacy practices serve as symbolic capital that indexes individual's social and material positions in a society (Lam & Warriner, 2012).

These diverse theoretical frameworks and positions are brought together by one coherent research project and shared research methods. Individually, each chapter is qualitative and ethnographic with multiple data sources such as interviews and observations, and collectively these case stories complement each other and shed light on the historicity and complexity of agency and identity among L2 learners in transnational processes.

Diverse Students and Diverse Orientations

The chapters in this volume also delve into the diverse experiences of students from a variety of home countries. It is probably no coincidence that two (Ma & Green-Eneix; Zhang) of the six case report chapters in this volume focus exclusively on international students from mainland China. Based on the most recent statistics, students from China account for 34% of all international students in the US. This phenomenon has a close relationship with China's one-child generation, Chinese parents' heavy investment in their (most likely) only child's education, as well as the neoliberal aspirations for flexible citizenship in the developed world (Fong, 2011). This new educational landscape also presents particular challenges to the design and implementation of English writing instruction on many US college campuses, and Great Lake University is no exception. As mentioned in almost every other chapter in the volume, Chinese students account for a sizable portion of Great Lake's international student population.

Meanwhile, these two chapters focusing on Chinese students also capture the diverse orientations within this group. The chapter by Ma and Green-Eneix describes two Chinese students (Andy and Sarah), who socialized in what the authors referred to as a cocoon community exclusively with other Chinese students. Inside the writing classroom, they almost always seated themselves with other co-nationals and as far away as possible from non-Chinese students. Even though Sarah's writing instructor attempted to break this pattern by assigning seats and groups, Sarah viewed the effort as a 'waste of time' because she believed that English was less efficient for peer communication in the classroom. Meanwhile, outside the classroom, their socialization frequently took place on the internet using a China-based social media platform: WeChat. China's social media landscape is somewhat unique, as most of its platforms are based within China and not used widely overseas, while most social media sites that are not China based are not accessible from mainland China. Language learners often maintain interactions on social media sites that they are already familiar with and with friends and family to whom they are already connected (Reinhardt & Zander, 2011). Thus, as shown in Ma and Green-Eneix's chapter, China's Great Firewall can still effectively separate Chinese students from other students in the virtual world even after they have left the country.

One factor that has likely contributed to the phenomenon, as pointed out by the authors, is a test-centered approach used in their high school English classrooms prior to their arrival in the US. Both Andy and Sarah attended high school programs that were intended to prepare Chinese students to study abroad. In both cases, the decision was made long before they left China to avoid the intense pressure of China's national college exam. Yet, both students ended up focusing on another exam – the TOEFL – rather than actually preparing themselves to become capable of communicating with others using English in the academic context. This phenomenon reveals the conundrum that many Chinese study abroad students experience – they opt out of China's own higher education to avoid the highly competitive and exam-focused high school experience but they end up participating in another exam-focused education for TOEFL. This contradiction reveals how agency, even in the form of resistance, can be also shaped by the very social structures and institutions that it is intended to oppose (e.g. Block, 2015).

Zhang's chapter, however, showcases a very different kind of Chinese student. Unlike Andy and Sarah, Charles in Zhang's chapter described his co-nationals as 'poor' basketball players, and he sought out opportunities to interact with 'funny' American students. He also adamantly resented being positioned as an English language learner and thus resisted visiting the writing center, where he tended to receive corrective feedback for his non-native use of English grammar and vocabulary. Charles' story complements those of Andy and Sarah and showcases the diverse orientations among Chinese study abroad students toward their co-nationals when being abroad. While many of them may choose to internalize the cultural logic that emphasizes an ethnicity-based Chinese fraternity across national borders (Fong, 2011; Ong, 1999), other Chinese students overseas may also rebel against this norm and seek out an alternative.

In addition to these chapters focusing on students from China, the remaining chapters present case studies of students from many other countries in the world: Bolivia (Fraiberg), Botswana (Son), Ghana (Straayer-Gannon & Wang) and South Korea (Son). Indeed, as mentioned by Fraiberg in this volume, international students at Great Lake University came from many parts all over the world. Thus, in many cases, L2 English socialization becomes *lingua franca* socialization in this context. This is particularly evident in Son's chapter, in which the two focal students, Minji and Carter, both chose to frequent the non-native English tutors at the writing center. Son's analysis shows that this was because these international students perceived the non-native tutors to be more patient and sympathetic towards their difficulties. This result shows how *lingua franca* socialization may be qualitatively different from L2 socialization; in the former, language learners' experience more often than not challenges and transcends the ideology of native-speaker-ism that has been prevalent in language teaching research and practices. *Lingua franca* socialization is also common not only between first-year international students and their writing tutors: it is also the case for more senior undergraduate and graduate students across disciplines, where their professors, mentors and supervisors of other kinds are often not English native speakers either (see, for example, the engineering lab team in Burhan's 2020 doctoral thesis). I believe that a continued focus on *lingua franca* socialization among international students in Anglophone academic contexts can generate new understandings of how we organize our social and professional lives through our engagement in academic discourse.

Conclusion

As I write these remarks, many of us – particularly those who live in the US, where Great Lake University is located – are still living through the once-in-a-century pandemic of COVID-19. As part of containment measures, travel restrictions are being imposed by national and local institutions, and transnational movement has been literally halted. After decades of continued growth (Institute of International Education, 2019), international education is witnessing severe disruptions in this global health crisis. While this rare but important context is a powerful reminder that language learning and teaching are closely connected to institutional and societal contexts (Douglas Fir Group, 2018) – a point that has also been a central theme throughout this volume – it also brings many new questions for applied linguists interested in study abroad, identity and literacy transnationality. Some of the questions are expected to remain even after the crisis. For instance, as virtual classes have been set up to facilitate social distancing, universities across America are exploring the possibility of increasing their online offerings of courses and degree programs. It may soon be not uncommon for international students to take online classes and have virtual appointments with writing centers without leaving their home countries. This change could constrain and alter socialization patterns for many – both the students and their instructors and tutors. How will writing programs, writing centers and students renegotiate and reconstruct their relationship when their interactions are limited to the online space exclusively are certainly questions to be yet explored. Communication that relies exclusively on the internet, furthermore, also entails questions regarding privacy, surveillance and censorship. These concerns are increasingly the reality as the pandemic has forced people across the world to shift the modality of their interactions to online. More qualitative stories exploring individual cases of agency, conformity and resistance will help us better understand identity in online literacy practices in the age of 'Big Data' and algorithms.

This health crisis has also led to more prevalent misinformation and has exacerbated exclusivist sentiments such as nationalism, ethnocentrism and racism in many parts of the world. Many international students are on one hand stuck in the places where they are because of travel restrictions, but on the other hand they may also face legal and institutional challenges that further marginalize them as outsiders who do not belong. The identity struggles of international students in their L2 academic socialization processes documented in the chapters throughout this volume are not only more relevant to this time of a global crisis: I suspect that they will likely also be more multimodal, more intricate, and more contested.

Wenhao Diao
University of Arizona

References

Block, D. (2015) Structure, agency, individualization and the critical realist challenge. In P. Deters, X. Gao, E.R. Miller and G. Vitanova (eds) *Theorizing and Analyzing Agency in Second Language Learning: Interdisciplinary Approaches* (pp. 17–36). Bristol: Multilingual Matters.

Burhan, E. (2020) Understanding multiple layers of practice: A study on academic discourse socialization in engineering research teams. Unpublished doctoral thesis, University of Arizona.

Caglar, A.S. (2001) Constraining metaphors and the transnationalisation of spaces in Berlin. *Journal of Ethnic and Migration Studies* 27 (4), 601–613.

Canagarajah, S. (2013) Negotiating translingual literacy: An enactment. *Research in the Teaching of English* 48 (1), 40–67.

Diao, W. and Trentman, E. (eds) (2021) *Language Learning in Study Abroad: The Multilingual Turn*. Bristol: Multilingual Matters.

Douglas Fir Group (2016) A transdisciplinary framework for SLA in a multilingual world. *Modern Language Journal* 100 (S1), 19–47.

Duff, P. (2012) Identity, agency, and SLA. In A. Mackey and S. Gass (eds) *Handbook of Second Language Acquisition* (pp. 410–426). London: Routledge.

Duff, P. (2015) Transnationalism, multilingualism, and identity. *Annual Review of Applied Linguistics 35*, 57–80.

Engeström, Y. (1987) *Learning by Expanding: An Activity-theoretical Approach to Developmental Research*. Helsinki: Orienta-Konsultit.

Fong, V. (2011) *Paradise Redefined: Transnational Chinese Students and the Quest for Flexible Citizenship in the Developed World*. Palo Alto, CA: Stanford University Press.

Institute of International Education (2019) *Open Doors 2019 Report on International Educational Exchange*. Retrieved 30 July 2020 from http://opendoorsiie.wpengine.com/annual-release/.

Lam, W.S.E. and Warriner, D.S. (2012) Transnationalism and literacy: Investigating the mobility of people, languages, texts, and practices in the contexts of migration. *Reading Research Quarterly* 47 (2), 191–215.

Ochs, E. and Schieffelin, B.B. (2011) The theory of language socialization. In A. Duranti, E. Ochs and B.B. Schieffelin (eds) *The Handbook of Language Socialization* (pp. 1–21). Oxford: Blackwell.

Ong, A. (1999) *Flexible Citizenship: The Cultural Logics of Transnationality*. Durham, NC: Duke University Press.

Park, J.S.Y. and Bae, S. (2009) Language ideologies in educational migration: Korean jogi yuhak families in Singapore. *Linguistics and Education* 20 (4), 366–377.

Reinhardt, J. and Zander, V. (2011) Social networking in an intensive English program classroom: A language socialization perspective. *CALICO Journal* 28 (2), 326–344.

Tardy, C. (2011) Enacting and transforming local language policies. *College Composition and Communication* 62 (4), 634–661.

Telles, E., Flores, R.D. and Urrea-Giraldo, F. (2015) Pigmentocracies: Educational inequality, skin color and census ethnoracial identification in eight Latin American countries. *Research in Social Stratification and Mobility* 40, 39–58.

Vygotsky, L.S. (1978) *Mind in Society: The Development of Higher Psychological Processes*. Cambridge, MA: Harvard University Press.

Index

Note: Page numbers in **bold** refer to information in tables, those followed by 'n' refer to notes.

CPSIA information can be obtained
at www.ICGtesting.com
Printed in the USA
JSHW041521070922
30174JS00004B/43

9 781800 415546